Folens

GCSE
Applied
ICT

DOUBLE
AWARD

Maggie Banks • Colin Harber-Stuart • Dave Parry

Contents

Contents

How to use this book

What you will learn in each topic is clearly shown at the beginning.

Words in **bold type** can be found in the Glossary, at the end of this book.

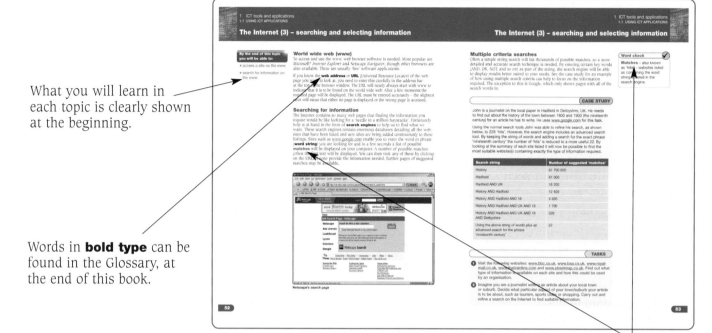

Important words are shown in **bold type** and their meanings explained in Word check boxes.

Clear pictures and diagrams illustrate the text.

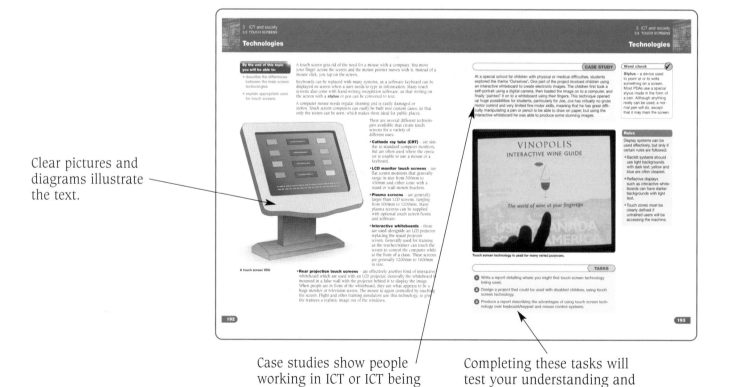

Case studies show people working in ICT or ICT being used in everyday life.

Completing these tasks will test your understanding and knowledge.

Welcome to GCSE in Applied ICT (Double Award)

This book has been written to help you gain the knowledge, skills and understanding that you need to obtain a GCSE in Applied Information and Communication Technology (ICT) (Double Award). As this is a vocational course, as well as studying this book, you should also gain first-hand experience of how ICT is used in organisations and society by making visits, listening to speakers or watching videos. Some of the activities included will help you to do this.

The book is not designed to be read from cover to cover. You will probably need to dip into different sections at different stages of the course. The book has been organised to help you to do this.

There are three main sections that correspond to the three main areas of study in the qualification. These are: ICT Tools and Applications; ICT in Organisations; ICT and Society.

Each section is divided into sub-sections that match the main headings within each area of study. Each sub-section is made up of a number of topics each taking up a double page. There is an introduction to each section that tells you what it is about. The introduction also lists the sub-sections included.

Each double-page topic starts with a list of what you will be able to do when you have finished studying it. It is headed 'By the end of this topic you will be able to:'. Important words that you need to understand as part of the topic will be explained in 'Word check' boxes in the margin. Other terms will be explained in the glossary on pages 248 to 251. You should look there if you are not sure what a particular term means.

Each topic may have other boxes containing different types of information. There may be short case studies telling you about a real-life application; there may also be other interesting facts, instructions or examples. Each topic will also have tasks or activities that you should carry out to reinforce what you have learnt, to find out more about it or to apply it. You may be able to use some of these tasks as part of the portfolio that you will have to produce for assessment.

Towards the end of the book, on pages 246 to 247, there is a detailed case study of an organisation. You can use this to carry out some of the tasks or to help you produce your portfolio if you are unable to visit organisations to gain first-hand information.

There are four main awarding bodies offering the GCSE in Applied Information and Communication Technology. You will need to produce a portfolio, which your teacher will assess, this will then be checked by the awarding body. There will also be some assessment that is set and marked by the awarding body. Your teacher will tell you which awarding body's qualification you are taking and how it will be assessed.

The way that the three main areas of study, listed above, are labelled will also depend on the awarding body.

1 ICT tools and applications

Contents

Organisations use ICT for many different tasks, which you will learn about later in this book. ICT provides organisations with a range of tools and applications that enable these tasks to be carried out. In this section you will learn about these ICT tools and applications so that you can understand how they meet organisations' needs. What you learn in this section will help you to understand how ICT is used by organisations and its effect on everyday life.

Many of the applications may be familiar to you – you will almost certainly have used word processing software, for example – but you will probably only have used them for your own purposes. You need to make sure that you can use all the tools and facilities of the software described in the following pages. You will also learn what needs are met by particular applications software and when to use the tools and facilities offered.

Nearly all organisations use word processing software to produce letters, reports and other documents. The marketing departments in some organisations may use publications and presentation software to produce publicity materials. Finance departments use spreadsheet software to predict future cash flow. Libraries use database software to keep records of books and members, and track the location of books. For example, some organisations may use multimedia software to produce interactive training materials. Most organisations will communicate using email, both within the organisation and externally, and many will use the Internet both to locate information they need and to provide information on the organisation's website.

ICT is used all the time in our everyday lives. Below, a surgeon performs surgery using equipment operated by voice commands.

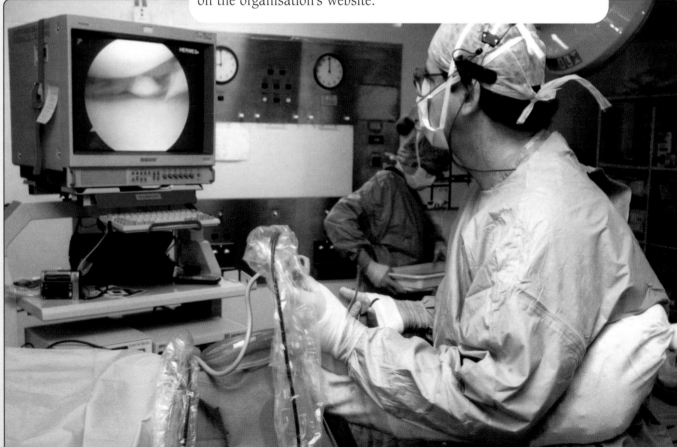

Some organisations use specific applications to meet their particular needs. A graphic design company or a television production company may use software that allows graphic images to be captured, manipulated and enhanced. A manufacturing company may use applications such as **CAD/CAM (computer aided design/computer aided manufacture)** to automate and control the production process. The National Weather Centre uses applications to monitor and record physical and environmental data that can be analysed and interpreted so that an accurate weather forecast can be given.

As well as learning about these applications and how they meet organisations' needs, you will consider the different types of documents that organisations use to communicate information. You will learn about the factors that contribute to the effectiveness of these documents and how to produce your own business documents.

Finally in this section you will learn about the standard ways of working when using ICT so that you can keep yourself and your work safe.

Word check

CAD/CAM (computer aided design/computer aided manufacture) – a system that uses a computer package to design an item. The output from the design package is linked directly to control the machinery that produces the item.

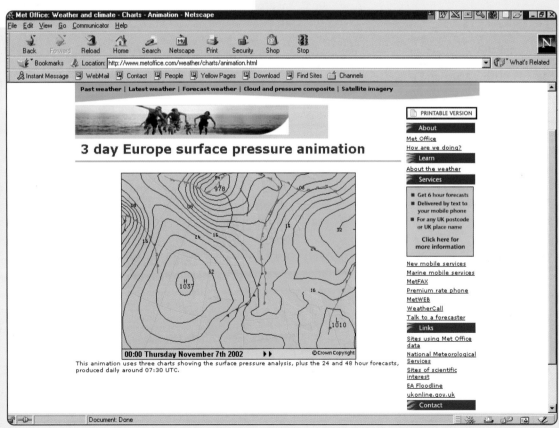

The Meteorological Office website, www.metoffice.com, shows you weather forecasts for around the world.

Presentation of information: using word processing software (1)

By the end of this topic you will be able to:

- enter, cut, copy, paste and move text
- format text – justify and change font or size attributes

Office applications

Word processing software is the most frequently used of all the main types of 'office' application. It is used to create a wide range of business documents such as letters, questionnaires, worksheets, memos, reports and **CV**s.

Text is usually entered letter by letter using the keyboard. However, text can also be imported from other sources such as web pages or scanned documents.

Keys with special functions

When entering text using the keyboard there are a number of keys that have special functions.

Key	What it does	When to use it
Shift	Capital letter or upper symbol on some keys, e.g. >	Single capital letters and always for symbols
Caps Lock	Capital letters	Whole words in capitals
Tab	Lines up text vertically	E.g. when typing a list
Enter	Moves cursor down a line	To start a new paragraph
Backspace	Deletes to the left of the cursor	To edit text as you enter it
Insert	Switches on overtype mode	To replace a section of text
Delete	Deletes to the right of the cursor	To edit text after it has been entered
Home	Moves cursor to the beginning of a line	To insert something at the start of a line
End	Moves cursor to the end of a line	To continue typing after editing

The Page Up, Page Down and arrow keys allow you to move the cursor while editing. It may seem easier to use the mouse to position the cursor but using the keyboard is often quicker as you do not need to move your hand from the keyboard to the mouse and back.

Did you know ...

Using the shift key with the arrow keys allows you to select a block of text rather than **dragging** the mouse pointer over it.

Moving text

Once text is entered it can be processed very easily. A section of text can be selected and then **cut** to remove it. Cutting text is not the same as deleting it because the cut text can be pasted in a new position. Text can also be **copied** and pasted elsewhere. This leaves the text in its original position as well as copied somewhere else. When text is cut or copied it is held in a temporary storage area called the **clipboard**.

When you cut and paste text you move it from one position to another. This can also be achieved by dragging the selected text to its new position using the mouse.

Presentation of information: using word processing software (1)

The main advantage of word processors compared to typewriters is that text can be entered and then edited to create the effect desired.

They also provide spelling and grammar checkers to help make your work accurate although it is still important to proof-read.

There are many different effects and changes that can be made.

It is important not to use too many effects in any document – it should be kept simple for most impact.

Fully justified

Left aligned

Centre aligned

Right aligned

The various forms of alignment.

Formatting text

As well as moving text around it can be formatted, which includes changing the font style, size and/or attributes (**bold**, *italic*, <u>underline</u>) of all or part of the document. It is important that the font you choose is appropriate to the purpose of the document. A decorative style such as this may be suitable for an invitation but not for a business letter. A large font size may be suitable for a notice that needs to be read from a distance but not for a business report. Emboldening text for emphasis is effective if used sparingly but **loses its effect if too much text is emboldened**.

Formatting can also determine how the text is aligned or justified. Text can be left, right or centre aligned, or fully justified which is where all the lines of a paragraph are the same length and wider spaces are automatically placed in between words to stretch out the text.

Word check

CV – short for curriculum vitae. This is a document that summarises a person's educational qualifications and employment experience. It is used when applying for a job.

Dragging – moving the mouse while holding down the left mouse button. This is used to select an area or to move an object on the screen.

TASKS

1. Make sure you can use the tools and facilities described above using the word processing software available to you.

2. Collect a range of business documents and list the formatting features used in each one. Are they appropriate and effective?

3. Use word processing software to produce a letter. Enter, edit and format the text to give the letter impact.

Presentation of information: using word processing software (2)

Inserting images in a document

'A picture paints a thousand words' – one advantage of modern word processing software is the ability to include graphic images. This may be a piece of ClipArt, a graph or chart imported from a spreadsheet package, an image created in painting or drawing software or one captured using a scanner or digital camera. Microsoft® *Word*, for example, even has its own drawing tools that you can use to create an image.

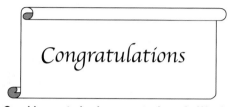

Graphic created using an autoshape in *Word*.

Before including an image you must make sure that it is appropriate to do so and that it helps to get the message across.

Wrapping text

When combining text and graphics a number of wrapping options are available. These can allow the text to wrap around the graphic in various ways, separate the text from the graphic or allow them to overlap.

Tables

Another way of making information easier to understand is to put it in a table. The table below is part of an **itinerary**.

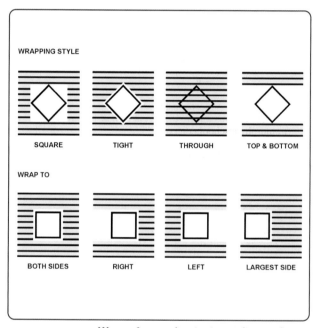

Ways of wrapping text are shown above.

Flight no.	Day	Date	From	To	Depart	Arrive
QF002	Sat.	07 Dec.	London (Heathrow)	Sydney	22:00	06:30 2 days later
QF449	Fri.	13 Dec.	Sydney	Melbourne	16:30	17:50
QF612	Sat.	21 Dec.	Melbourne	Brisbane	08:05	09:10
QF637	Sat.	28 Dec.	Brisbane	Melbourne	17:45	21:00
QF387	Tue.	07 Jan.	Melbourne	London (Heathrow)	17:45	05:55 1 day later

Bullets

When you want to include a list of points in a document you can use bullets, like the list at the start of each topic in this book. When the points have a particular order, or you want to be able to refer to each point, you can use numbered bullets, like the tasks at the end of this topic.

Presentation of information: using word processing software (2)

Headers and footers

Headers and footers are usually used in documents that have more than one page. A header is one or more lines of text that appears at the top of each page of a document. A footer is usually at the bottom of each page.

By using special symbols in the header and/or footer, changing values such as page numbers, date or time, can be used. For example, in a 12-page report the use of the page number symbol (usually #) will ensure that the correct number is printed on each page. It is also useful to include the filename in the footer of a document, especially if it is a standard letter or form that will be used again.

Word check

Itinerary – details of the stages of a journey.

Page 1 of 2 Bring and buy sale — Header showing page numbers in document and title of document

The school bring and buy sale will this year be held on 25 June at 10:30 am, in order to help raise funds for new equipment in the chemistry laboratory.

Volunteers are required to run the stalls and I would be grateful if you could let me know either in person or by email (m.murphy@school.edu.com) if you would be available to help.

We require the following types of goods to sell on the stalls:

• Antiques
• Books
• Bric-a-brac
• Computer games
• Home-made cakes and pastries
• Old school uniforms (clean and in good condition)
• Ornaments
• Models
• Records, music cassettes and DVDs
• Toys
• Videos

Bullet points assist in drawing the reader's attention to important information and make the document easy to read

Please bring your goods for the bring and buy sale to the gym on the day before the sale (24 June), or on the day itself.

The following page shows future fundraising events.

Footer showing who created the document and when, also the filename

Created by Mary Murphy on 25/05/03 12:18PM Fundraising.doc

TASKS

1 Find out how to include graphics and tables and how to use bullets, headers and footers in the word processing software available to you.

2 Collect a range of business documents that include graphics, tables, bullets, headers and footers. Describe what these features are used for and whether they make the document easier to understand.

3 Produce a page for a travel brochure. Include a picture or a graph (for example of temperatures), a table and a bulleted list. Include your name and the filename in the footer.

Presentation of information: using word processing software (3)

By the end of this topic
you will be able to:

- use mail merge facilities

Mail merge

Many organisations need to send out similar letters to a number of people. The **recipients** of these letters are more likely to take notice of the content if the letter is addressed to the recipient personally. Mail merge facilities allow you to produce a standard letter and print it out with different names, addresses and other details. These details may come from an existing database or a table of data may be set up for the purpose. You will learn about databases later in this section. Here we will look at how to create a mail merge document using a table of data. The software will probably have a mail merge helper to guide you through the process.

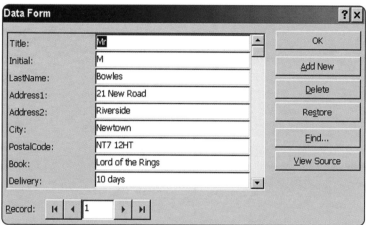

Entering variable data in a data form.

Table of data

The table of data will contain the items of information that will change in each document. These are called fields. Each field must have a name called the fieldname. These are entered in the document where you want the item to appear.

The first stage is to enter the text of the standard letter. You then need to select or create the data source for the variable data to be included. To create a data table you set up the fieldnames you need to include and then enter the data.

Next you need to insert the fields into your standard letter. The fieldnames are usually shown with « » around them.

The Book Place
Wood Lane
Anytown
AN1 6GH

7 December, 2002

«Title» «Initial» «LastName»
«Address1»
«Address2»
«City»
«PostalCode»

Dear «Title» «LastName»

Thank you for your order for «Book». Unfortunately, this book is out of stock at the moment. We are expecting a delivery in «Delivery». Rest assured we will send your copy to you as soon as the new stock arrives.

Yours sincerely

Jack Dawes
Manager

Presentation of information: using word processing software (3)

The final stage is to merge the two files. You can either merge to a new file or directly to the printer. Merging to a file means that you can check that everything is correct before you print, but this may be impractical if the data file has a large number of **records**.

Word check

Recipient – the person who will receive a letter or other communication.

Record – one complete set of fields, in other words one row in a data table or all the variable data for one letter.

> The Book Place
> Wood Lane
> Anytown
> AN1 6GH
>
> 7 December, 2002
>
> Mr M Bowles
> 21 New Road
> Riverside
> Newtown
> NT7 12HT
>
> Dear Mr Bowles
>
> Thank you for your order for Lord of the Rings. Unfortunately, this book is out of stock at the moment. We are expecting a delivery in 10 days. Rest assured we will send your copy to you as soon as the new stock arrives.
>
> Yours sincerely
>
>
> Jack Dawes
> Manager

Mail merge facilities can also be used to produce address labels or for any other document where only certain items change.

TASKS

1. Create a standard letter to inform parents of the grade achieved by their child in ICT. As well as the parents' names and address you will need to include fields for the child's name and their grade. Create a data table and enter data for some of your classmates. Merge the files and print out the personalised letters.

2. Keep a record of all the personalised 'junk' mail received at your home in a week.

3. In a group, discuss and draw up a list of other purposes for which mail merge facilities could be used.

Did you know ...

Direct marketing companies use mail merge facilities to send out advertising material addressed to individuals. They buy lists of names and addresses of people who meet particular criteria, which are supplied in electronic form and can be merged directly with standard documents. This targeted advertising is more effective than material that is not addressed to an individual.

Presentation of information: using publications software

Desktop publishing

Publications software is often called 'desktop publishing' (DTP). The main purpose of DTP is to create professional looking page layouts, combining text and graphics. Although modern word processor applications now have very similar features to DTP, page layout is more easily changed in DTP software.

DTP software is usually **frame-based**. This means that pages are built up as a series of frames – each frame containing one type of data – for example, text, photo, drawing, WordArt. These frames can be accurately positioned using **rulers** and **layout guides**.

Creating text and graphics

Text and simple graphics can sometimes be created within the DTP application. However, it is usually best to create the page content in software more suited to the purpose. For example, a line drawing may be created in a CAD program and then imported into the DTP application. The text should be created in a word processing package, which often offers more text editing features, before being imported into a text frame.

Care is needed when importing graphics to ensure that the frame has the same proportions as the graphic you want to import. If they do not match the graphic will be distorted.

When a multi-page document is to be produced it is important that there is a consistent page layout. This is achieved by creating a master page. The margins, column and other layout guides are set on the master page so that objects can be positioned consistently on all the pages.

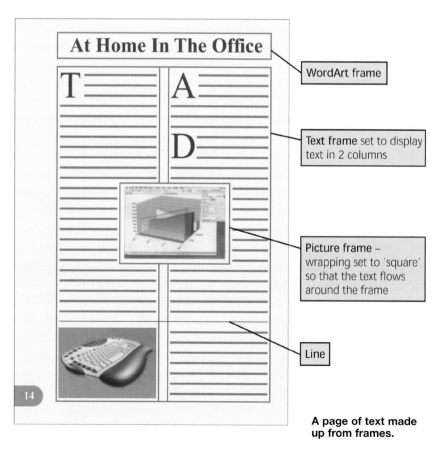

A page of text made up from frames.

Presentation of information: using publications software

Layout

The first step to creating a good published document is to plan the layout of the pages. You will need to consider things like the balance of text and graphics and the position of a graphic relative to the text it relates to. Other considerations will be covered in more detail in the section on developing business documents later in this book.

Producing documents in-house

DTP software is often used by organisations to produce documents 'in-house' that they would previously have had to pay a specialist publisher to produce. Such documents include brochures, newsletters, advertising flyers and even magazines. Newspaper and magazine publishers use this type of software to lay out the pages of their products. The layout of the pages in this book will also have been created using DTP software.

A balanced page (left) and an unbalanced page (right)

TASKS

1. Collect some brochures, catalogues and magazines. In a group, discuss the layout features of each one. Decide which layout works best and which do not work as well.

2. Create a two-page newsletter for your school, college or club using publications software.

3. Create a similar newsletter using word processing software. Which was the easiest to use in order to create a professional looking document? Why?

Presentation of information: using presentation software (1)

Creating presentations

Presentation software is often used to illustrate a talk or to communicate information to people. The presentation can be designed to be shown to an audience on a large screen, as a continuously running presentation in a public place such as a post office, or as an interactive presentation for a single viewer. This type of software can also be used to create and print a set of overhead transparencies that can be used with an overhead projector (OHP) when access to computer equipment is not possible.

Modern presentation software allows sound and video clips to be included in presentations along with buttons and **hotspots** to move between slides creating multimedia presentations. This will be covered in the topics on using multimedia software.

All presentations are made up of slides. Most presentation software provides a range of 'themes' or design templates that can be used on all the slides. This will determine the background style and colour, the text style, size and colour of headings, sub-headings and various levels of body text and the style and indentation of bullets. You can adapt these themes to suit your presentation or create your own theme from scratch.

Master slides

The theme should be applied to a master slide. This will ensure that all slides in the presentation have a consistent appearance. The master slide can also include any information such as the date, a footer or the slide number that you want to appear on every slide – just like the header and footer described in the topic on word processing software.

Click to edit Master title style
Title Area for AutoLayouts

- Click to edit Master text styles
  - Second level
    - Third level
      - Fourth level
        - Fifth level

Object Area for AutoLayouts

‹date/time›
Date Area

‹footer›
Footer Area

‹#›
Number Area

A master slide ensures that all the slides are consistent.

Presentation of information: using presentation software (1)

Presentations are used to illustrate talks.

Rules

1. Try not to mix typefaces – maximum three per slide.

2. Use dark backgrounds for on-screen presentations with contrasting text colours.

3. Use light backgrounds (or none) for OHP slides.

4. Use short bullet-point type sentences for ease of reading.

5. Avoid complicated text: explanation should be given by the presenter, or through clear on-screen explanations.

6. Use ClipArt sparingly – it detracts from the message you are trying to convey.

The use of frames

Like DTP software, presentation software often uses frames to position the different elements. As well as text, these frames can include pictures, charts or graphs, tables and **organisation charts**. These can be imported from other packages or created in the presentation software. Unlike DTP software, text is usually typed directly into the presentation software. This is because the amount of text is limited and usually consists of a bulleted list. These bullets should simply highlight the main points of the presentation, especially when it is being used to illustrate a talk. The software can then be used to produce and print out more detailed notes for the speaker.

As well as notes for the speaker, the slides can be printed out as handouts for the audience. These usually have three or six slides on a page.

Word check

Hotspot – an area on a screen display that responds to a mouse click. This may be a piece of text or a graphic which will take the user to another page or screen.

Organisation chart – a diagram of the management structure of an organisation.

TASKS

1. Find out what themes or design templates are available in the presentation software available to you. Find out how to set up a master slide.

2. Design and create a short presentation to illustrate a talk on the different types of software used to present information, the differences between them and for what tasks each type of software is best suited.

3. Produce a short report detailing an investigation into how businesses use presentation software. Include your name and the filename in the footer.

Presentation of information: using presentation software (2)

By the end of this topic you will be able to:

- edit a presentation

- apply transition, timing and animation effects

In the last topic you learnt how a consistent and professional looking presentation can be created using the inbuilt themes, or design templates, provided by the software and by the use of a master slide. As with any other software used to present information, it is possible to edit your presentation to improve it.

Editing presentations

Many of the same facilities for editing are available in presentation software that are used in word processing software. It is possible to insert, delete, cut, copy, paste and move the text or graphics, just as you would do in a word processed document. As well as this you can resize or move frames to reposition objects. You need to be careful when doing this, however, as you may spoil the consistency of your presentation.

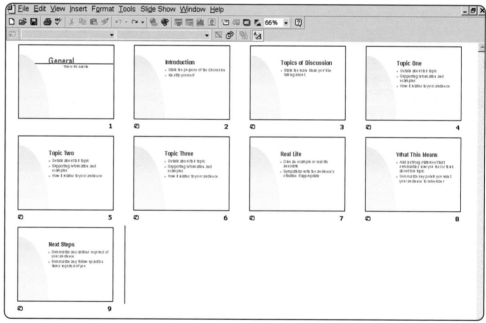

Slide sorter view

Slide order

The main editing feature available in presentation software that is not available in word processing software is the ability to change the order of the slides. Presentation software usually has a number of different views in which the slides are presented on the computer screen. Individual slides are usually created and edited in slide view, with one slide shown filling most of the screen. Another view is slide sorter view. This shows a **thumbnail** of all the slides in order, along with any transition timings and effects (see later). In this view it is possible to drag a slide from one position to another with the mouse.

Timing the presentation

Presentation software can be set up so that a mouse or keyboard click is required to move on to the next slide or the software can be set to move on automatically after a specific time. When the presentation is to be used to illustrate a talk, careful rehearsal is needed to make sure the presentation keeps pace with the presenter and vice versa. An unattended presentation that loops through a series of slides must have timings set that give sufficient time for people to read each screen.

Presentation of information: using presentation software (2)

Transition and animation effects

Other facilities are available to make the presentation more interesting to watch. Different transition effects can be applied. This is the way that the software moves from one screen to the next. Effects such as 'dissolve' and 'fade through black' can be used.

It is also possible to control the way that objects appear on screen. Often when giving a presentation, the presenter wants to address one point at a time. When using slides on an overhead projector, this usually means that part of the slide has to be covered so that each point can be revealed as required. With an on-screen presentation, each point can be made to appear when it is needed by clicking. Also, different animation effects can change the way that the text appears. Lines of text can be made to 'crawl in from right' or 'fly in from top', for example.

Word check

Thumbnail – a greatly reduced copy of an image that allows many images to be fitted on a single screen so that they can be quickly previewed and selected.

Applied ICT
- Presentation software
- Spreadsheets

Applied ICT
- Presentation software
- Spreadsheets
- Databases
- Multimedia
- The Internet
- The world wide web
- Business documents

One point at a time can fly onto the screen, so that each may be separately addressed (left). The screen showing all the points is on the right.

TASKS

1. Find out how to edit a presentation and how to apply timing, transition and animation effects in the software available to you.

2. Edit the presentation you produced in the previous topic to improve it. Add timing, transition and animation effects to the presentation. Don't forget to rehearse the presentation so that the timings match the pace of your talk.

3. Produce a presentation about the Applied ICT GCSE course that could be left to run automatically, using automatic timing, on a school open evening. Don't forget to make sure people have enough time to read each slide.

Spreadsheets (1) – entering data

A spreadsheet is a type of program that can process numbers in a structured and efficient way. A user enters data into different parts of the spreadsheet – called cells. Calculations can then be performed by using formulae and functions. The spreadsheet program can be used to search for particular items of data and to sort the data into order. This type of software can also be used to create graphs and charts that help the user understand the data.

Entering data

Data is entered into cells which are organised into columns and rows. This grid is called a **worksheet**. Each cell has an address which consists of the column letter followed by the row number. So the cell shown below in green is cell B4.

Columns

	A	B	C	D
1				
2				
3				
4				
5				
6				
7				
8				

Rows

A worksheet with cell B4 highlighted in green.

Types of data

There are basically three types of data that can be used in a spreadsheet – number, text and formulae. Each cell must only contain one type of data. If the user enters numbers and text into one cell the spreadsheet software will treat it all as text.

Number data

Number data can include date, time and currency. Each item of data is converted to and stored as a number, but the cell(s) can be set to display the data in the format required. For example, 17th December 2003 is stored as a number (37972) but can be displayed in many different data formats such as: 17/12/03; 17-Dec-03; December 17, 2003, and so on.

Examples of number data		
174.325	numbers	the user can set the number of decimal places to be displayed
£211.20	currency	can be displayed without pence
17.6%	percentages	can be displayed without decimal point
14/07/2003	date	can be any other acceptable date format
16:25; 4:25:00 pm	time	can be any other acceptable time format

Text data

Text data may be product descriptions, names, colours or any other variable data as well as titles, headings and labels for columns and rows, which help to make the data easier to understand and use. Cells that include text data cannot normally be used in formulae. They can, however, be searched for and used to sort the data into alphabetical order.

Spreadsheets (1) – entering data

Formulae

Cells can display the results of automatic calculations. The user enters a formula in the cell and the cell displays the result of the calculation. Even if the numbers are changed the formula cells will always display the result correctly. Modern spreadsheet software provides a wide range of inbuilt formulae – functions – to perform many different types of calculation. Probably the most useful is the SUM function which will add up a column or row of data.

Examples of formulae

=B3+C3+D3 (addition)

=B3-B2 (subtraction)

=B3*B2 (multiplication)

=B3/B2 (division)

=SUM(B3:D3) (using the SUM function)

=AVERAGE(B3:B8) (using the AVERAGE function)

CASE STUDY

Deepak Patel has decided to set up his own company to service computers. He needs a loan from the bank to buy equipment and to rent a workshop. He must convince the bank manager that his business will make money so that he can pay back the loan. To do this he must produce a business plan. This business plan will include a cashflow forecast and a projected profit and loss account, showing the money he expects to pay out each month and the money he expects to receive. The projected profit and loss account shows the **profit** (or loss) that Deepak expects to make after a certain period. Deepak creates both of these documents using spreadsheet software. By doing this Deepak can change the figures to see what will happen if he finds cheaper premises or if he increases his charges.

TASKS

1 Find out how spreadsheets are used in your school or college.

2 Create a simple spreadsheet to show what money you receive and what you spend in a typical week. Put the amount you receive from different sources in different rows, such as pocket money and part-time job. Don't forget to add row labels. Enter a formula to find the total money you receive. Then put the amount you spend on different things in different rows – such as sweets, CDs or magazines. Enter a formula to find the total amount you spend. Finally enter a formula to calculate how much money you have left at the end of the week – if any.

Word check

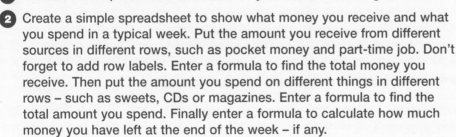

Profit – the money a business makes after all expenses have been paid.

Spreadsheets (2) – editing the spreadsheet

By the end of this topic you will be able to:

- cut, copy, paste and move data between cells, columns and rows
- insert and delete rows and columns

Worksheets and workbooks

In the last topic you learned that data is entered into a grid of cells called a worksheet. Modern spreadsheet software allows you to create a number of linked worksheets. These linked worksheets are known as a workbook. For example, the sales figures for four different salespeople in a company could be kept on separate worksheets. These could then be summarised on a fifth worksheet to show the overall sales for the company; a further worksheet could show these figures in a chart. All six worksheets would be saved as a workbook in the same file. You can move from one worksheet to another in a workbook by clicking on the appropriate **tab**.

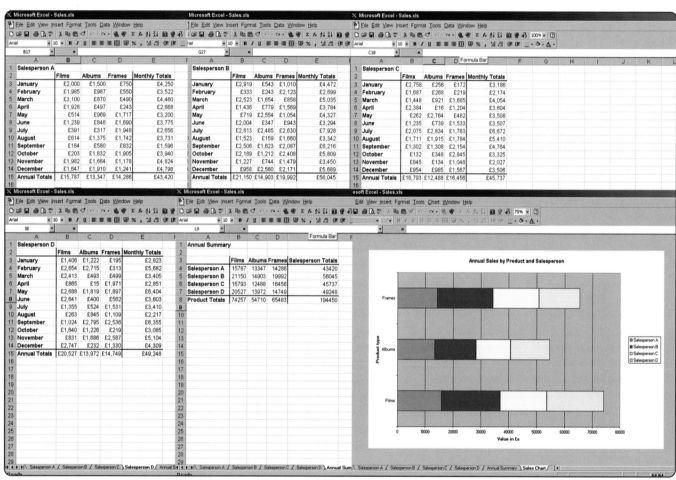

A workbook composed of six separate worksheets.

Spreadsheets (2) – editing the spreadsheet

Copying and pasting data between cells, rows and columns

You can select a single cell or a group of cells – called a range. You can then copy these cells and paste them to another cell or cells on the same worksheet or to another worksheet in the same workbook. They can even be pasted into a different workbook or other type of document such as a word-processed report. One very useful feature is where the cell or cells are pasted as a link into the other workbook or document. Whenever a change is made to the original data, the new result will be displayed automatically in the document that has been linked.

When designing a spreadsheet it is a good idea to plan the design first on paper, so that all the necessary columns and rows can be included. The spreadsheet should be given a title and each column should be given a heading so that its contents can be easily recognised. Labels should also be used for rows where they help to make the meaning clearer.

Inserting and deleting columns and rows

However well you design the spreadsheet, you may need to add further columns or rows after the spreadsheet data has been entered. Most spreadsheet applications make the inserting and deleting of rows and columns simple. To insert a row, just select the row immediately below the position of the new row and insert a complete row. Inserting columns is similar – select the column immediately after the position of the new column and insert the new column. You can insert more than one row or column by selecting that number of rows/columns before inserting. To delete a row or column simply select it and use the 'delete column' or 'delete row' command in the Edit menu.

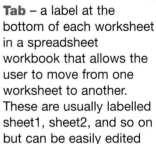

A new row will be inserted above row 6.

Spreadsheets (3) – working with formulae

Entering a formula

In the example shown below the user should first enter a formula in cell D3 that will subtract the cost price of Mars from the selling price to give the profit margin. This formula must begin with an '=' sign so that the spreadsheet software will know that the result should be displayed after the calculation has been carried out. In this case the formula entered in cell D3 will be '=C3–B3' and the result '12' will be displayed in cell D3.

	A	B	C	D	E	F
1	Shop sales – Week beginning 22/09/03					
2		Cost price	Selling price	Profit margin	Number sold	Profit
3	Mars	35	47		437	
4	Twix	35	48		602	
5	Kit Kat	40	52		32	
6	Dairy Milk	45	55		868	
7	Polos	25	32		225	
8	Starbursts	30	35		415	
9					Total profit	
10						

Shop sales spreadsheet

Replicating a formula

Instead of keying in a formula for each of the other products, it is much more efficient and accurate to **replicate** the formula down the column. There is usually a 'fill' command for this. Many spreadsheet applications have shortcut methods to replicate formulae. Microsoft® *Excel* displays a small black button in the bottom right-hand corner of the selected cell – you drag this button down the column and the formula is copied. In the example, the formula in each row will be slightly different – in cell D4, for example, the formula will look like: =C4–B4 – the cell addresses in the formula will have the same column letter but a different row number. The spreadsheet application has used relative cell references to correctly replicate the formula in each cell. You will learn more about cell references in a later topic.

TASK

❶ What formula is needed in F3 to calculate the profit? (This is the number sold multiplied by the profit margin.) Key in the information from the above spreadsheet into your spreadsheet software and enter and replicate the formulae to display the totals as shown in Number sold and Total profit.

Spreadsheets (3) – working with formulae

Using functions

The spreadsheet's built-in functions were mentioned in Spreadsheets (1).

In our example, the formula in cell F9 would be =SUM(F3:F8). This tells the spreadsheet software to add together all the cells in the range F3 to F8. The SUM function is much better to use than a formula that adds together all the individual cells, especially when there are a lot of cells to add.

TASK

2 Enter the SUM function in your spreadsheet in cell F9. What is the total profit for the week?

There are many other very useful functions built in to all spreadsheet software. Many involve highly specialised calculations – but these are always done automatically by the spreadsheet software.

'What if' query

One of the most useful features of spreadsheet software is the ability to recalculate automatically when a change is made to the data. The user can enter or edit the data and look immediately to see the effect of the change. There is no need to start again each time – once the hard work of setting up the spreadsheet has been done it can be used over and over again! For example, the weekly shop sales spreadsheet shown above can be used every week – the formulae will always calculate the results using the new data entered. If a change has to be made to a price all the calculations will be updated automatically and the new results displayed.

TASK

3 The cost price of Mars has gone up by 2p. The shopkeeper does not want to pass this increase on to the customers. Use your spreadsheet to find out how many more Mars would have to be sold to make a similar profit.

Some of the types of sweets sold in your shop.

Spreadsheets (4) – charts and graphs

- create charts and graphs

- select an appropriate chart or graph to display data

- correctly label a chart or graph

A well designed chart or graph is an excellent way to present information in a visual format – it can tell the reader at a glance what you want them to know about your data. Creating a chart or graph is a task which can be readily carried out by all spreadsheet applications, although careful thought is needed about what you want the graph to show.

	A	B	C	D
9				
10			Number Sold	
11		Mars	437	
12		Twix	602	
13		Kit Kat	32	
14		Dairy Milk	868	
15		Polos	225	
16		Starbursts	415	
17				
18				
19			Profit	
20		Mars	£52.44	
21		Twix	£78.26	
22		Kit Kat	£3.84	
23		Dairy Milk	£86.80	
24		Polos	£15.75	
25		Starbursts	£20.75	
26				
27				

Spreadsheet showing the number of sweets sold and the profit made.

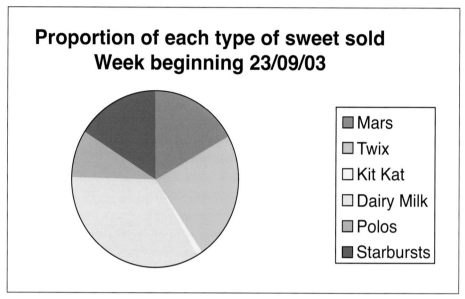

Pie chart created by the spreadsheet application.

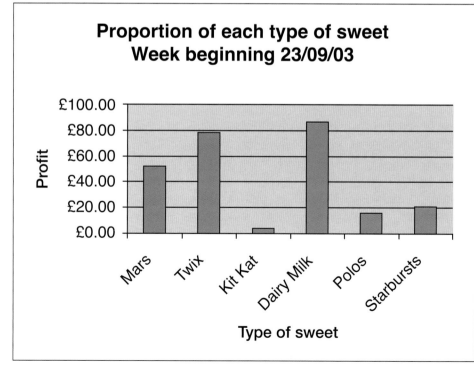

A column, or bar, chart created by the spreadsheet application.

Pie charts and column charts

The two charts shown have been produced from the shop sales spreadsheet you met in Spreadsheets (3). The first one is a pie chart. This shows the proportion of each type of sweet sold during the week. It is not possible to tell from this type of chart the actual number sold in each case. The column (or bar) chart, on the other hand, allows the viewer to get an idea of the actual values. It shows the actual profit made from each type of sweet during the week.

Spreadsheets (4) – charts and graphs

When creating a chart you need to be careful what you select. In the example, the row labels have been selected so that they appear on the chart, but not the column heading. It is sometimes helpful to copy and paste the data to a blank part of the spreadsheet so that the data you need to use is in columns (or rows) next to each other as shown. However, if the values are produced by a formula – like the Profit column on the facing page – you will need to make sure that you paste the values, not the formula.

Labels, legends and keys

It is very important that charts are properly labelled and have a title that states clearly what the chart shows. Pie charts must have a **legend** or **key** to tell the viewer what each segment represents. Column or bar charts and line graphs need **axis labels** – Profit and Type of sweet in the example. Some spreadsheet software may automatically insert a legend. This is not needed when there is only one series (column or row) of data and should be deleted.

Charts, other than pie charts, can be produced using more than one row or column of data. The example opposite shows the breakdown of annual sales for a company by product and salesperson. In this example, both the column headings and row labels have been selected, but not the row or column containing the totals. You can choose whether the rows or columns are plotted on the axis. The same data could be plotted with a bar for each salesperson, with sections of the bar representing the different products. A legend is essential for this type of chart.

Choosing the appropriate format

You must take care when deciding what type of chart or graph is most suitable for the data you want to display. If your graph is to be printed in black and white you may need to use patterns rather than colours for the different segments.

	A	B	C	D	E	F
1	Annual Summary					
2						
3		Films	Albums	Frames	Salesperson Totals	
4	Salesperson A	15787	13347	14286	43420	
5	Salesperson B	21150	14903	19992	56045	
6	Salesperson C	16793	12488	16456	45737	
7	Salesperson D	20527	13972	14749	49248	
8	Product Totals	74257	54710	65483	194450	
9						

Row labels are selected on this spreadsheet so that they appear on the chart.

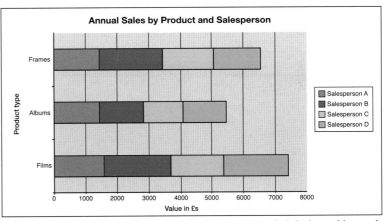

A column chart showing axis labels and legend.

TASKS

1. Find out how to produce the charts shown above for the shop sales spreadsheet in your spreadsheet software. Try other types of charts or graphs. Decide which type produces the best representation of the data.

2. Create three more worksheets and enter sales data for the following three weeks. Some of the sales will go up and some will go down over the three weeks. Alter the data according to you and your friends' favourite sweets. Produce a summary sheet showing the profit for each type of sweet for each week. Calculate the total profit for each sweet and the total profit for each week. Produce a chart to show the profit made on each sweet in each week.

Spreadsheets (5) – cell referencing and printing

By the end of this topic you will be able to:

- use relative and absolute cell referencing

- print selected areas of a spreadsheet

Relative and absolute cell references

In Spreadsheets (3) you learnt that when a formula is replicated, the cell addresses in the formula usually change to match the row or column. This is called a relative cell reference. Most formulae use relative cell references.

Sometimes you need to always use the same cell in a formula regardless of which row or column the formula is in.

In the example below, showing the **sales commission** paid to car salespeople, the formula used to calculate the commission for Frain in cell C3 will be '=B3*B10'.

If this formula was replicated down column C the formula in cell C4 would be '=B4*B11'. We want it to be '=B4*B10', as cell B10 contains the data we want to use in all the formulae used in column C.

	A	B	C	D
1	Car sales commission			
2	Salesperson	Car sales	Commission	
3	Frain	£17,600	£211.20	
4	Daley	£24,256	£291.07	
5	Johnson	£48,650	£583.80	
6	Chaudry	£19,284	£231.41	
7	Machin	£59,365	£712.38	
8	Misevic	£15,542	£186.50	
9				
10	Commission	1.20%		
11				

An absolute cell reference has been used in this spreadsheet to calculate commission.

To do this we must use an **absolute cell reference**. To make a cell reference absolute, simply put a $ sign in front of each part of the cell address you want to stay the same (the formula should look like =B4*B10) – then when the formula is replicated it will always keep the cell address as B10. There will usually be a shortcut key – F4 in Microsoft® *Excel* – so you don't need to type in the $ signs.

Absolute cell references make it easy to ask 'what if' questions as you only need to change the value in one cell. For example, to see the effect of a change in the commission rate, only the data in cell B10 needs to be changed.

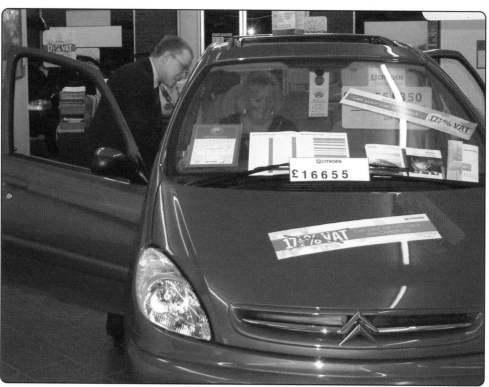

Car salespeople earn commission on the cars they sell.

Spreadsheets (5) – cell referencing and printing

Printing selected areas of the spreadsheet

Many spreadsheets can be very large which may present a problem if you need to print the spreadsheet. There are different ways to overcome this problem.

Always use the print preview facilities where available so that you can check what the spreadsheet will look like when it is printed and adjust it if necessary. Try to avoid having it print on different pages if there is any way to fit it onto one page. Changing the page from **portrait** to **landscape** may help if the spreadsheet is wider than it is deep. Page breaks can also be moved so that they occur in sensible places.

Most spreadsheet applications have an option to scale the whole spreadsheet to fit to one page. However, the printed data may be very small and anyone trying to read it will probably need a magnifying glass.

All spreadsheet applications provide ways to print only certain parts of a spreadsheet. To do this you select the area of the spreadsheet that you want to print and use the 'Set print area' command in the File menu.

When printing a spreadsheet, you can include a suitable title as a header and useful information such as the date, the filename, the page number and your name in the footer, just as you can with word processing software.

Annual Summary

	Films	Albums	Frames	Salesperson Totals
Salesperson A	15787	13347	14286	43420
Salesperson B	21150	14903	19992	56045
Salesperson C	16793	12488	16456	45737
Salesperson D	20527	13972	14749	49248
Product Totals	74257	54710	65483	194450

The Annual Summary spreadsheet prints on to a portrait page (left). If another column is added it must be printed landscape so that it fits on one page (below).

Annual Summary

	Films	Albums	Frames	Salesperson Totals	Salesperson Totals for Previous Year
Salesperson A	15787	13347	14286	43420	42800
Salesperson B	21150	14903	19992	56045	44251
Salesperson C	16793	12488	16456	45737	47328
Salesperson D	20527	13972	14749	49248	55521
Product Totals	74257	54710	65483	194450	189900

TASK

1 Try keying in the example shown on the opposite page, or one similar, and experiment until you get the formula replicated correctly down column C. Think of other examples when an absolute cell reference would be needed.

Databases (1) – types of database

A database is a collection of information organised in such a way that a computer program can quickly select desired pieces of data. It is best to think of a database as an electronic filing system.

There are several types of databases – flat file, relational and hypertext.

Flat file database

This is a relatively simple database system in which the data is contained in a single table. An example of a flat file database is an address book stored on a computer. Names and addresses can be entered, together with telephone numbers. These are stored in a single table.

Firstname	Lastname	Address	Telephone
John	Smith	12 New Road, Anytown	01234 567890
Mohammed	Ahmed	25 Old Road, Newtown	01345 123456
Lee	Chan	13 Station Road, Anytown	01234 987654

Computer databases have now replaced the card index system for sorting information, as shown in this picture of a library.

Databases (1) – types of database

Relational database systems

This type of database can use several tables to store information, and each table usually has a different **record structure**. They are widely used in business and commerce. For example, a public library may use a database system with multiple tables to store information about members, books, videos, tapes, loans and so on. The loans table will be linked to the other tables so that when a member borrows a book, all their details and the details of the book do not need to be entered again. The membership number links to the member's record in the Members table and the book's ID number links to the book's record in the Books table.

Members table	Loans table	Books table
Membership number	Loan number	Book ID number
First name	Membership number	Title
Last name	Book ID number	Author
Address	Date borrowed	ISBN
Telephone number	Return date	Category
Date of birth	Returned?	Subject
	Overdue fine	

Hypertext database

This is a special type of database system in which objects (text, pictures, music, programs, and so on) can be linked to each other. When you select an object, you can see the other objects that are linked to it. It is very easy to move between one object and another even though they might be very different types of object. For example, in a CD-ROM article about the piano, hypertext links (the icons that you select to view linked objects) can be included which will open photographs of different types of pianos or play piano pieces to illustrate how they sound.

Did you know ...

What is the difference between data and information?

Data is factual information. Data on its own has no meaning, but becomes information when it is put into context.

Information is a collection of facts or data.

For example: '37' is data whilst 'Chocolate bar 37p' is information.

TASK

 In a group think about and research the different tasks that databases could be used for. Decide whether a flat file, a relational, or a hypertext database would be needed in each case. Present your results in a table.

Databases (2) – structure of databases

Databases are organised by **fields**, records and **files**. A field is a single piece of information; a record is one complete set of fields, and a file is a collection of records. For example, you can think of a telephone book as an example of a file. The telephone book contains a list of records (one for each person or company that subscribes to the phone service), each of which consists of three fields: name, address and telephone number.

Database structure

Before you can enter data in a database you must set up its structure. Each field must be given a name, called the **fieldname**. In addition, each field must be set to store a certain type of data (see Databases (3)) and have the field length set. This should always be long enough to fit the longest entry likely for the field, for example, a surname field must be set to allow the longest surname possible! One field should hold data that is **unique** to each record. This is called the **primary key**.

Fields can be required, optional or calculated. A **required field** is one where data must be entered by the user. The user will not be able to continue until they have entered a value. An **optional field** is one that may be left blank. Data should not be entered into a **calculated field**; the database system will automatically determine the correct value from the formula entered by the database designer.

If you are designing a relational database you will also have to decide what tables or **entities** are needed and which fields (often called **attributes** in relational databases) belong in each. There are rules for doing this but they are beyond the scope of this book and qualification.

ISBN	Title	Author	Category	Subject
0-571-20987-4	True History of the Kelly Gang	Peter Carey	Non-fiction	Biography
0-571-16833-7	Cabal	Michael Dibden	Fiction	Detective
0-906-21221-9	Kaleidometrics	Sheillah Shaw	Non-fiction	Graphics
0-140-51437-6	The New Penguin Dictionary of Computing	Dick Pountain	Non-fiction	Computing
0-862-00070-0	Learn to Use Websites	Christopher Dillinger	Non-fiction	Computing
0-906-23317-0	Lord of the Rings Reader	Jean McCarthy	Non-fiction	Education
0-140-56372-9	Elementary Physics	Hans Kasper	Non-fiction	Science
0-576-53210-X	Multimedia	Fred de Vries	Non-fiction	Computing

Information in a database is stored in fields.

Databases (2) – structure of databases

The example shown on page 32 is an extract from a database **file** used to store information about books and their categories. Each book has a separate **record** (shown as a row in the table), which is divided into suitable **fields**. The ISBN field is the **primary key** as every book has a unique ISBN.

Once the database structure has been set up you can begin to enter data. This can be entered directly into the table, or you can set up a form to enter the data, as in the Car Dealer example below. This is usually quite easy to do as there are **wizards** available in the software to help you. It is easier to enter data into a form than directly into the table as you only have one record on screen at a time.

Word check

Unique – not the same as any other, in other words the primary key must contain a different value for each record.

Wizard – a set of screens that lead the user through a complex process in a step-by-step way. The user is able to select options on each screen and then move on to the next.

Car Dealer Entry

```
┌─────────────────────────────────────────────────────────┐
│ ▣ Car Dealer Entry                              _ □ ✕    │
├─────────────────────────────────────────────────────────┤
│   Car Dealer Entry                                        │
│   ─────────────────────────────────────────────          │
│ ▶                                                         │
│     NAME            [                    ]                 │
│                                                           │
│     ADDRESS1        [                    ]                 │
│                                                           │
│     ADDRESS2        [                    ]                 │
│                                                           │
│     TOWN            [                    ]                 │
│                                                           │
│     COUNTY          [                    ]                 │
│                                                           │
│     POSTCODE        [                    ]                 │
│                                                           │
│     TELEPHONE       [                    ]                 │
│   ─────────────────────────────────────────────          │
│                                                           │
└─────────────────────────────────────────────────────────┘
```

Form used to enter data

TASKS

1. List the fieldnames, data types and field lengths that may be used in a database of customer details kept by a software supplier.

2. Set up a database structure to store this data.

3. Create a data entry form and enter some suitable records, including your school or college and other organisations that use software.

Databases (3) – data types and validation

By the end of this topic you will be able to:

- understand the different data types

- know the difference between verification and validation

- set up validation rules

Data types

There are different data types that can be used to store the data in a database file. Text (correctly called alphanumeric) data can be used for any mixture of text and numbers – for example, addresses and telephone numbers (see Hint below). Examples of other data types are shown in the table.

Data type	Example
Text/character	Blake; 23, Turnberry Road
Memo	Used for large amounts of text
Number	16.45; 736413
Autonumber	Automatically gives a unique number to each new record created
Logical (Yes/no)	Yes/no; True/false
Currency	£36.28; $125
Date/time	27/05/2003; 14:27; 7.45pm

Hint

Database fields used to store telephone numbers must normally be set to **text** data type. If you set the data type to number, the 0 at the start of the number will NOT be displayed.

A field set to accept one type of data will not accept anything entered that is in the wrong format. For example, an error message is shown if the user tries to enter a name into a field set for currency. This is an example of the database's built-in validation rules (see below).

Validation and verification

Many errors can be avoided by **validating** data as it is entered. To do this a **validation rule** is used for each field. All data entered will be checked to see if it conforms to the rule; if it doesn't, the user will be asked to correct the error and won't be able to continue data entry until it has been fixed.

One form of validation rule is a range check. For example, all the employees in an organisation must work for a minimum of 16 hours but less than 48 hours each week. 'Hours worked' is a field in the organisation's personnel database. The validation rule is:

>=16 AND <48

(greater than or equal to 16 and less than 48). If a figure outside this range is entered an error message will appear.

Databases (3) – data types and validation

Microsoft Access ⊠

ⓘ **The value you entered isn't valid for this field.**

For example, you may have entered text in a numeric field or a number that is larger than the FieldSize setting permits.

[OK]

Validation error message

Another type of **validation** check allows a mask to be applied. This is used when the data must have a particular format, such as a postcode. The mask ensures that only the correct pattern of letters and numbers can be entered. When only a limited number of values will be entered in a field, a rule can be set up so that only these values can be entered.

Verification

Verification simply means checking. Data that has been entered into a database record must be checked by comparing it with the original data. It is possible for data to be validated by the database but still be incorrect. For example, an employee works 32 hours. The value 23 is entered by mistake. This would pass the **validation test** but is clearly wrong. This error could be avoided if the user verified the data entered.

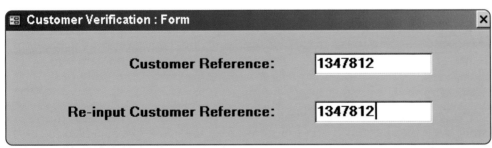

⊞ Customer Verification : Form ⊠

Customer Reference: 1347812

Re-input Customer Reference: 1347812

One way to verify data is to enter it twice. The dialogue here shows stars so that no-one else can read the password.

TASKS

❶ Collect information about products that might be sold by a software supplier. For each product find out the program name, cost, typical client, and any other useful information. You can use computer magazines, catalogues or the Internet to research this information.

❷ Set up a database to store details of the goods sold by a software supplier; using the software programs you collected in Task 1. Make sure that each field has the correct data type. Are there any other fields that are required? Set up a validation rule for at least one of the fields.

❸ Enter the data you found in task 1 into your database. Make sure you verify the data as you enter it.

Databases (4) – sorting, searching and relationships

By the end of this topic you will be able to:

- establish a **relationship** between fields in two tables

- sort data in a table

- search data in both flat file and relational databases

We have mentioned relational databases in both Databases (1) and Databases (2). We will now consider these in more detail. Most databases used in organisations are relational – some of them very complex.

In order to understand how they work we will return to a simplified version of the library database introduced in Databases (1). This database has three tables – members, loans and books.

Members table	Loans table	Books table
O╥ Membership number	O╥ Loan number	O╥ Book ID number
First name	Membership number	Title
Last name	Book ID number	Author
Address	Date borrowed	ISBN
Telephone number	Return date	Category
Date of birth	Returned?	Subject
	Overdue fine	

The diagram shows the fields in each of the three tables. Each table has a **primary key** labelled with a O╥. The Loans table has a field that matches the primary key of the Members table and a field that matches the primary key of the Books table. These are called **foreign keys**. They are the fields that are used to link the tables as shown by the lines. The fieldnames do not have to be the same in both tables but the format of the fields (data type, length) must be. You will need to find out how to link tables in the database software available to you.

It is pointless going to the trouble of setting up a database unless you are going to process the data in some way. This usually involves **sorting** data into alphabetical or numerical order (either **ascending** or **descending**), or **searching** for records that match certain criteria.

You can search on one criterion only or more than one. When searching on more than one criterion you use **logical operators**. You can also use **relational operators**. Some examples of logical and relational operators are shown in the table below.

Examples of operators

A simple search:
Category = Fiction

A complex query:
Return date < today's date
AND Returned? = No

Logical operators	Relational operators
AND	= equal to/is the same as
OR	> greater than/comes after
NOT	< less than/comes before

The way that sorts and searches are carried out will depend on the database software you are using. It may be possible to sort and carry out simple searches on a single table using the tools available in 'table' view. However, for more complex searching of related tables and the ability to present the results as a report, it is usually necessary to initiate a query. You will learn more about creating queries and producing reports in the next topic.

Databases (4) – sorting, searching and relationships

The Video Hire Shop

CASE STUDY

Patels Corner Shop

Video Title   The Matrix III

Date Purchased   10/4/03

Price   £17.95

Date	Customer Name	Amount Paid
12/4/03	Bill D	£2
13/4/03	Jayesh	£2
15/4/03	Angie Smith	£2
17/4/03	Bob?	Will pay later
19/4/03	Sue	£2
22/4/03	Tanya	£1.50
23/4/03	?	£2

Jalpur and Amina Patel own and run a corner shop. Recently Jalpur bought ten videos so that they could be rented to their customers. He decided to create a book with each film on a single page. The name of the person hiring the film, the date, and how much they had paid would be written when someone hired a video. One of the pages is shown here.

This system worked quite well for a few weeks – until Jalpur decided to add 30 new video titles to the collection. This meant a big increase in the amount of data that must be stored and used. They have a computer and decided that they could use this to manage the business.

TASKS

1. Describe how using a relational database could help Jalpur and Amina with their video hire system. Give details of the data that would need to be collected, stored and processed.

2. Plan (first on paper) a relational database with three tables (videos, members and loans). Your plan must state the fieldnames, field lengths, data types, primary keys and clearly show the relationships between the tables.

3. Create the database system using suitable software.

4. Check that your database system is working correctly by entering data. You must enter at least 40 video titles. In addition, you must enter at least 40 'customer records'.

5. Run your database system over a period of (an imaginary) week. Loan videos to members; make sure that some videos are loaned several times during the week. Also make sure that some customers hire several videos while others do not loan any.

Word check ✓

Relationship – the links between tables or entities in a relational database.

Ascending – smallest first or a to z.

Descending – largest first or z to a.

Did you know ...

The links between tables or entities in a relational database are called relationships.

Databases (5) – queries and reports

By the end of this topic you will be able to:

- initiate queries to sort and search data
- produce reports from queries

Queries

When setting up a **query** you must first select the table(s) that you want to use. If you select more than one table they must be linked (see Databases (4)). You can then select which fields are to be used in the query and which are to be displayed in the results. With a relational database you can select fields from one or more of the tables.

The next stage is to enter the criteria for sorting and searching the data. You can also choose not to display some fields.

Using the library database, the librarian wants to contact members who have overdue books. She needs to know their name, telephone number, the book title and when it should have been returned. The records need to be in date order so that the members with the most overdue books can be contacted first.

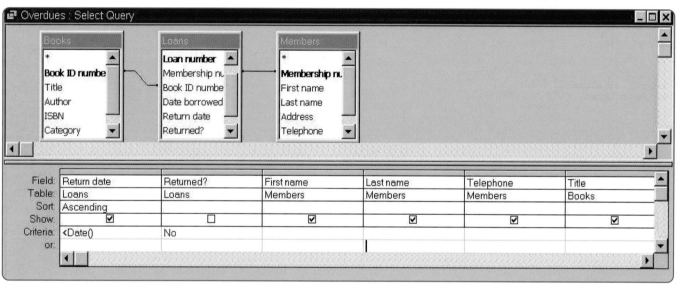

Set-up of a query with results to be shown in date order.

The data will be searched to find records where the Return date is before today's date AND where the 'Returned?' equals 'No'. The records are then sorted in ascending order of Return date (earliest first). The Returned? field will not be displayed as all records will contain the same data, 'No'.

Reports

The results of a query can be displayed in a table but it is often better to use the query to produce a **report**. You can then decide how you want the data to be displayed. You can change the font style and size, and add lines and borders to divide up the data and make it easier to read and understand. You can also add headers and footers just as you would in a word processed report.

You can design the layout of a report from scratch, but the software usually provides a report wizard to help you. You may still need to make adjustments to the design to try to ensure that the data is not split between too many pages and that all the data is visible.

Databases (5) – queries and reports

NAME	COMPANY	ADDRESS	PHONE	FAX	MOBILE	EMAIL
Gary Hart (sales)	Easton	51 The High St Cambridge CB3 4GH	0234 457835	0234 457834	0994 365829	ghart@eastons.com
Ranjit Singh	Eliman	The Maltings Dorton Newbury NW7 8PO	0653 835556		0234 457835	r.singh @eliman. hotmail.com
Charles Draper	Graham Supplies	Unit 34 Able Ind Est Burfield KO23 5YT	0123 987675	0123 987665	09997 526449	c.draper@demon.co.uk
Sandra Compton	B K Knights	34 Lower Bridge Rd Ecton Cambs CB35 7TC	0654 364950	0654 364765	0997 5763488	
Mark/ Sally	Marlton Repro	124 London Rd Marlton Bedford BE34 6RE	0456 957844	0456 957855	0889 998776	m.thompson@ mrepro.co.uk
Tony Hill/ Tony Parker	Two Tones Lighting	26 Market Square Bishop's Thornley Yorkley YR8 5TU	0192 932845		0666 445447	
Natasha	Dispatch it	Unit 12 Able Ind Est Burfield KO23 5RU	0234 457543	0234 876644	0994 365829	tash.dispatch@ hotmail.com

Entries in a typical database

CASE STUDY

Jalpur and Amina have found that their video hire database has helped them keep track of all the video rentals. They want to extend its use, find out more about the patterns of borrowing to help them identify which customers hire which type of video, which type are most popular, etc. They also want to be able to produce reports.

TASKS

1 Carry out some queries listing information that may be useful for Jalpur and Amina. For example:

- a list of all the videos hired to one particular customer
- a list of customers who have hired videos of one particular type (genre) – e.g. science fiction or horror
- a list showing all videos with a 15 certificate that are also science fiction or horror.

2 Create a report showing all the videos of a chosen genre – with a list for each showing the members who have borrowed that video.

3 Create a report in the form of a letter to send to members who have overdue videos.

Multimedia (1) – planning a presentation

Twenty years ago, personal computers could display text and numbers in a single colour on a **monochrome** monitor. Computer sound was restricted to a single **monotone** 'beep' from a tiny speaker inside the main system unit. Now, for example, images can be displayed in true colour, and the computer can be used for multi-track sound recording and playback.

The availability of multimedia tools and authoring software enables the user to create highly effective presentations for a variety of purposes. Presentations can be created combining text, graphics, sounds, animations, videos, and so on. These can be interactive (where the user chooses from on-screen options using buttons or hotspots) or linear (where the slides are set up to run automatically or to be displayed in time with the presenter's own explanations). Modern presentation software, as described earlier in this section, can be used to produce these presentations but specialist multimedia authoring software is also available.

CASE STUDY

A software writing company offers free days, where members of the public can attend a demonstration of the latest software. By using a multimedia projection system the presenter is able to carry out a demonstration on a laptop computer, which is then projected onto a large screen in front of the audience. This means that over 100 people can view the demonstration.

The professionalism of the presenter and the quality of the demonstration help to promote the new software. Many of the people attending the demonstration leave with the intention of purchasing the new software.

Multimedia presentations are used by organisations for many purposes. They can be used for staff training, for providing instructions to users of a product and for promotional purposes.

Producing a multimedia presentation is a relatively simple operation with modern software. The skill is in making the presentation lively and interesting, as well as communicating the intended message.

Although there are a number of different software applications available for carrying out this activity, they all rely on two simple principles: the presentation is made up from a number of slides or screens, which have a structure through which the presenter can navigate.

Planning a presentation

The key to producing an effective multimedia presentation is planning, which involves deciding the answer to a number of questions.

- What is the purpose of the presentation?
- How will it be used?
- What will it contain?
- How will the content be organised?
- What will appear on each slide/screen?
- What routes will there be through the presentation?
- How will the user move from slide to slide?
- What **multimedia components** need to be found or created?

There are tools that can help with the planning of a presentation. Two of these are a **storyboard** and a **structure diagram**.

A storyboard consists of a series of boxes that represent the slides/screens in the presentation. You use the boxes to indicate what will appear on each slide/screen.

A structure diagram is used to show how the slides/screens link together. This can be linear, hierarchical or a more complex mesh structure.

Multimedia (1) – planning a presentation

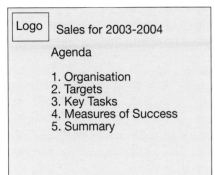

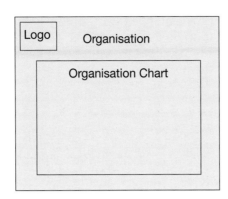

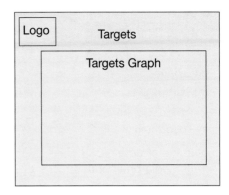

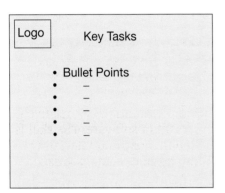

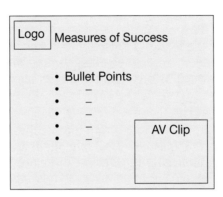

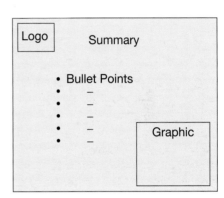

A storyboard

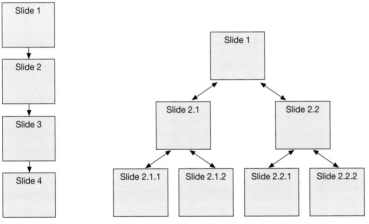

A linear structure diagram **A hierarchical structure diagram**

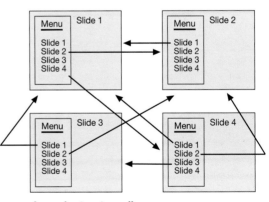

A mesh structure diagram

TASK

1 Design a multimedia presentation to promote a product. This may be an existing product or one you make up. Answer the questions posed on the opposite page and produce a storyboard, structure diagram and task list for the presentation.

Multimedia (2) – finding and creating components

By the end of this topic you will be able to:

• find and create multimedia components for a presentation

Once you have planned your multimedia presentation, the next step is to begin creating it. In your planning you will have decided what multimedia components you need for your presentation, now you must go about finding or creating them.

When you find existing materials that you want to use in your presentation you must consider and respect copyright. You will learn more about copyright later in this section.

You will need to ensure that all the files that you find or create are saved in a format that can be used by your multimedia software, and in a suitable directory/folder. This will ensure they can be located easily, as will the use of meaningful filenames.

Text files
Much of the text in a presentation, such as headings, sub-headings, bullet points and so on, will be directly input onto the slides. However pre-prepared text files such as organisation charts may be imported and displayed.

Image file
Images can be obtained from many different sources and be of different types. Libraries of clipart are available on CD-ROM, the Internet or are packaged with software applications. Some of these are free. These libraries contain different types of images from simple line drawings and cartoons to high quality photographs of a wide range of subjects. Other sources of images include those scanned by an optical scanner or photographs taken with a digital camera.

Sounds may be recorded through the sound card, by using a microphone.

Sound files
Sounds can also be obtained from many different sources and be of different types including music, speech and special sound effects. All of these can be obtained from any sound source and recorded via the sound card onto a computer file. Many can also be downloaded from the Internet. If you have access to a microphone you can also record sound files.

Midi sound files take up little space compared with recorded sounds. These midi files store music data in a similar way to how a word processor stores text. Like a music synthesiser, the computer's sound card and processing power are used to play the notes stored as data.

Video and animation
It is possible to include video clips and animation in presentations – though great care must be taken not to overdo it! As with graphics files, video files can be in different formats, and can take up huge amounts of storage space. Several things will affect how large the final video file will be including the number of frames per second (fps), the **resolution** of the video clip, and the number of colours used in the clip.

Animations (such as those created using Macromedia® *Flash*) usually take up less space than video clips.

Multimedia (2) – finding and creating components

Using *Flash*, interactive animations can be made, such as this 'Christmas card'.

Word check

Resolution – the number of pixels in each frame. This relates to the quality of the image.

Pixel – one of the dots that make up an image on a computer screen.

Did you know ...

The video or animation format must be recognised by the presentation software used. Special programs – called CODECs – must be installed to handle computer video and sound. If the correct CODEC isn't installed the video or sound file will not work!

Did you know ...

The size of the image file will depend on the format and the quality of the saved image. A 640 x 480 **pixel** image saved in 24-bit colour as a bitmap (.bmp) will occupy about 900KB. The same size image saved as a JPEG in optimised 8-bit colour will occupy only 40–50KB.

Sound files can also take up large amounts of disk space – a standard audio CD track can take up 40Mb of disk space – whilst a compressed MPEG version (the widely used MP3 files) may be just 4Mb (taking up only 10 per cent of the original file space).

TASKS

1. Locate or create the components you need for the presentation you planned in Multimedia (1). Make sure all the components are in the correct file format and save all the files in a new folder with meaningful filenames.

2. Scan a photograph into the computer. Save the file as a bitmap (.bmp). Save it again as a JPEG. What is the difference in the size of the two files?

Multimedia (3) – slides, backgrounds, frames and layers

Slides

A presentation is made up of any number of slides, and can look very unprofessional and clumsy if the slides all look different. In a document such as a newsletter there may be good reasons for using a wide range of different font sizes, styles and layouts. However, in a slide presentation a very important rule is to 'keep it dead simple' (KIDS).

It may be a good idea to create a **template** for your slideshow – so that all the slides will follow a similar style. Decide on a suitable font and style for headings and sub-headings and keep with this throughout. Save the template so that all your slides can follow this style.

Backgrounds

Background colours can be added to the slide template – it is also possible to add background images – either a single image to cover the whole slide or a pattern that can be 'tiled' to fill the background so that it adds texture. It is important when selecting a background to ensure that text and images will be clearly visible against it.

Frames

Within each slide the different items of text and image are generally held in frames. These frames can be used to resize and position the items on each individual slide. Frames can also be used to ensure consistent positioning of common items such as logos on each slide.

Various layout guides are available for use in most software applications – the user can modify these guides to help them create the layout they want.

This slide uses frames to position the multimedia components. They are not visible when the presentation is run.

Multimedia (3) – slides, backgrounds, frames and layers

Layers

Each frame can be set on a different layer within a slide from the back to the front. The layers are used to position items relative to the depth of the slide. For instance, they can be used to ensure that a description of a picture appears in front of the graphic image. Layers are also used to hide buttons and links if you do not want them to be visible to the audience during the presentation. With some software, when you import a sound file or video file into a slide it is shown by an icon which can be hidden in the same way.

Word check

Template – a master pattern for a document that includes layout details and items that will be the same on every page/slide.

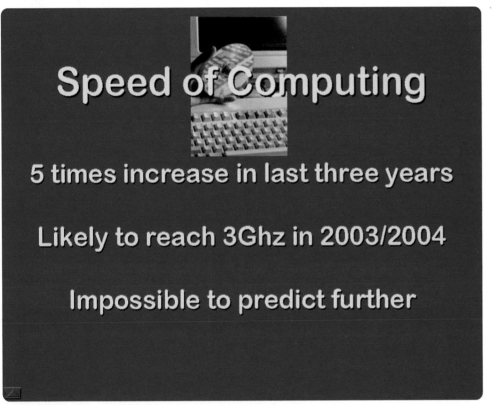

The use of layers allows the text to show over the pictures.

TASK

1. Create a slide template for your presentation. Choose a suitable background and decide on the text style for headings and sub-headings. Create and position frames for any items that will appear on every slide, such as a logo.

Multimedia (4) – creating and editing the presentation

By the end of this topic you will be able to:

- assemble a multimedia presentation

- edit the presentation and its components

Now that you have planned the presentation, found and saved all the required components and defined the format that will be used, you can start to build the final product. Essentially the steps below represent a proven sequence to follow.

Creating the slides

Start by creating each slide in order following your storyboard or structure diagram. The amount of information on each slide should be kept to a minimum. If there is too much for one slide, then split it over two or three. Provide interactive buttons to move between these linked slides, or set the timing carefully to provide the viewer with just enough time to take in all that they need to. When all of the slides have been created you can move on to the next stage.

Interactive presentations

You should use buttons or hypertext links to enable you to move between the slides. Should you be producing the presentation for someone else, you will need to show the user how to navigate through your presentation – this can either be in a user guide or through on-screen prompts, whatever is most suitable for the presentation. It is best to start with a title slide that also contains a menu of options. Alternatively the menu may follow the title slide. Also you should consider providing a summary slide to conclude the presentation, re-emphasising the major points covered.

The person giving the presentation needs to know how to navigate through an interactive presentation.

Multimedia (4) – creating and editing the presentation

Custom animation and slide transition

Each object on a slide can be controlled so that it appears in a particular way. This is usually referred to as 'custom animation'. For example, text can appear in one block at the same time, or be timed to appear point by point, images can be faded in and out, video clips can be played automatically or after a button has been clicked.

When the presentation is completed with the required slides in the correct order you may decide to create special 'slide transition' effects, where, for example, one slide changes to another in a pre-set manner, and set the time for each slide to remain on the screen.

Testing and editing the presentation

When your presentation is complete you will need to run through it to test that it works properly. You must make sure that you test all the routes through the presentation so that all links and buttons work as they should and that any sound or video clips play. You also need to check that the timings set are appropriate and that any slide transitions are effective. If you find any problems you will need to edit the presentation, perhaps by re-establishing a link or by trying a different slide transition.

You should also check any text carefully to make sure it is spelt correctly and that it makes sense. You will probably be able to edit the text in the multimedia software.

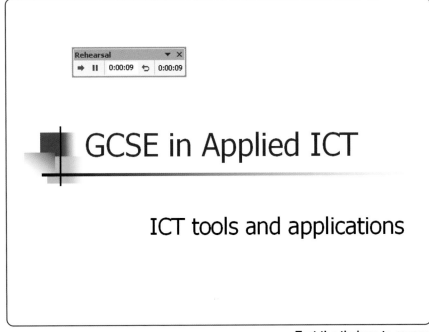

Test the timings to ensure that you have sufficient time to discuss each point.

Finally, you should make sure that the images, and any sound and video clips, are suitable and effective. If you need to edit these you will have to do so in the appropriate software and re-import them into the presentation.

TASK

1 Create your presentation. Test it and make any changes necessary.

The Internet (1) – sending emails

- understand what is required to communicate using email
- send an email to an individual and a group

The Internet is a huge Wide Area Network (WAN) where millions of computers are linked using a variety of different connections. Connection to the Internet is made through an **Internet Service Provider (ISP)**.

You will learn more about the Internet and Internet technologies in Section 3 of this book.

The Internet has many different uses. In this section we are going to consider two of the main uses of the Internet: electronic mail (email) and the world wide web (www).

Email

To use email you need a program called an email client. The most commonly used email client software packages are Microsoft® *Outlook* or *Outlook Express* and Netscape *Communicator*. Using this software you will be able to send and receive emails, reply to emails, forward emails to other addresses and keep an address book of email contacts. The software will also provide a folder structure for storing emails.

You also need a unique **email address**. Most email addresses are of the form: your.name@domain name. For most individuals the domain name is the name of their ISP, for example 'aol.com'. Most organisations have their own domain name, for example 'folens.com' or 'qca.org.uk'.

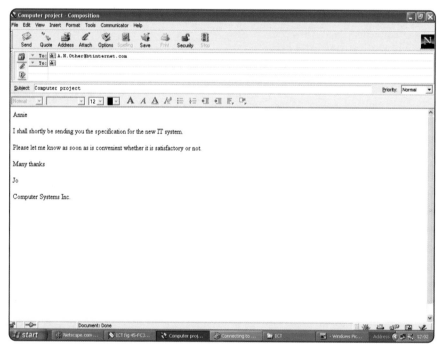

Sending an email message in Microsoft® *Outlook*.

The Internet (1) – sending emails

Sending an email

A standard form is used to create an email. First you must enter the email address of the person you are sending the email to – the recipient. This must be entered correctly or your message will not reach its destination. If the recipient is in your email address book you can simply select the address from there.

You can send an email to more than one recipient by entering each person's email address, or you can set up a group of addresses in your address book. Selecting the group name will send the email to all members of the group.

You should also enter a subject for the email. This is not compulsory but it allows the recipient to know what the email is about. The email can be created as a simple text message or in a format similar to a web page that can include a range of fonts and graphics. You can also attach a file to the email. This can be any type of file – text, graphics, sound, video, and so on – but the recipient will need to have the correct software to access the file. There may also be a limit on the size of file that can be sent or received.

Word check

Internet Service Provider (ISP) – a company that sells access to the Internet and provides Internet services such as hosting websites.

Online – connected to the Internet so that data can be sent and received.

Did you know ...

You will find other options as well as 'To:' when addressing an email. These are 'cc:' and 'bcc:'. These allow you to send copies of the email to other people. The difference is that 'cc:' shows the copy address on the email when it is opened, 'bcc:' (blind copy) does not.

When you have completed the email you must send it to the recipient – to do this the computer must be **online**. Some software sends the email as soon as the Send button is pressed; other software puts the emails into an Outbox to be sent later. You can set a priority flag so that the recipient knows whether it is urgent or not.

The recipient's ISP will store the email in a mailbox so that when they connect to the Internet (and run their own email client software) the email will be downloaded to their own computer and can then be read.

TASKS

1. Find out what email client software is available to you and the facilities it offers (how to delay sending an email, how to address it to more than one person, and so on).

2. Enter the email addresses of your friends, family and any business contacts you have made in an email address book. Create groups in the address book.

3. Compose and send an email to an individual and to a group.

The Internet (2) – receiving, replying to and forwarding emails

By the end of this topic you will be able to:

- receive emails
- reply to emails
- forward received emails to others

Communication is a two-way process and will only occur if you can also receive emails sent to you. How you do this will depend on the system you are using and how it is connected to the Internet.

Receiving emails

If your system has a permanent connection to the Internet, your messages may be automatically downloaded onto your computer as they arrive, providing the email client software is open. Alternatively you may get a pop-up message to tell you that there is new mail for you. You will then need to use the software's facility to download the messages into your Inbox. If you use a **dial-up connection** you will usually have to select the **download** facility.

Once your emails are downloaded you will be able to read them. If an email has a file attached it is best to save it to disk rather than open it from the email client software. Attached files can carry computer **viruses**. If the file is saved to disk it can be checked for viruses before it is opened.

Replying to emails

To reply to an email you simply click the Reply button and enter your reply before sending it in the normal way. The sender's email address is automatically used and Re: is put in front of the original subject. When the email has been sent to other people as well as you, you can choose to reply just to the sender or to all the other recipients as well.

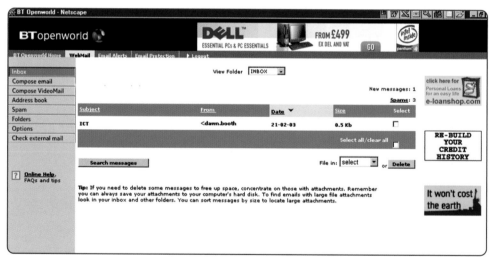

Checking for messages using web-based email.

Forwarding an email

You can send an email you receive to someone else. To do this you click the Forward button. You will need to enter or select the recipient's email address. The letters FW: will appear at the beginning of the subject. You can then add your own message – perhaps explaining why you are forwarding the email.

The Internet (2) – receiving, replying to and forwarding emails

Web-based email

Some email is web-based. This means that the email address is obtained from a website (such as www.hotmail.com) and the user must be online to make use of the email facilities. The advantage of web-based email is that it can be checked from any location in the world, providing the user has access to a computer with an Internet connection.

Some advantages and disadvantages of email

Advantages	Disadvantages
It is quick and simple to use	Beware of spam – when a user is bombarded with emails offering goods or services
It can be cheap, especially when the email is composed off-line	Some attachments to emails can contain viruses. All attachments should be checked with up-to-date virus checking software before they are opened
Sending an email to more than one person is easy	
The email client software is able to store details of many email addresses	
A file can be attached to an email, for example, digital photos or an important business document	

Word check

Dial-up connection – a connection to the Internet using a modem and the telephone line. The modem has to dial the telephone number of the ISP server to make the connection.

Download – transfer data from an ISP's server to a user's computer.

Virus – a small computer program that can copy itself from one computer to another. Viruses are usually written with malicious intent and cause damage to computers they infect.

TASKS

1. Find out how to receive an email on the computer system you have access to.

2. Send a reply to an email you receive. If you receive an email that has been sent to others, reply to the sender only and then to all the other recipients.

3. Forward an email to someone else. Include a message explaining why you are forwarding it and ask them to reply to you.

4. Find out how a local business uses email and write a report on the advantages and disadvantages to the company of using it.

The Internet (3) – searching and selecting information

World wide web (www)

To access and use the www, web browser software is needed. Most popular are Microsoft® *Internet Explorer* and Netscape *Navigator*, though other browsers are also available. These are usually 'free' software applications.

If you know the **web address** or **URL** (Universal Resource Locator) of the web page you want to look at, you need to enter this carefully in the address bar at the top of the browser window. The URL will nearly always start with www to indicate that it is to be found on the world wide web. After a few moments the required page will be displayed. The URL must be entered accurately – the slightest error will mean that either no page is displayed or the wrong page is accessed.

Searching for information

The Internet contains so many web pages that finding the information you require would be like looking for a 'needle in a million haystacks'. Fortunately help is at hand in the form of **search engines** to help us to find what we want. These search engines contain enormous databases detailing all the websites that have been listed and new sites are being added continuously to these listings. Sites such as www.google.com enable you to enter the word or phrase (**word string**) you are looking for and in a few seconds a list of possible matches will be displayed on your computer. A number of possible matches (often the first ten) will be displayed. You can then visit any of these by clicking on the URL. If none provide the information needed, further pages of suggested matches may be available.

Netscape's search page

The Internet (3) – searching and selecting information

Multiple criteria searches

Often a simple string search will list thousands of possible matches, so a more detailed and accurate search technique is needed. By entering certain key words (AND, OR, NOT, and so on) as part of the string, the search engine will be able to display results better suited to your needs. See the case study for an example of how using multiple search criteria can help to focus on the information required. The exception to this is Google, which only shows pages with all of the search words in.

CASE STUDY

John is a journalist on the local paper in Hadfield in Derbyshire, UK. He needs to find out about the history of the town between 1800 and 1900 (the nineteenth century) for an article he has to write. He uses www.google.com for this task.

Using the normal search tools John was able to refine his search, as shown below, to 228 'hits'. However, the search engine includes an advanced search tool. By keeping the string of words and adding a search for the exact phrase 'nineteenth century' the number of 'hits' is reduced to a more useful 22. By looking at the summary of each site listed it will now be possible to find the most suitable website(s) containing exactly the type of information required.

Search string	Number of suggested 'matches'
History	61 700 000
Hadfield	61 000
Hadfield AND UK	16 200
History AND Hadfield	12 400
History AND Hadfield AND 18	4 830
History AND Hadfield AND UK AND 18	1 790
History AND Hadfield AND UK AND 18 AND Derbyshire	228
Using the above string of words plus an advanced search for the phrase 'nineteenth century'	22

TASKS

1. Visit the following websites: www.bbc.co.uk, www.baa.co.uk, www.royalmail.co.uk, www.thetrainline.com and www.streetmap.co.uk. Find out what type of information is available on each site and how this could be used by an organisation.

2. Imagine you are a journalist writing an article about your local town or suburb. Decide what particular aspect of your town/suburb your article is to be about, such as tourism, sports clubs or shopping. Carry out and refine a search on the Internet to find suitable information.

The Internet (4) – browser software and navigating websites

Using browser software

When you find a useful website it is important that you can visit it again without carrying out long searches. Browser software allows you to **bookmark** the site by adding its URL to a list of **favourites**. To do this you select the **Add to favorites** or **Bookmark this page** option. It is usually the actual page you are viewing that is bookmarked. To visit the site again, you simply have to select it from the list.

You can organise these favourites into groups. This makes it even quicker and simpler to find a specific website again. For example, you may store all URLs concerning holiday flights in a single group, so that you can readily visit these sites to check them for special bargain deals!

Favorites list

Bookmarks Tools Window Help	
Bookmark This Page	Ctrl+D
File Bookmark...	Ctrl+Shift+D
Bookmark This Group of Tabs...	
Manage Bookmarks...	Ctrl+B
Personal Toolbar Folder	▶
Netscape Netcenter	
Search	▶
Business and Finance	▶
Computers and Internet	▶
Directories	▶
Entertainment and Lifestyles	▶
News and Sports	▶
Shopping and Classifieds	▶
Travel and Leisure	▶
What's New and Cool	▶
Personal Bookmarks	▶
Dales Holiday Cottages	
Sykes Cottages	
Netcenter	
The British Tourist Authority Web Site	
Royal Mail	
Jobworld UK - Jobs and employment vacancies opportunities!	
Yorkshire Dales Walks Pathfinder Guide - Adventurous Traveler Bookstore	
Yorkshire Dales, Northern England - accommodation and attractions guide	
Expedia.co.uk Travel	
Hong Kong - City of Life - All About Shopping - Map of the Main Shopping Areas	
Welcome to DART-Tag online	
RealPlayer Home Page	
Media	▶
Imported IE Favorites	▶
Lloyds TSB - Home page	

Browser software also provides facilities for you to **navigate** within and between websites using the **forward** and **back** buttons. When following hyperlinks between web pages you may want to return to an earlier web page or site. This is possible using the back button to go backwards along the chain of sites visited. It is then also possible to go forward again along the chain. You can simply click the button to go back or forward one page, or you can list the pages and select the one you want to return to.

Another useful facility is the history listing. Each website visited will be stored in the history listing in the browser software, which can be set to store the URLs automatically for future use.

Large websites

Like a printed encyclopaedia, very large websites can sometimes contain many thousands of pages of information. Looking for something specific on one of these websites can be as much of a problem as finding a topic in an encyclopaedia. The site owners will, however, provide the necessary tools to find the information you require, such as a search facility or an index. Sometimes this may take the form of a site map, with guidance on what information can be found on each page.

The Internet (4) – browser software and navigating websites

Some sites provide an alphabetical index. You select the first letter of what you are looking for and a page listing all the topics beginning with that letter is displayed. Clicking on a topic may then bring up a further menu to narrow down the subject area.

Most large sites are well designed and provide links back to previous menus and the home page. They also often show the location of the page you are viewing, for example, home/britain/kent/towns. However, care is sometimes needed if the site contains links to **external websites**.

Word check

Navigate – move purposefully through the pages of a website or from one website to another.

External websites – a large website may have links to websites created by other organisations – these are external websites. The original website may provide a warning that the link will take you out of the site.

TASKS

1. Visit the BBC website - www.bbc.co.uk. Use it to access revision information on word processing and desktop publishing software. Return to the home page and find out about the weather in your local area.

2. Visit the British Tourist Association website – www.travelbritain.com or www.bta.org.uk. Use it to find information about tourist attractions in your local area.

Home page of the British Tourist Authority website.

How standard applications meet an organisation's needs

There are very few organisations today who do not rely on some form of computer system to manage aspects of their daily operations. Whilst large organisations may have implemented **custom-built software**, many smaller companies make use of standard software packages to do a similar job. Mixtures of word-processing, DTP, spreadsheet, database, email and Internet software are nowadays sufficiently flexible and powerful to meet all of the needs of many such companies.

You will learn more about organisations and how they use ICT in the next section, but the case study opposite shows how the software you have been learning about meets the needs of one organisation.

Typical page from one of Tourismo Espagnol's magazines, showing ⅛, ¼ and ½ page advertisements.

How standard applications meet an organisation's needs

CASE STUDY

Tourismo Espagnol Publishing started life producing advertising magazines for the travel industry. To do this they use DTP software based on three Mac computers. DTP software is used to create each page for the magazines. With this software the production staff can input text, insert graphics and images and lay out the items on the page. Many of the pages in the magazines consist entirely of advertisements of $\frac{1}{8}$, $\frac{1}{4}$, $\frac{1}{2}$ or full pages. These are created in standard text frames to make page layout easier.

More recently they have started producing their own magazines for distribution in Spain and the UK. These magazines are primarily for people who own holiday properties for rent in Spain, in order that they may advertise those properties. The production costs for these magazines is paid for entirely by the charges that Tourismo Espagnol apply for the advertisements. Airlines, ferry operators and other travel industry companies also advertise in the magazines.

The company employs three part-time **telesales staff** to sell advertising space. They have recently implemented a database that runs across a local area network of PCs and includes details of all of their customers, and all the people that they have contacted to try to sell advertising to. The database also provides a system to remind staff to make a telephone call back to a customer. The sales staff also make extensive use of fax and email to correspond with customers.

Currently all order-processing is based on hand-written documents and invoicing is carried out using a word-processing package. Order processing and invoicing will soon be added to the database system.

The company uses a spreadsheet system to maintain records of sales and to run a basic sales and purchase system.

Tourismo Espagnol are associated with a company that provides a website for people to advertise properties, and they sell these services as well. They also often use the Internet to download photographs for use in the magazines.

The Managing Director of the company has a number of presentations that he maintains on a laptop computer. He uses these presentations when he attends exhibitions and when he visits some of his larger customers to sell the services of Tourismo Espagnol.

A typical small office, like Tourismo Espagnol has to produce its invoices.

Word check ✓

Custom-built software – is software that has been written especially for the organisation to meet their specific needs. This is also known as bespoke software.

Telesales staff – staff who sell a product or service over the telephone rather than face-to-face.

TASKS

1. Find out which software applications are used in your school or college and the needs that each application meets.

2. Visit a local company or use case study material from this book to find out how ICT meets their needs.

Organisations that manipulate graphic images

By the end of this topic you will be able to:

- understand how software can be used to capture, manipulate and enhance graphic images
- identify the type of organisation whose needs are met by this type of software

Many organisations now use the power and flexibility of **bitmap graphic software** to manipulate images as part of their everyday processes. With such software these images may be simply resized, cropped, coloured, or, as the example opposite, re-coloured (enhanced), or they may be drastically modified or distorted.

For example, a photograph can be modified by placing one person's head on another person's body or an image can be set onto a totally different background. Many of the photographs that you see in magazines may have been changed from the original in some way.

The images that are changed may have been captured using digital cameras and scanners or from libraries of photographs.

CASE STUDY

Image Revolution is a small graphics design organisation associated with a larger printing company. Image Revolution uses DTP and bitmap graphic software based on Mac computers to produce flyers, advertisements and brochures for a variety of different projects.

A recent project involved producing a sales brochure for a marketing company where all the images had to be in monochrome (black and white). The marketing company already had all of the images that were to be used, some of these were in computer based files, some were original photographs, but all were in colour.

Firstly, all the required images were loaded onto a Mac computer by scanning or importing as appropriate. The images were then converted to 16-bit greyscale using the bitmap graphic software.

Brochure in colour and then converted to greyscale.

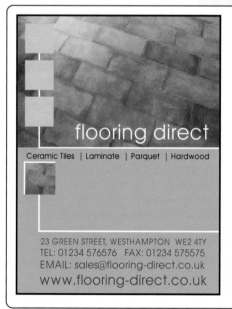 

After these images had been laid out with the associated text on the pages of the brochure, a **proof** of the brochure was printed and sent to the customer. The customer decided that several of the images needed resizing, a number of others needed cropping and many of the images needed to be enhanced.

The resizing and cropping was carried out simply using the bitmap graphic software. Image Revolution used a variety of techniques to enhance the selected images, including adjusting the brightness, contrast, lightness and tones of each image. A draft was produced after each technique had been applied and again sent to the customer.

Organisations that manipulate graphic images

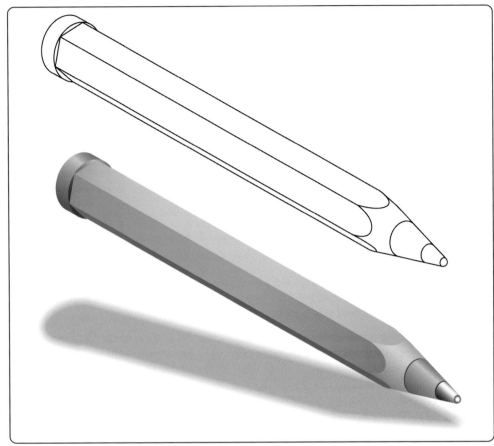

The pencil below has been enhanced.

CASE STUDY (Continued)

The customer selected the variation of each image that they liked, these were laid out in the brochure and it was sent for printing.

During a similar project one of Image Revolution's customers decided that, in a particular photograph, there were a number of trees in the background that they wanted to be 'removed'. In the same bitmap graphic software, the trees were carefully erased by copying areas from the surrounding parts of the image and pasting these over the trees. The customer then decided that the sky in the photograph was not sufficiently blue, so the hue and saturation of this area of the image was enhanced until a satisfactory result was achieved.

TASKS

1. Find out what bitmap graphic software is available to you so that an image looks better, for example brighter or clearer. Scan in a photograph, possibly of your family or pet, and use the software to manipulate the image. Crop the unnecessary edges.

2. Find out about other companies that use this type of software and the way that they use it.

Organisations that use ICT for automation, control and monitoring

Automation and control

Since the early 1970s, computers have been used to automate and control processes that originally required human intervention. The software applied to such automation and control was generally expensive, highly specialised, and required large micro computers to run it. Nowadays much of this type of software is readily available and can be run on most modern PCs.

This software can be used to automate everything from simple **entry control systems**, through automatic printing systems, to full CAD/CAM (computer aided design/computer aided manufacturing) systems. CAD/CAM is where a product is designed using a CAD/CAM package and the output from the package is used to control the machinery that produces the product.

CASE STUDY

SupaSoft plc is a large company that produces tissue products for the retail trade.

Some of their products are sold using their own name and others are sold using a number of other brand names. The tissue papers used in these products are essentially the same, only the packaging varies.

In order to automate the various machines used to manufacture, cut, roll and package their product, SupaSoft have a comprehensive computer control system.

The stages of production that this system controls are as follows:

- All production starts from a mix of paper pulp, but depending on the quality of the final products, this mix varies.

- When the correct mix has been achieved, a defined quantity of tissue is produced on huge rollers and dryers. The width of the roll of tissue so produced is generally standard, but the length and thickness can vary.

- The final roll of paper can also be used for a number of products so the cutting machines are automated. Thus, for example, they can produce toilet rolls, and a variety of sizes of facial tissues from the same basic roll of tissue.

- Finally, the packaging machines are also controlled to select the appropriate types and brands of packaging.

Paper is made on huge machines which are driven by computer controlled processes.

Organisations that use ICT for automation, control and monitoring

Monitoring and recording

Computer systems are invaluable when an organisation requires to record and monitor large volumes of data, and then use the data for complex analysis and interpretation. Different types of **sensor** are used to collect the data.

Examples of data, analysis and interpretation include:

- traffic flow and roadwork data for road design or journey planning systems
- traffic speeds to make sure that drivers are driving within the speed limit
- temperature, air pressure, rainfall, and so on, data for weather forecasting systems
- data on the chemical content of water for pollution monitoring systems.

CASE STUDY

Throughout the UK, the flow of traffic on many roads is recorded and monitored on a continual basis. Around towns you will often see cables laid across busy roads attached to a grey box on the pavement. On major roads and motorways electronic sensors are installed in many places. These devices record the number of vehicles passing in each direction through that location.

The data collected from this monitoring can be used for a number of purposes. Within towns it can be used to analyse the bottleneck areas, perhaps resulting in the adoption of a new one-way system. On a section of the M25 motorway to the west of London, this information is used to impose a variable speed limit system to attempt to limit traffic jams and queues.

Speed cameras use sensors to detect when cars are travelling too fast.

TASKS

1. Use the Internet and other sources to find out about other organisations that use automation and control. Write a report on your findings. Don't forget to acknowledge the sources you use.

2. When you are travelling, try to take note of any traffic monitoring sensors you see.

3. Find out more about weather forecasting and environmental monitoring. Produce a presentation for your classmates.

Word check

Entry control system – an automated system that opens a door or barrier in response to a specific combination of keys being pressed or data being read from an identity card.

Sensor – a device that converts a physical property such as temperature into an electrical signal that can be input into a computer system.

Purpose, audience, style and tone

By the end of this topic you will be able to:

- understand the different purposes of business documents
- identify the target audience
- recognise different writing styles and tones

In the first part of this section you learned about, and how to use, the different software tools that businesses use to organise and present information. In this and the following topics you will learn about the various documents produced – both on paper and on screen – and how to create your own effective business documents.

There are a number of factors that must be considered when creating documents or deciding whether a document is effective. These include the purpose of the document and the intended audience. These will determine the writing style and tone.

Purpose

Businesses use documents for many different purposes. Some of these are:

- to inform the reader
- to persuade the reader
- to create a good impression
- to summarise information
- to collect information
- to attract attention
- to explain details
- to set out facts clearly.

For example, the purpose of a letter to existing customers telling them about a change of address is to inform the reader; the purpose of a letter to prospective customers encouraging them to buy the company's goods is clearly to persuade the reader; the purpose of a poster or flyer is to attract attention; while the purpose of a database report is to set out facts clearly.

Styles vary for the age group of the audience that the information is aimed at.

Purpose, audience, style and tone

Target audience

Documents may be produced for an audience within the organisation (**internal**) or outside it (**external**). An example of a document for an internal audience is a memo (short for memorandum). Even within the organisation there are different audiences. These could include the general workforce on the one hand and senior managers on the other.

Audiences outside the organisation will include other businesses and the general public. Some documents may be targeted at certain age groups, for example, teenagers or retired people. The audience for some documents will be an individual and for others a group of people.

Sporting Times   2 The Avenue
Wellington
Shropshire
WE11 9LL

6 December 2003

Miss J Agbenyega
4 New Hill
Wellington
Shropshire
WE14 8XZ

Dear Miss Agbenyega

Please be aware that your account is now overdue. Payment of £25.65 should be paid by return. Payment should be received by ourselves by the 1st of each month.

Should you have any queries on your account, please contact the undersigned to discuss the matter.

Yours sincerely

Harold Wiggs
Accounts Department

Sporting Times   2 The Avenue
Wellington
Shropshire
WE11 9LL

6 December 2003

The Occupier
10 The Lane
Wellington
Shropshire
WE11 9LL

Dear Sir or Madam

Have you heard about our one-day Christmas bonanza? On Wednesday 17 December we shall be giving every person who walks through our door a glass of wine or sherry and a mince pie.

As if that wasn't enough, we shall also be giving a 10% reduction off everything in the shop. Yes – EVERYTHING!

We look forward to sharing our Christmas festivities with you.

Yours faithfully

Andy Slade
Sales Manager

A formal letter requesting payment (left). A slightly less formal letter advertising a special offer (right).

Writing style and tone

As mentioned above, the purpose and audience for a document determine the writing style and tone. For example, the writing style can be formal or informal; tone can be informative, persuasive or argumentative. Most external business documents, such as letters, are formal in style. However, the purpose of the document will determine the tone. Returning to the letters described above, the letter to existing customers will aim to set the facts out clearly, while the one to prospective customers will use persuasive language to encourage the reader to buy the products.

An informal writing style is what you would use when writing a letter to a friend. Some external documents, such as posters and flyers, may use an informal style, particularly if they are aimed at a younger audience. However, on the whole, it is internal documents such as memos, emails and notes that will have a less formal style.

TASKS

1. What is the main purpose of: a letter responding to a job advertisement; a glossy advertisement for a new car; a letter offering a new credit card; a table of football results; an online order form?

2. Collect as many different types of business documents as you can. For each one, try to decide what the purpose is and who the target audience is. Identify the writing style and tone of the document. Decide how effective each document is. Use your findings to produce a set of guidelines on how to match writing style and tone to the purpose and audience of a document.

Presentation and layout

By the end of this topic you will be able to:

- consider issues of presentation and layout

- understand the importance of accuracy, clarity, consistency and house style

In the last topic you learned about some factors that contribute to the effectiveness of business documents. In this topic we will consider aspects of presentation and layout.

It is possible to enhance documents by using **colour** and **images**. These can be very useful in improving the impact of the document and in helping to get the message across. However, too much colour or too many images can have the opposite effect. For example, putting a coloured background in the row of a spreadsheet that shows the results can serve to draw the reader's eye to the most important information, but shading alternate rows in different colours will do little to enhance understanding. Also, the use of colour and images is not always appropriate, for example in a formal letter.

Layout too can enhance or detract from the effectiveness of documents. Certain documents have particular layout requirements. For example, a web page may use frames so that links to other pages can be displayed consistently on every page. You will learn about specific layout requirements for different documents on the following pages.

Documents that are for an external audience convey an image of the organisation. It is important that this image is a good one. Readers will not have a good image of the organisation if the documents they receive contain spelling, grammar or layout errors. It is vitally important that all documents are checked for errors – using both spelling and grammar checkers and by careful **proof-reading**. It is also important that the message is clear and that a consistent style is used.

	A	B	C	D	E
1	Holiday Accounts				
2					
3		Income			Expenditure
4	Maggie	£110.00		Deposit	£310.50
5	Ron & Tina	£220.00		Balance	£292.00
6	Pat	£110.00		Booze	£100.00
7	Paul	£110.00		Food	£101.19
8	Alan	£45.00		Meat	£74.23
9	Roger	£110.00		Fresh food	£65.22
10	Dave	£110.00		Fuel	£20.00
11	John and Sheila	£220.00		Tina (wine/juice)	£68.00
12	Sylvia	£35.00		Shopping	£12.00
13	Greg	£50.00		Veg	£2.50
14	Whip Kitty	£14.78		Maggie	£1.74
15				Black pudding	£7.50
16				Bread & Buns	£3.55
17				Bread	£0.82
18	Totals	£1,134.78			£1,059.25
19					
20				Balance	£75.53
21					

	A	B	C	D	E
1	Holiday Accounts				
2					
3		Income			Expenditure
4	Maggie	£110.00		Deposit	£310.50
5	Ron & Tina	£220.00		Balance	£292.00
6	Pat	110		Booze	100
7	Paul	110		Food	101.19
8	Alan	45		Meat	74.23
9	Roger	110		Fresh food	65.22
10	Dave	110		Fuel	20
11	John and Sheila	220		Tina (wine/juice)	68
12	Sylvia	35		Shopping	12
13	Greg	50		Veg	2.5
14	Whip Kitty	14.78		Maggie	1.74
15				Black pudding	7.5
16				Bread & Buns	3.55
17				Bread	0.82
18	Totals	£1,134.78			£1,059.25
19					
20				Balance	£75.53
21					

Limited use of colour in the spreadsheet (left) draws the eye to the important information, but too much colour (right) loses the effect.

Presentation and layout

House style

Many organisations develop a **house style** that is used for all types of external documents. The house style ensures that all documents produced have a consistent style and are instantly recognisable as coming from the organisation. Some organisations spend millions of pounds having a new corporate image and house style developed for them.

The house style will determine:

- the font style, size and colour to be used for different purposes
- where and how a logo is used, if an organisation has one
- the exact layout of different types of documents
- the type of paper to be used for printed documents, and so on.

Some organisations will provide document templates for staff to use. Others will provide a guide for employees to follow.

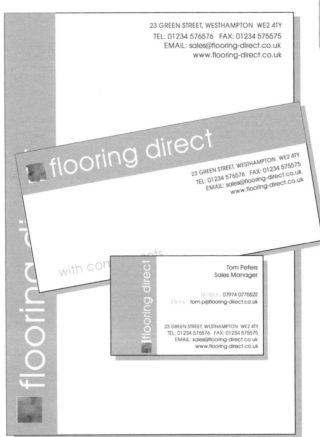

Typical stationery with a house style throughout.

TASKS

1. Using the documents you collected for the last topic, consider the use of colour and images in the different documents. Decide whether the colour and images have been used appropriately. Draw up a list of questions that you should consider before using colour and images in documents.

2. Collect examples of all the different types of documents your school sends out. Do they have a house style? Produce a set of rules to create or update a house style for your school or college.

Memos, letters and faxes

By the end of this topic you will be able to:

- recognise examples of memos, letters and faxes
- understand the different purposes of memos, letters and faxes
- identify the layout requirements of memos, letters and faxes

Memos

A **memo** is an internal document. As such it does not need to include the organisation's address, telephone number or other contact details. Most organisations have a standard memo form (see the example). Some information such as From:, To: and Date: will always be included. Other information such as CC: (copied to) or Circulation: (a list of all the people who will receive it) and Time: may also appear. The last point is particularly important if an urgent reply is needed. It is usual to include a subject before the message itself. The message may be written in an informal style, as it will only be read by employees within the organisation. Nowadays, emails are replacing memos for sending messages.

Memo

To:	All Staff
From:	John Bridges
CC:	
Date:	27/09/03
Re:	New Health and Safety Policy

The company is introducing a new Health and Safety policy to ensure we comply with all UK and EU regulations. A copy will be sent to each department. Please make sure you read it and act on it.

John

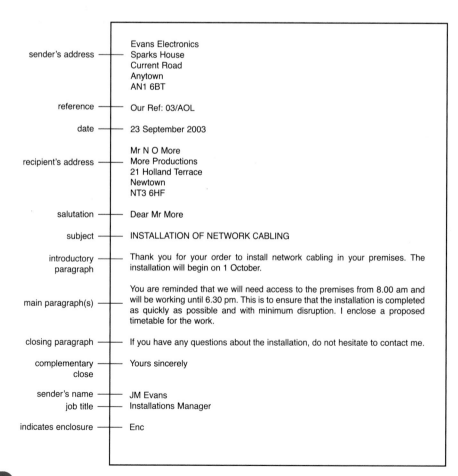

sender's address	Evans Electronics Sparks House Current Road Anytown AN1 6BT
reference	Our Ref: 03/AOL
date	23 September 2003
recipient's address	Mr N O More More Productions 21 Holland Terrace Newtown NT3 6HF
salutation	Dear Mr More
subject	INSTALLATION OF NETWORK CABLING
introductory paragraph	Thank you for your order to install network cabling in your premises. The installation will begin on 1 October.
main paragraph(s)	You are reminded that we will need access to the premises from 8.00 am and will be working until 6.30 pm. This is to ensure that the installation is completed as quickly as possible and with minimum disruption. I enclose a proposed timetable for the work.
closing paragraph	If you have any questions about the installation, do not hesitate to contact me.
complementary close	Yours sincerely
sender's name	JM Evans
job title	Installations Manager
indicates enclosure	Enc

Letters

A **business letter** is an external document. It will usually be printed on the organisation's headed paper. Many letters are now fully blocked. This means that every line starts at the left-hand margin. No punctuation is included, for example in the address, except that needed in the body of the letter. This body text may be fully justified. It is very important that letters are clear and accurate so they create a good impression of the organisation.

The example, left, shows the layout of a business letter and what it should include.

Memos, letters and faxes

Faxes

A **fax** is an external document that is sent via the telephone lines. As such it is pointless using colour, as it will always be printed in black and white. Faxes usually start with a fax header sheet. This may include the organisation's logo or letterhead. It will also include details of who is sending the fax, including their telephone number and fax number, and who is to receive it. This will usually include their name and department as well as the name of their organisation and their telephone and fax numbers. Most importantly, the fax header will state how many pages are being sent. It may also include the subject.

The fax header sheet will have a space for a message such as 'Please find the attached order'. Sometimes faxes are used to send a brief message on the fax header sheet, but usually other documents are attached.

Did you know ...

Salutation and complementary close: if you know the name of the person you are writing to, use Dear (their name) and Yours sincerely. If you don't know the person's name (or it is a very formal letter), use Dear Sir or Dear Madam and Yours faithfully. Word processing software may offer you the option Yours truly. This is an American expression that is not usually used in the UK.

Word check

Fax – this is short for facsimile which means an exact copy. The sending fax machine converts the document into a signal that is sent along the telephone wires. The receiving fax machine then converts the signal back to a printed page that is a copy of the original.

MORE PRODUCTIONS

21 Holland Terrace
Newtown
NT3 6HF
Phone: 01345 987654
Fax: 01345 987655

Fax

To:	John Evans	**From:**	Neil More
Fax:	01234 567899	**Date:**	27/09/03
Phone:	01234 567800	**Pages:**	2
Re:	Network installation	**CC:**	

☐ Urgent   ☒ For Review   ☐ Please Comment   ☐ Please Reply   ☐ Please Recycle

•**Comments:**

Please find attached map of our location.

TASK

1 Collect examples of memos, business letters and faxes from different organisations. Use a table to compare different examples of each type of document. Identify the things that are the same and the things that are different. Decide which one of each type of document is most effective. Try to explain why you find it the most effective.

Agendas and minutes

Agenda

All businesses have meetings, some may have too many! To help structure what is going to take place at the meeting a plan is needed, which is called an agenda.

The agenda should be circulated at least 24 hours before the meeting, so that all of the people who will be attending have time to prepare for it. They will then be able to take an active part in the meeting.

An agenda usually contains a number of items arranged in a particular order. One point should lead on to the next point in a logical way, although this is not always possible.

The first item on the agenda should always be 'apologies'. This is the point where people who were expected to attend the meeting, but are unable to be there, can be noted as absent. People who are unable to attend should send their apologies and, if they have given a reason for not attending, it is usually recorded in the minutes.

The second item on the agenda is usually asking everyone to agree that the minutes taken at the previous meeting are a true and correct record of the proceedings. This then leads to the third item which is 'matters arising from the minutes of the last meeting'.

After these preliminary items, various points for discussion can be added. If the agenda has been circulated prior to the meeting, other people may put forward items for inclusion, otherwise the main points tend to come from the person who called the meeting – usually the **chairperson**.

The final item on the agenda is usually 'any other business' or AOB. It is at this point that anyone at the meeting, who feels that something has been omitted, can include it. A time limit for AOB is often set at the beginning of the meeting, so that the meeting will not run on too long and people know when the meeting is due to finish, or 'close'.

The start time and the venue of a meeting must be circulated prior to the event. Everyone then knows at what time they must be there and note the time as busy in their diary. It is also important to set the finish time, as meetings may tend to drag on!

A term sometimes used to describe the finish of, not only, the meeting, but also, items on the agenda is 'guillotine', as it conjures up the idea of a swift and final action!

Minutes

Alongside the agenda, a second important document is the minutes.

The minutes are a record of what is said and agreed at the meeting. It is not usually a word-for-word account, but it should give a clear view of what happened, so that anyone not attending the meeting is clear on what was discussed, the outcome of those discussions and who is responsible for carrying out any required actions. The minutes also act as a reminder to people who were at the meeting, of what was said and done.

Agendas and minutes

It is important to arrange before the meeting who will be taking the minutes. In some businesses there may be a designated person, such as a secretary, who will take the minutes and then type them up and distribute them to whoever needs a copy. In many places however, such as schools, there is no spare time for secretaries to attend meetings which do not directly relate to their job. In these cases the minutes are usually taken by someone who attends the meeting anyway.

The Houses of Parliament

Before the minutes are distributed after the meeting, they are usually checked by the chairperson, who will make sure that they are as true a record as possible. They are then copied and distributed. A copy should be kept on file for future reference, particularly if financial matters were discussed as the accounts department may want to check what was said at a later date.

CASE STUDY

Parliament recently held a vote on altering the structure of the day for meetings in The House. For many years the business of the day, which is one long meeting, started around lunchtime and went on until everything on the agenda was finished. This sometimes meant running on into the early hours of the morning!

The MPs got fed up with this and decided to guillotine the day's work in the evening. In order to get through all of the agenda, the day will start a bit earlier.

This seems reasonable, but many people are concerned that some things as important as those that are discussed at The Houses of Parliament shouldn't be stopped, just because it is time to finish!

TASKS

1 Collect an agenda and a copy of the minutes from a recent meeting and compare the two documents.

2 Produce a report summarising what you think happened at the meeting and present this to someone who attended it.

3 Collect their comments, did you summarise it correctly? If not what did you get wrong? Is this a fault of the documents, or your lack of understanding?

Word check

Chairperson – often altered to chairman or chairwoman, this is the person in charge of the meeting, usually a manager of some sort, but it could be anybody.

Posters, flyers, advertisements and business cards

Posters

Posters are used to publicise events or products. They can also be used to display important information. Posters can be used for both internal and external purposes. For example, a poster may be used internally to remind employees of the Health and Safety procedures they must follow, while an external poster may advertise a concert that an organisation is presenting.

The most important feature of a poster is that it must be eye-catching. Colours and images can be used to good effect and the text must be large enough to read from a distance. The amount of text should be kept to a minimum but all necessary details must be included.

Flyers

A flyer is an external document, often used for publicity purposes. Flyers are designed to be handed out to people or put through their letterboxes. Some flyers simply use black ink on white or coloured paper; others are printed in full colour on glossy paper. They may be a scaled-down version of a poster or a sheet folded in half or three. They need to grab the recipient's attention so they will be read.

A flyer (right) can be a scaled-down version of the poster (left).

Posters, flyers, advertisements and business cards

Advertisements

Advertisements come in all shapes and sizes. Large advertisements on billboards and other places are just like posters. Full or half-page advertisements for products in magazines and newspapers also follow similar styles. Job advertisements need to provide sufficient information to encourage the right type of **applicant** to apply – such as the experience required, the job location and the salary offered. They also need to create a good impression of the organisation. Small ads selling second-hand goods tend to be short and to the point as advertisers are often charged extra for more than a certain number of words.

Business cards

Business cards can also be thought of as advertisements for an organisation. They are designed to be given out by **employees** to people they do business with. It is vital that a business card creates a good impression. Most business cards are of a similar size so that they fit easily into a wallet, purse or pocket. They are usually printed on card so that they don't get damaged easily – some are printed on plastic similar to a credit card. The card will include at least the company name and contact details and usually the employee's name and job title.

A business card

In this case the advertisement is selling the Disney Channel.

<table>
<tr><td>

TASKS

1. Keep a record of any posters you see. Note down the purpose of each one, the target audience, the presentation and layout used, and how well they meet the purpose and the needs of the target audience.

2. Make a collection of any flyers that come through your letterbox or that are handed to you. Use a table to compare them. Which features are similar and which are different? Suggest how the differences relate to the purpose and the target audience.

3. Look in the jobs section of a local or national newspaper. Choose a range of different advertisements from large whole page ones to the smallest. What information do they all contain? Apart from size, how do they differ? What impression does each give you about the organisation?

4. In a group, collect as many business cards as you can. Make a note of what each one contains and the presentation techniques used. Decide which gives the best impression of the organisation.

</td><td>

Word check ✓

Applicant – a person applying for a job.

Employee – a person who works for an organisation.

</td></tr>
</table>

Magazine layouts, web pages and presentations

Magazine layouts, web pages and presentations all share similar features. All three can be used to provide information about an organisation and to promote its products or services. All three usually incorporate colour and images – and, in the case of web pages and presentations, can include sound, video and animation. Also, all three use frames to position different elements.

A typical magazine page, with a banner headline

Magazine

Magazine **layouts** often display text in columns. They may include a banner headline – a title in a large font that goes the full width of the page. Individual stories will have headings and sub-headings. These will usually be in different font sizes and may use different font styles. It is important, however, that not too many font styles are used to achieve consistency throughout the document.

Pictures may be positioned anywhere on the page and the text may wrap around it or sometimes even flow over it. Colour should be used with care so that it does not detract from the articles. However, this may depend on the audience.

Web pages

Using frames in a **web page** is like having two separate web pages in one. Usually, one frame contains a table of contents and menus, which allow links to all the other pages on the site. The second frame contains the pages of information.

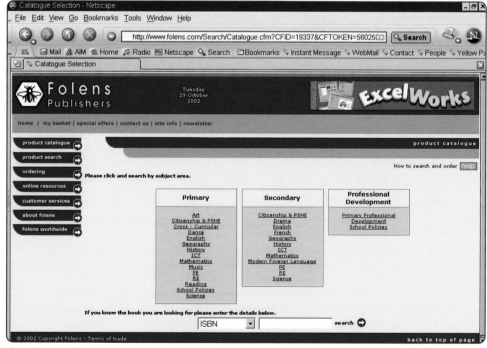

A web page that makes good use of frames.

Magazine layouts, web pages and presentations

The advantage of using frames is that the menu frame can always be present on the screen so, although the content changes, the navigation system does not. This makes it much easier to navigate the site.

The balance of text, pictures and other effects will depend on the audience for the website, as will the use of colour. Also, while it may seem desirable to include many features such as pictures, video clips and animation to make the site exciting, this may make the site slow to download, which could be frustrating for the user.

Presentations

The golden rules for **presentations** are consistency and simplicity. All slides should have the same basic layout, with consistent use of colour (for both background and text), font style and font sizes. The minimum amount of text should be used and graphic images should be limited to one per slide in most cases. Each slide will usually have a title frame; there will also usually be a footer possibly including the slide number and date. The main part of the slide may include a text or graphic frame, or both. If the presentation is interactive, there will also be hotspots and navigation buttons to allow the user to move through the presentation.

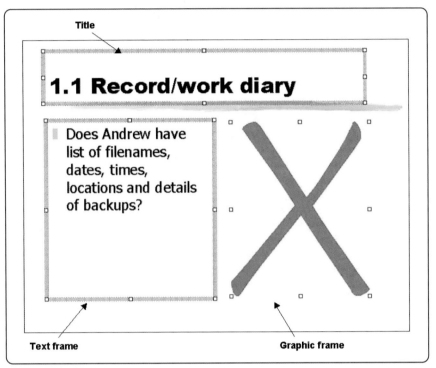

Typical components of a presentation slide

TASKS

1. Make a collection of different types of magazines that are produced for different audiences. These might include computer magazines, teenage magazines, magazines for particular professions, hobbies or interests and possibly 'in-house' magazines from organisations. Study the layout of these magazines. Identify the features that are the same. Consider how each uses layout, pictures and colour and how they meet the needs of their particular audience. Summarise your findings in a presentation.

2. Visit a number of different websites. Make notes on the use of frames, colour, images and other features. Give each website a rating for time to download, ease of navigation, visual impact and quality of information. Which website do you consider the most effective overall and why?

Data capture forms, financial plans and database reports

Data capture forms are used to collect data for input into a computer system. Examples are passport application forms and driving licence application forms. Considerable care is needed in the design of data capture forms so that the data can be easily and accurately entered. This may be done using a **data entry screen**, which closely matches the design of the data capture form.

Data capture forms contain a series of questions or labels such as 'name'. The person completing the form may be required to write in a box, for example when entering their name. They may be required to choose an option by putting a ✓ or ✗ in a box, circling or underlining a choice, or crossing out options that do not apply. Where the person has to write in a box, it may be divided up into a number of small boxes so a single letter is written in each.

5   Your health

You must complete either Part A or Part B – otherwise your application will be sent back to you.

If you have already told us about a medical condition that could affect your fitness to drive – and you have no new medical condition – miss out Part A and go on to Part B of this section.

Part A

Have you ever had, or do you currently suffer from any of these conditions?   Yes   No

If you have answered Yes, please tick ✓ all the appropriate boxes.

1. Epilepsy
2. Fit(s) or blackouts
3. Severe and recurrent disabling giddiness
4. Diabetes controlled by insulin
5. Diabetes controlled by tablets
6. An implanted cardiac pacemaker
7. An implanted cardiac defibrillator (ICD)
8. Angina, (heart pain) **which is easily provoked by driving**
9. Persistent alcohol misuse or dependency
10. Persistent drug misuse or dependency
11. Parkinson's disease
12. Narcolepsy or sleep apnoea syndrome
13. Stroke, with any symptoms lasting longer than one month, recurrent "mini-strokes" or TIAs
14. Any type of brain surgery, severe head injury involving **in-patient** treatment, or brain tumour
15. Any other chronic neurological condition
16. A serious problem with memory or episodes of confusion
17. Severe learning disability
18. Serious psychiatric illness or mental ill-health
19. Total loss of sight in one eye
20. Any visual condition affecting **both** eyes or remaining eye if one eye only **(excluding short/long sight or colour blindness)**

You must provide, when appropriate:

- your last licence and counterpart (if applicable) ....
- your test pass certificate (if applicable) ....
- a medical report form D4 (see notes F) ....
- your fee (remember to sign your cheque).........................
- D750 photocard application form (if applicable)...................

Your fee

Check the fee on leaflet INS115. Do not send cash to DVLA. Please write the applicant's name, address and date of birth or driver number, if known, on the back of the cheque/postal order.

Amount

£

Cheque or postal order number(s)

This declaration must be signed by the person applying for the licence.

I understand that it is a criminal offence if I (or anyone) make(s) a false declaration in order for me to obtain a licence and can lead to prosecution and a fine of up to £2500. I also understand that it is an offence to fail to provide information and can lead to prosecution and a fine of up to £1000.

I declare that I have checked the details I have given and to the best of my knowledge believe they are correct and I am entitled to the licence for which I apply.

Signature

Date

If you send the form to: DVLA, Swansea use the appropriate postcode from this list:

- First provisional licence **SA99 1AD**
- First full licence for cars and motorcycles **SA99 1BJ**

Part of a data capture form. The information provided will be input into a computer system.

Financial plans are usually produced using spreadsheet software. They include cashflow forecasts and predicted profit and loss accounts. These were described in Spreadsheets (1). Financial plans will be used within an organisation to identify the effects of any increased costs; to identify when the organisation might be able to invest in new equipment, or to identify when they might be short of money. They will also be used externally, for example, to obtain financial loans from banks.

Data capture forms, financial plans and database reports

Financial plans must be clearly set out with titles, headings and labels so that it is clear what the document shows and the period of time to which it applies – plans may be short, medium or long term. Lines and borders and white space may also be used to separate different areas of the document. Graphs and charts may be used to present the information visually. These too must be clearly and accurately labelled.

Database reports are used to display the results of queries in a way that is easier to understand than a simple table. The data can be organised in different ways such as in columns or record by record. The data can also be grouped so that, for example, all sales records relating to a particular region are displayed together. Calculations can also be carried out so, for example, the total sales for the region could be shown. Headings and sub-headings, graphic lines and borders, and headers and footers are all used to make the document easier to read and understand.

Word check

Data entry screen – an on-screen form used to enter data, for example, into a database. The form may have drop-down lists of options or radio buttons that can be selected to reduce the need to type in data entries, hence reducing keying errors.

	A	B	C	D	E	F	G	H
1	Cashflow Forecast January to June							
2								
3		Jan	Feb	Mar	Apr	May	Jun	
4	**Income**							
5	Sales	£2,500	£2,225	£1,000	£1,750	£2,000	£2,000	
6	Consultancy	£0	£0	£500	£250	£250	£500	
7								
8	Total Income	£2,500	£2,225	£1,500	£2,000	£2,250	£2,500	
9								
10								
11	**Expenditure**							
12	Rent	£300	£300	£300	£300	£300	£300	
13	Heating	£125	£125	£100	£75	£50	£50	
14	Lighting	£25	£25	£25	£25	£25	£25	
15	Telephone	£175	£175	£175	£175	£175	£175	
16	Raw materials	£1,500	£1,500	£1,500	£1,500	£1,500	£1,500	
17								
18	Total Expenditure	£2,125	£2,125	£2,100	£2,075	£2,050	£2,050	
19								
20	Brought forward		£375	£475	-£125	-£200	£0	
21	Cash at Bank	£375	£475	-£125	-£200	£0	£450	
22								

A cashflow forecast is an important part of the financial plan.

TASKS

1. Collect some examples of data capture forms, such as questionnaires or guarantee forms. List the purpose of each one and the techniques used. Comment on how easy each is to complete.

2. Use the Internet to discover more about the types of documents used for financial planning. Hint: There are a number of sites that offer help in creating business plans for those wishing to set up a small business.

Creating a portfolio of business documents

Over the last six topics you have learned about many different types of business documents and what makes these documents effective. Earlier in this section you learned about the tools and facilities offered by applications software to process and present information, and how to use them. It is now time for you to put what you have learned into practice and create your own business documents.

Ideally you will create documents for a real organisation. This may be for a local small business, a local charity, a club or society, or even your school or college. You may be required to develop a house style for the organisation and use it to produce a range of documents. Alternatively, you may be required to produce specific documents, perhaps conforming to an existing house style.

After you have found out which documents you are to produce, the next step is to identify the exact purpose of each document. Will it be required to:

- inform the reader
- persuade the reader
- create a good impression
- summarise information
- collect information
- attract attention
- explain details
- set out facts clearly?

Who will the audience be? Will it be:

- internal or external
- an individual or a group
- another organisation or the general public
- young or old?

Having identified the purpose and the audience for each document you will need to consider the writing style and tone that is appropriate to the purpose of the document and the target audience.

Certain documents have particular presentation and layout requirements. You will need to consider these requirements for each document you are to produce. You will also need to apply what you have learned about what makes a document effective and what does not.

Finally, you will need to consider which applications software package and which tools and facilities are best suited to creating each document. For example, word processing software would be most appropriate for creating letters and memos, but publishing software would probably be more appropriate for creating a flyer or magazine layout.

Creating a portfolio of business documents

The video hire business run by Jalpur and Amina Patel from their corner shop has become more and more popular. They have decided to rename their shop Patel's Video Hire and to concentrate solely on this aspect of the business.

To do this, Jalpur has decided that he will need to advertise the business. He has suggested that they put posters in the shop window telling customers about the latest videos and DVDs they have in stock. Amina thinks that they should also place a quarter-page advertisement in the local newspaper and hand out flyers to passers-by in the town centre.

With the increase in the number of people hiring videos and DVDs, Jalpur has decided that a membership scheme is needed. Customers will have to complete a membership form so that their details can be easily entered into the database which will then produce a membership card showing their name and membership number. Letters will be sent to members who have not used the service for several weeks. These letters will tell the members of new arrivals that might be of particular interest, based on the type of film they prefer. Letters will also be sent to members with overdue videos.

Jalpur and Amina will also need to increase the number and range of videos and DVDs in stock. They will need a loan from the bank to buy these. The bank manager requires financial plans for the business to check that it will make enough profit to pay back the loan.

Many 'corner shops' now hire out videos. This one has neon signs to advertise the fact.

1 Create the documents that Jalpur and Amina need for their business. Create a suitable logo and use it to develop a house style that will create a good impression of Patel's Video Hire and make the documents instantly recognisable.

Security and confidentiality

By the end of this topic you will be able to:

- understand the importance of following standard ways of working
- keep information secure
- protect confidentiality

It is important that you follow standard ways of working when you are using ICT. This can range from keeping backup copies of your files to making sure that the layout of your work area is safe and healthy. It is important to follow standard ways of working to prevent problems caused because information in ICT systems can easily be lost or misused. It is also important to prevent sickness or injury to yourself and others. In the last few topics of this section we will be considering the different aspects of standard ways of working that you should know about and follow.

Keep information secure

This means ensuring that information stored on an ICT system cannot be corrupted, lost or stolen. There are many different threats to this information. These include viruses and **unauthorised access**.

One way of protecting against viruses is to install anti-virus software. This can be set up to scan all the files on the system at regular intervals and also to scan all new files before they are opened. However, the software must be regularly updated as new viruses are being developed every day. Other measures to reduce the risk of virus problems include, reducing or avoiding the use of floppy disks in more than one computer and taking care when downloading and viewing attachments to emails, particularly if you do not know the sender.

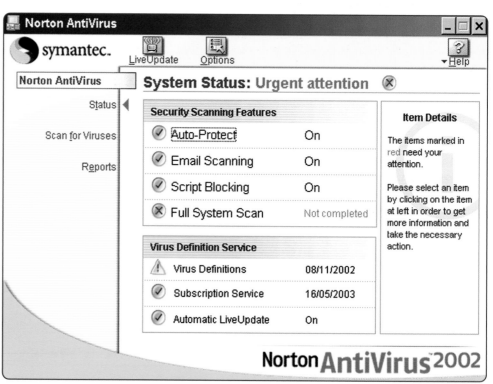

Anti-virus software helps protect against viruses. *Norton AntiVirus* and *SystemWorks* are a couple of the more popular programs.

Security and confidentiality

Most users will be required to log on to a computer system or network with a username and password. You will almost certainly have to do this to gain access to your school's or college's network. This is a useful security measure to protect data from unauthorised access. It is important that your password is **kept confidential**. The choice of password is also important. Many people choose a memorable date, such as a birthday, or the name of a family member or pet as a password. Unfortunately, these are very easy to guess and so are not very secure. You should choose a password that is a random set of letters and numbers. Do not write your password down. You should also change your password regularly, particulary if you think someone else knows it.

Another important way of preventing unauthorised access is physical security. This means keeping computer rooms, and sometimes the computers themselves, locked when they are not in use.

The log on screen

Protect confidentiality

Organisations frequently store data about individuals that is personal and sensitive. For example, medical records are increasingly stored on computer systems. Whilst this is of great benefit to the doctors and medical professionals providing treatment, the information must not be seen by others. It is important that such information is stored in secure conditions to avoid access by unauthorised people. It is also important that the employees who have access to the information do not discuss it with unauthorised people.

> ### Word check
>
> **Unauthorised access** – when someone who is not entitled gains access to a computer system. The person may find out information they should not know or may change or destroy the information stored.
>
> **Kept confidential** – kept to yourself, not told to anyone else.

CASE STUDY

In some organisations, employees are required to change their passwords after a certain period of time. This system displays a change password dialogue box and the employee cannot access the system until they have entered and verified (typed in a second time to avoid errors) a new password.

TASKS

1. Make a list of different types of information that need to be kept confidential.

2. Produce a poster for use in your school or college, explaining how to choose and use passwords to improve security.

3. Write a report explaining how to protect your system at school or college against viruses.

Copyright, saving work and backups

By the end of this topic you will be able to:

- respect copyright
- save work regularly using different filenames
- keep dated backup copies of files in another location

Respect copyright

Copyright relates to an author's ownership and control of the work they produce. If a file is copyrighted it is illegal to copy it without permission from the original owner. This may include downloading and using text, images, video or sound from the Internet, as well as scanning pictures from books and other sources. Some material can be copied for personal or educational use but not if the final product is to be sold. It is not always clear what copyright exists on a piece of work. If in doubt, it is best to seek permission from the copyright owner before using the material. You should also acknowledge the source of any material you copy and use.

Copyright also applies to software. It is illegal to use software without a **licence** – either by making pirate copies of software bought by other users or, for example, using software on a network that is licensed for use on a stand-alone computer.

Save work regularly using different filenames

Many software applications have built-in facilities to save work regularly whilst you are working. Others have pop-up reminders that prompt you to save work regularly. This is a simple but very effective way to prevent the loss of data through, for example, a computer system failure or network problem. It is also important to save files regularly using a slightly different filename. For example, if you are creating a presentation, the first time you save the file it could be saved as 'mypres1.ppt'. If, having done some more work, you simply save the file without changing the filename it will overwrite the earlier version. By choosing 'Save as' and changing the number '1' to '2' at the end of the filename the earlier version will remain. If the final version (for example 'mypres6.ppt') is accidentally damaged through a software or hardware problem, you can go back to version 5 of the file and only have a small amount of work to do to complete it. Also, if you try to amend the presentation but get in a mess, or decide you don't like the changes, you can simply go back to an earlier version.

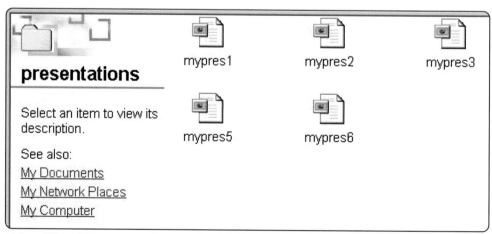

Using different filenames to keep earlier versions of a presentation.

Copyright, saving work and backups

Keep dated backup copies of files in another location

Keeping backups may be as simple as saving work onto both the hard disk (or your network storage area) and also onto a floppy disk which can be taken home. An organisation's network will have backup software and hardware installed to save work files regularly. Two copies may be made so one can be kept off-site in case of a fire, for example. The backup policy will include occasional full system backups that are also stored off-site. It is important that all backups are dated so that you know which version is being **restored**.

Did you know ...

The level of backup an organisation has depends on how vital the data is to the running of the organisation. Some organisations have mirrored systems. This means that data is saved on two identical systems. If one fails the other can still be accessed. Banks' data are so crucial that they have second systems in secure locations in the country well away from the main system. This means that they can continue to operate if the main system is destroyed.

Word check

Licence – permission to use a piece of software under certain conditions. For example a 10-user licence allows up to ten people, within the organisation that has bought the licence, to use the software at the same time.

Restore – replace lost or damaged data with a copy retrieved from a backup.

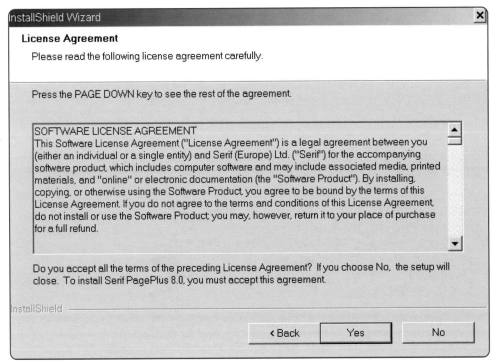

A typical licence agreement

TASKS

1. Do some research on the Internet to find out more about the laws of copyright. Produce a guide on copyright for computer users in your school or college.

2. Find out about your school's or college's backup policy and how to go about getting a lost file restored.

Physical methods of protecting data

All business data should be kept securely. Most company networks have password protection and each individual user has their own logons. On top of these security measures, though, there should be consideration given to securing the data physically.

Making sure a company's premises are secure is essential in all industries and all companies make sure that their windows and doors are securely locked at night. But many companies do not think about securing their information, beyond software passwords.

It is important that data is backed up and stored away from the computer, in a safe or secure room, or preferably off the premises. If a burglar then steals the computer, or the building burns down, some of the data may be lost, but at least there will be a second copy of the majority of the data which can be used by the company.

Data, such as employee records, wages, bank details and so on, are crucial for the running of a business. If they are lost, through theft or a fire, a company may collapse, causing the employees to lose their jobs.

Many institutions routinely back-up their systems, but the back-up media, usually a tape or CD, is often stored with the computer. If something does happen, such as a fire, the original and the back-up are lost.

There are many companies offering safe storage of data on a web-based server. This system allows the organisation to rent space on a machine somewhere else in the world. Each time a back-up is made, usually daily, the files can be uploaded to the server, where it is stored until it is needed.

This has many advantages: the organisation does not need to worry about the data being lost, they can upload at any time of the day or night; data can be downloaded easily, to replace lost information. It also means that they do not have to buy and maintain other back-up systems, such as **tape streamers**.

However there are also disadvantages: the data may not be as secure as storing it on tape or CD in a safe, as web-based systems can be hacked, although these servers are protected by firewalls and other systems. The connection to the server needs to be fast and reliable, a standard dial-up Internet account would probably not be sufficient. If the organisation's computer system is unavailable, through theft or fire, the upload and security information may also be lost. So although the data is secure, the organisation cannot retrieve it!

A relatively new idea in this field is the use of removable hard disks. Although these have been around for many years, recently companies have seen the benefits of using them to back-up and store essential information.

The computer can be used as normal, files can be backed up and the tape or CD stored in the safe. But on top of this level of security the hard disk can be removed from the machine and stored somewhere safe. This has the advantage of allowing the data to be transported to another machine relatively easily, with all of the programs, passwords and other information needed to access the data.

Physical methods of protecting data

The building that your computer system and backup tapes are in should be kept secure against burglary.

TASKS

1 Investigate the procedures used to securely store data in your school or college, or in a local company.

2 Make recommendations as to whether the security system used is sufficient.

CASE STUDY

Each evening a college backs up its financial information on to a tape via a tape streamer. The tape is then stored in a fireproof safe, where it is locked away until the next day.

There are seven tapes, each one is reused every seventh day, overwriting the data that was previously stored.

The system that was used to enroll students and to record all of the financial data developed a fault. Unfortunately nobody spotted it straight away, as it appeared to be a minor error.

The data continued to be backed up and everything seemed fine. At the end of the month the payroll was calculated using the same database. It was immediately evident that something had gone wrong as the staff wages were incorrect! No problem, thought the administration team, we will just run from the back up and maybe lose a day's data.

Unfortunately the error had also been backed up! And because they only used seven days worth of tape, and the error had been on the system for at least two weeks, there was no clean copy!

This meant an awful lot of re-entering data to try to sort out the mistake!

Working effectively and safely

By the end of this topic you will be able to:

- manage your work effectively

- work safely when using ICT

Managing your work effectively

It is easy to create folders and sub-folders in your file storage area, whether this is on a network or on a hard disk. A lot of time can be wasted searching for files that have been saved (and lost) somewhere, without any planning or organisation. You might create a folder for each subject with sub-folders for different units or topics. In addition, always save work with filenames that relate to the content – this will help you to locate them faster when you need them again. If you still have trouble finding work that you have stored carefully, there are built-in search facilities in most software packages to help you find file(s). You can search for the date and time the file was created, the filename or even some word(s) that have been used in the file.

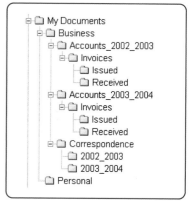

Folder structure

Working safely

There are a number of health and safety problems that can be caused by the use of computers, though the risks to the user can be greatly reduced by taking sensible precautions.

Eye-strain and **headaches** are problems that can be caused by working for long periods staring at a computer screen. One solution is to take regular breaks away from the computer. You should also refocus on something elsewhere in the room at regular intervals. A screen filter can also be useful, as can **diffuse lighting** in the room being used. It is also important that the screen is positioned to minimise glare from windows – blinds may be needed to reduce the light entering.

Repetitive strain injury (RSI) causes aches and pains, and possible damage to muscles and tendons due to repeating the same actions over and over again – for example using a mouse or keyboard. The solution is to use a well-designed keyboard, possibly including a wrist-rest. The height of the keyboard is also important. Your lower arm (from elbow to wrist) should be horizontal to prevent putting undue strain on your wrists. Taking regular breaks is also important.

Back and circulation problems are often caused by sitting for long periods using a computer. The solution is to sit correctly. You should use an adjustable chair with a suitable backrest. The chair should be adjusted so that your eyes are level with the top of the screen and your feet flat on the floor. If you are short you may need to use a footrest. You should also take regular breaks.

Trailing cables can cause people to trip and fall. This may also cause damage to equipment. All cables should be routed round the walls, preferably in suitable **conduit**. Cable ties should also be used to keep monitor and printer cables, for example, tidy. The floor and doorways should also be kept clear of bags and other objects that could be a trip hazard.

Working effectively and safely

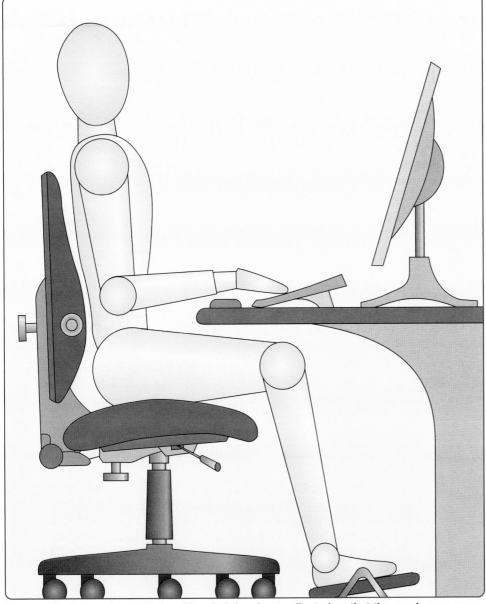

A correctly designed workstation. The chair has been adjusted so that the user's eyes are slightly above the top of the screen and a footrest and wristrest provided.

Word check

Diffuse lighting – lamps that are covered so that the light is spread out over a wider area, rather than coming from a point.

Conduit – a hollow tube fixed to, or channelled into, walls that can hold electrical and network cables.

TASKS

1 Look at your file storage area. How organised is it? Do you know what all the files contain? Re-organise your area. Create folders and sub-folders to organise your files. Check what is in any files you are not sure about. Rename them with a meaningful filename, or delete them if you no longer need them.

2 Produce a handbook for an organisation's employees, outlining health and safety issues.

Legislation and codes of practice

By the end of this topic you will be able to:

- take account of relevant legislation and codes of practice

The Data Protection Acts (1984, 1988 and **1998)** control the use of personal data stored on a computer. **Data users** must register with the Information Commissioner if they wish to store personal data on a computer system. In addition they must follow certain rules and codes of practice about:

- the type of data they can store
- how the data must be kept secure
- what they are allowed to share with others and who they can share it with
- the use to which the data can be put.

They are also required to make sure that the data is accurate and, where necessary, to update the data so that it remains accurate. Data subjects (the people whose information is stored by others) also have certain rights under these acts. More on the Data Protection Act 1998 in Section 3.

The Computer Misuse Act (1990) was introduced to control the problems caused by computer **hackers** and damage from computer viruses. It made it illegal for anyone to access areas of a computer network for which they had no permission. It also prevented people making illegal copies of computer programs and files. It made it an offence to alter computer files belonging to someone else, through deleting files or infecting them with a virus, for example. It also provided controls to prevent fraud and blackmail involving computers, such as where an organisation is threatened with a virus attack.

Hackers are people who access a computer system illegally. Unfortunately they can access other people's computers from their own computer. They do not always have to break into your office!

Legislation and codes of practice

The Copyright, Designs and Patents Act (1988) makes it illegal to copy a computer file without the permission of the owner of the copyright. When a user buys a software application they do not actually own the software – they buy a licence to use the software under certain conditions and restrictions. A single user licence, for example, only allows the software to be used by one user at any one time. They cannot make copies of the software to pass on to others unless the copyright owner gives them permission to do this. This also applies to downloading certain materials from the Internet and using them without the permission of the owners of the website.

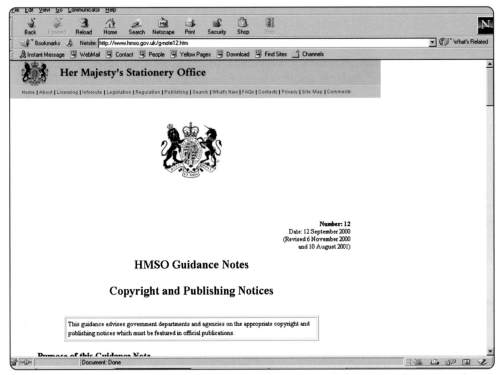

Her Majesty's Stationery Office provides information on copyright on **www.hmso.gov.uk**

Other codes of practice – All organisations that use computers have rules and codes about the use of computer hardware and software.
There may, for example, be restrictions on the use of the Internet or using floppy disks brought from home. It is important that these rules follow all the relevant laws – and also pay attention to the particular needs of the organisation. In some cases, staff who break any of these rules can be (and are) sacked on the spot!

> ### Word check
>
> **Data user** – an organisation that holds and processes personal information on a computer system – your school or college is an example of a data user.
>
> **Hacker** – a person who gains unauthorised access to a computer system or network.

TASK

1 Use the Internet to find out more about the legislation relating to computer use. Produce a presentation to summarise your findings.

2 ICT in organisations

Contents

In this section of the book we will explore how ICT is used by organisations.

Recent years have seen a revolution in the way that organisations carry out their operations. Until as recently as twenty years ago it was normal for most organisations to carry out most of their activities without the use of computers. Today it is unusual to find an organisation that does not use computers in its work.

This is a course in Applied ICT. It is about how ICT is used in the organisations where people work. In this section you will learn about a range of different types of organisation. During your studies you may have the opportunity to visit many different types of organisation and see many different types of ICT systems in operation.

Most organisations aim to make a profit, while others are funded by donations from charity or by the taxpayer. All organisations have to be careful about how much their operations cost them. All are seeking to find ways in which the use of ICT can make them more efficient.

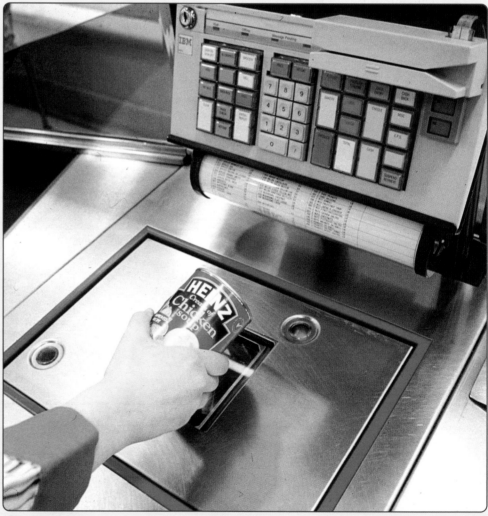

ICT is used in our everyday lives, even while shopping.

In the first section of this book you have been able to practice and develop your ICT skills across many different areas including word processing, databases, spreadsheets and graphics. You have begun to explore how business organisations can use this software to produce the documents that they need to be able to carry out their activities. In this section you will learn about the ICT systems that enable organisations to produce these documents.

You will learn about the ways in which organisations are structured. You will learn about the different ways that the various parts of an organisation make use of ICT. You will also learn about the main components of an ICT system.

Banking is reliant upon ICT to transfer funds between accounts.

Finally, you will learn how to build real ICT systems that will help organisations to become better at what they do. This, for many people, is the most interesting and rewarding part of ICT. You will learn how to think through the design and implementation of your own ICT system. You will also learn how to evaluate the effectiveness of your system.

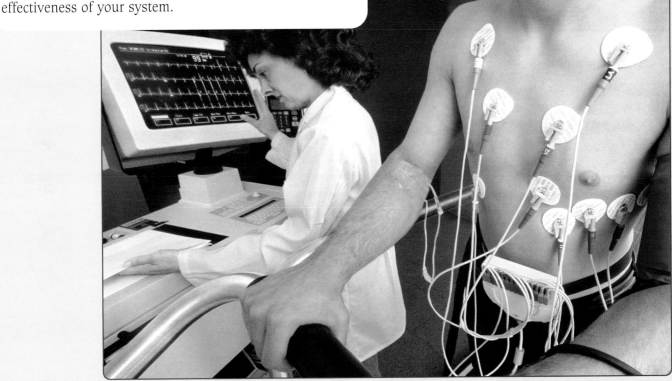

ICT even helps us to keep healthy.

Meeting the needs of the organisation

By the end of this topic you will be able to:

- understand that organisations use ICT for specific purposes
- understand that organisations make different uses of ICT depending on their specific needs

There are many different types of business organisation, all with differing needs. Some business organisations have as their main aim the desire to make a profit for their owners. Vodafone and the Royal Bank of Scotland are examples of large profit seeking businesses with branches in many different parts of the UK and abroad. They employ many hundreds of people. Other organisations can be very small, employing only one or two people.

CASE STUDY

Filmright Video Limited is a small video hire shop located in West Yorkshire. The shop hires out videos to people who hold a valid membership card. Membership is free. Customers wishing to have a membership card must present proof of their address before a card can be issued.

The business is owned by Mr Tariq Mahmood who employs two part-time staff who operate the shop in the evenings.

Mr Mahmood runs the business from a small office at the back of the shop which also doubles up as a storeroom for new and **surplus** stock. The backroom also has an area for staff to put their belongings and make tea and coffee.

The business has one personal computer. It has a small printer and is connected to the Internet using a 56kbps **modem**. The business has the following needs which are met by the use of ICT:

- to keep a list of all members, their membership numbers and home addresses
- to keep a list of which videos have been hired by which members
- to calculate the fines which are owed by members who fail to return a video on time
- to monitor which videos are the most popular and which ones should no longer be offered for hire
- to send letters to customers informing them of new videos and special offers.

TASKS

1 Which applications software could Mr Mahmood use to carry out these activities?

2 Mr Mahmood has decided that his business only needs to use one computer. Why do you think that he has made this decision?

Meeting the needs of the organisation

Non-profit making organisations

Some business organisations do not aim to make a profit. Schools and hospitals, for example, are often owned and run by the government. Their main aim is to provide an effective service for their users. However, they are usually still required to keep their spending within an agreed limit.

Word check

Surplus – something that is extra to your immediate needs.

CASE STUDY

The Holmchurch Hospital is a large National Health Service hospital based in the West Midlands. The hospital treats around 250 000 people each year and employs nearly 3000 workers.

The hospital has a number of separate computer networks which serve the various parts of the hospital. Over 80 per cent of all computer workstations are linked to the main hospital administration network. This enables files to be transferred from one part of the hospital to another.

The hospital has many differing needs which are met by ICT, including:

- to store the personal and medical records of every patient
- to transfer medical records between different hospital departments without risk of losing them
- to maintain an accurate record of the medical supplies used in the hospital
- to provide information to people who visit the hospital, for example directions to the hospital and a site map
- to monitor the health of patients.

TASKS

3 How could the hospital use computer systems to meet these needs?

4 Why do you think that a hospital makes much more use of ICT than a video store?

5 Visit the following website: www.nhsdirect.nhs.uk. How might this website, and others like it, change the way that hospitals operate in the future?

TASKS

6 Write a list of the needs of your school or college that are met by using ICT. You may need to carry out some research first.

7 Explain how ICT helps to meet these needs.

8 Are there any improvements that you could suggest to the way that these needs are met?

Using information

Computers are basically machines that store and process data. Data is the name for the **information** that is entered into and used by the computer system.

Main parts of a computer system

All computer systems have three main sections:

- *Input*: Information is turned into data and entered into the computer system.
- *Process*: Data is converted from one form into another.
- *Output*: The data is communicated back to a user as information.

The main parts of a computer system will be explored more fully in a later topic.

Sources of data error

Sometimes computer systems produce output data which does not make sense to the user. This is usually for one of two reasons:

1. There is something wrong with the computer program that processes the data.
2. There is something wrong with the input data. The computer may have carried out the correct processes but will still produce a 'wrong' result.

In this topic we look at the types of data that might be needed in a computer system. You will also learn the importance of making sure that the information collected is converted into a format suitable for the computer system.

The main parts of a computer system will be explored more fully in a later topic. However, it is important to stress that a computer system is made up of hardware which is connected together using cables. The cables are inserted into ports on each item of hardware. The computer system will also contain storage devices, such as floppy disk drives. Storage devices enable a permanent record of the data, used by the system, to be kept.

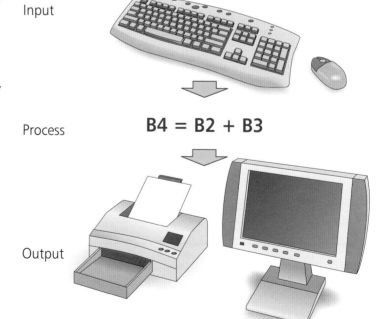

Input

$$B4 = B2 + B3$$

Process

Output

The three main parts of a computer system

Using information

TASK

 Mr Mahmood wishes to store information about his video shop's customers on a database.

There are three main reasons that he wishes to store customer information:

- to contact customers by post or telephone
- to identify customers who are not allowed to hire films they are not old enough to watch
- to keep records of which customers have hired which films.

List the main types of information that Mr Mahmood will need to collect about each of his customers.

Word check

Information – data that has a context and so makes sense to the user.

Data types and formats

Once the data that needs to be collected has been identified, the type and format of the data needs to be specified.

The data type describes the nature of the information that the data represents. For example, the data type could be **text** or **numeric**. The choice of data type is important. Some processes, for example performing calculations, can only be carried out on some data types and not others. The data format describes how the data will be displayed, for example the number 24.99 can be formatted as a currency so that it is displayed as £24.99.

- *Text*: the information that is entered is treated as text, even if it contains numbers. For example, it is not normally necessary to perform any calculations using a telephone number. Therefore telephone numbers are usually treated as text data by most databases.
- *Numeric*: this data can only contain the characters 0,1,2,3,4,5,6,7,8,9. The data can be presented in different ways on some programs. For example spreadsheets will allow the number 12.99 to be displayed as a currency with a £, $, or other currency symbol in front.
- *Date/time*: can be displayed in different formats. For example dd/mm/yy will display the date 25th December 2003 as 25/12/03. The format dd/mm/yyyy will display the same date as 25/12/2003.

TASK

 Mr Mahmood has decided to use the following types of information about his customers:

- Title, first name, last name, house name/number, street, town, postcode, telephone number and date of birth.

Which data type would be best to use for each type of information he wishes to collect?

The main functions of business organisations

By the end of this topic you will be able to:

- identify the four main functions of an organisation
- understand how large organisations are divided into smaller departments

As this is a course in Applied ICT you need to know how real business organisations use ICT to help them meet their needs. In order to do this you not only need to know about the different ways that ICT can be used, you also need to understand how organisations operate.

Over the next few pages you will learn how large organisations operate and what their main functions are. You will also learn how they are organised. Throughout this topic our main focus is on how organisations use ICT.

In an earlier topic you learned about a video shop and a hospital. One of the many differences between the two organisations is their size. The video store employed only three people, while the hospital employed nearly 3000.

Whatever their size, organisations all need to carry out the same four main functions. What is different is how those functions are organised.

Four basic functions of an organisation

All organisations need to undertake the following four functions:

1. Sales

All organisations usually provide a product or service for their clients or customers. Profit-seeking organisations, such as an Internet bookstore, will try to sell their products to customers in exchange for money. The money they receive from sales is the main income the business needs to pay its expenses. If the business' income is greater than its expenses then it will make a profit.

$$\text{Profit} = \text{Income} - \text{Expenses}$$

2. Purchasing

All organisations need to bring in the goods and services that they need in order to carry out their operations. A supermarket, for example, needs to purchase the food and other products that it then sells to its customers. A hospital needs to purchase the medicines and medical equipment that it needs to provide a service to its patients. All organisations need to purchase the services of the people who work for them. These people are called employees if they work for the business, or contractors if they are hired for a specific period of time.

TASKS

1. What are the main sources of income for your school or college?
2. What are the main items purchased by your school or college?

The main functions of business organisations

3. Finance
An organisation needs to make sure that it has enough money available to pay for its purchases and other expenses. If there is not enough money available from the sale of its own products then the organisation needs to find the money from elsewhere. The organisation also needs to account for its income and expenditure so that, for example, it pays the right amount of **taxation** to the government.

4. Operations
An organisation needs to be able to carry out the activities that it has to perform. For example, a business which makes pre-packed sandwiches needs to be able to turn its raw materials (bread, margarine/butter, fillings, packaging) into the finished sandwich products. The organisation may need to carry out its operations by observing certain laws, for example, health and safety, and food hygiene laws.

Dividing the organisation into departments
Most large organisations divide up the main functions of their business into different departments, as it is easier to manage the work of a smaller group of people.

One of the problems with dividing an organisation into different departments is that it becomes harder to co-ordinate the work of different departments. One reason for this is that people are very aware of the work of their own department, but sometimes find it difficult to see things from the point of view of other departments and of the business as a whole.

Word check

Taxation – money that has to be paid to the government, which is used to finance government spending.

CASE STUDY

Rawlinson's Haulage is a family-owned business which operates a large fleet of container lorries throughout the UK. The company's head office is based in Sussex but since 1998 most of the firm's lorries have operated from six different bases throughout the UK. The firm's main sales department is based in Sussex, but lorry operations are run from the firm's Newcastle lorry depot. This has caused problems for the firm as there have been several occasions when the sales department has agreed work which the operations department has been unable to fulfil because of a lack of suitable lorries.

The owner, Barry Rawlinson, is considering upgrading the firm's computer system to enable more effective communication to take place between the different parts of the organisation.

TASKS

3 How is your school or college organised?

4 Write a paragraph explaining how each of the main functions are carried out and by whom.

5 Are there any other important functions not covered by this list?

The work of the sales department

Key marketing issues

- What products should the organisation produce?
- What price should be charged for them?
- How will the organisation make customers aware of the products?

The sales department of an organisation is often the first one that a customer comes into contact with.

The main responsibility of the sales department is to make sure that the organisation sells its products to its customers. Unless the firm can bring in sufficient sales revenue it will not have a chance of making a profit.

The sales function is often combined with another important function called marketing. Marketing is the way in which the organisation presents itself and its products to existing and potential customers.

The sales department is generally responsible for the following activities:

- all day-to-day communication with customers
- taking customer orders
- **liaising** with other departments, for example the operations department, to check the availability of products
- maintaining a database of customer information
- keeping customers informed of the progress of their order towards completion
- providing after-sales service to customers once the product has been delivered.

CASE STUDY

Jameson and Jameson is a leading supplier of health care products to the medical profession. The firm sells its products throughout England and Wales.

Michael Rhodes is a Sales Manager at Jameson and Jameson. He is based at the firm's North Yorkshire sales office.

Michael is responsible for carrying out the following tasks:

- Making sure that sales staff have up-to-date information about products, prices and availability.
- Monitoring sales trends to identify products which are not selling as well as expected.
- Maintaining lists of active and potential customers. These are produced from the Sales Representatives' weekly reports.

TASK

1 Write a list of how the sales department could use ICT to carry out these activities.

The work of the sales department

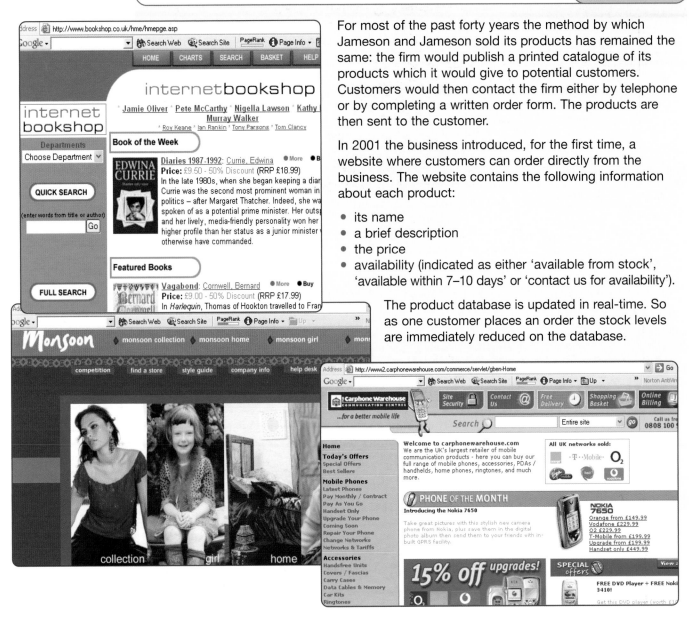

For most of the past forty years the method by which Jameson and Jameson sold its products has remained the same: the firm would publish a printed catalogue of its products which it would give to potential customers. Customers would then contact the firm either by telephone or by completing a written order form. The products are then sent to the customer.

In 2001 the business introduced, for the first time, a website where customers can order directly from the business. The website contains the following information about each product:

- its name
- a brief description
- the price
- availability (indicated as either 'available from stock', 'available within 7–10 days' or 'contact us for availability').

The product database is updated in real-time. So as one customer places an order the stock levels are immediately reduced on the database.

Visit the websites of the following retailers:

WH Smith: www.bookshop.co.uk
Monsoon: www.monsoon.co.uk
Carphone Warehouse: www.carphonewarehouse.com

2 Apart from what they sell, how are the websites similar and different to each other?

3 How do businesses which sell products online ensure that data is kept secure?

Word check

Liaising – the process of making contact with other people. For example to check the progress of an order.

How the sales department uses ICT

By the end of this topic you will be able to:

● understand how and why a sales department uses ICT to carry out its main activities

Sales departments use a wide range of information and communication technologies to help them carry out their main activities. In the previous topic we saw how businesses are increasingly using the Internet as a location to market and sell their products. In this topic you will learn about some of the other ways that the sales department uses ICT.

ICT used in sales

Customer databases

It is important that organisations keep up-to-date records of their customers. It is important to know who has purchased which products, how much they have spent and when they last purchased a product. This information provides the organisation with important marketing knowledge which they can use to target their products at the right customers.

TASK

1 Why would a business not use a person's SURNAME as the key field in a customer database?

Keeping accurate customer records is an important part of customer service. Many businesses identify their customers by a unique customer code. The customer is given the code and they use it whenever they contact the business. The code is the primary key which identifies the customer's details in the organisation's database. The sales assistant enters the customer number into the database and the customer's details are then displayed. This saves time for both the customer and the business when placing orders. Websites that have an online order form sometimes use a combination of the customer's email address and a secret password to extract the customer details from the database.

Computerised order systems

Most large organisations use computer systems to enter and process customer orders. The computer system usually consists of a **relational database** containing a customer data file and a product data file. The key field is either the customer number or the product code. Once entered onto the system the order details are sent to the production department's computer system.

Interflora sell flowers on the Internet.

Many businesses now allow customers to enter orders directly onto their computer system. This is often done via the Internet using a **secure server**. Airlines and online bookstores are examples of organisations that do this.

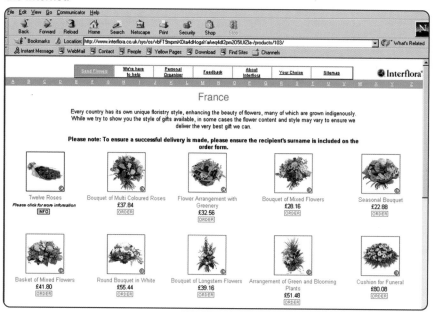

TASK

2 Visit the following two websites:

www.amazon.co.uk
www.interflora.co.uk

How do they differ in the way that they enable customers to place orders?

How the sales department uses ICT

Analysis of sales patterns and trends

The marketing function of a business relies upon having accurate information of customer sales patterns and trends. One source of this information is the organisation's own computer database files of customer transactions.

One of the reasons for the introduction of **loyalty cards** by large retailers such as supermarkets has been the need to match information on product sales to the records it has of each customer. The diagram opposite explains how a loyalty card scheme helps the supermarket keep a database of customer purchases.

The customer database can be **interrogated** to produce reports on a yearly, monthly or even daily basis. The reports can provide a summary of sales figures and can be produced as tables or graphs. The reports are analysed by senior managers. This helps them to market their products more effectively.

Buying goods at the supermarket checkout

The cashier uses a *scanner* to read the unique code for each product contained on the *bar code*.

The till extracts the price of the product from the product database and adds this to the sales total recorded on the till.

The system keeps a list of all the products bought by the customer.

The cashier then *swipes* the customer's loyalty card through a *card-reader*. The loyalty card contains details about the customer on a magnetic strip.

The customer's details are then matched to the details of their purchases. A permanent record is then saved of the items bought by the customer. This information is stored on a customer database.

TASK

RG Foods Ltd is a leading manufacturer of crisps. It currently produces two main products: Hiker's Crisps, a standard product aimed at the mass market and Gourmet Traditional, aimed at the luxury end.

The sales manager has provided you with the following sales figures for the past 12 months:

Total monthly sales (thousands of bags)												
Product	Jan.	Feb.	Mar.	Apr.	May	Jun.	Jul.	Aug.	Sep.	Oct.	Nov.	Dec.
Hiker's Crisps	128	125	122	135	132	130	129	129	120	121	118	114
Gourmet Traditional	56	53	52	51	52	51	49	50	47	46	46	44

3 Use the above data to produce a report for the sales manager. The report should contain the data, at least one graph and a written summary of the main trends. You may need to use different software to produce each part of the report then combine them into a single document.

Word check

Interrogation – the process of searching a database, using certain search criteria, to extract specific information.

The work of the purchasing department

The work of the purchasing department is no less important to the business than the sales department. While the sales department is ultimately responsible for winning the orders that will enable the business to survive, the purchasing department is responsible for making sure that the organisation has the supplies that it needs to carry out its operations.

No business makes everything that it needs itself. Computer manufacturers, for example, purchase **components** such as microprocessors from specialist manufacturers. Most of the components found inside a PC will not have been made by the company whose name appears on the front of the computer.

Customer requirements

Most organisations face two conflicting pressures from their customers: customers want to buy high quality products but want to pay as little as possible for them. Customers also want products to be delivered as quickly as possible after placing their order.

As a result, the purchasing department needs to obtain high-quality raw materials but pay as little as possible for them.

The purchasing process

Identify the product required

↓

Identify possible suppliers

↓

Compare price, quality and availability of different suppliers' products

↓

Place an order with the best value supplier

↓

Monitor the order to check when it will be delivered

↓

Take delivery and put into stock or production

CASE STUDY

Phillipa Johnson is the purchasing manager for Stamford Audio Limited. The organisation makes a range of quality speakers for music systems. The firm's products cost between £250 and £2000 for each pair of speakers. Phillipa is responsible for buying the components that the production department needs to make the speakers.

Each time a new product is designed the engineers specify the type of components needed. The firm also has a budget for the overall cost of the components. The total cost of the components needed for the Exemplar 50 speaker range, for example, must not be greater than £85.

Phillipa orders components from suppliers who can offer the best combination of price, delivery and performance. All components must meet a minimum level of performance; this is set by the engineers. If two or more suppliers can meet the performance levels set by the engineers then it is up to Phillipa to decide which of them is given the order to supply the components.

The work of the purchasing department

Stock control

Managing stock is an important activity of the purchasing department. All firms need to carry a stock of raw materials and office supplies. For example a restaurant needs to carry a stock of the foods it needs to make its meals.

If the restaurant does not have enough stock then it will run out of ingredients and be unable to make certain meals. This might lose the restaurant income if customers are unhappy and decide to eat elsewhere.

On the other hand, having too much stock can also be expensive. If the restaurant has too much stock of fresh ingredients they may become unusable and so represent a waste of money. It also costs money to find the storage space to keep surplus stock.

In an ideal world an organisation would not need to keep any stock. The supplies that they need would arrive from suppliers at the exact moment they were needed in the right quantities. This would help keep costs to a minimum and so make the business more competitive. This is the aim of a system called *just-in-time* stock control.

CASE STUDY

Jill Andrews is a production worker at Noisecraft Electronics. The firm manufactures a range of computer controlled sound recording and mixing systems. The market for these products is very competitive, especially at the low-cost end of the market. The firm faces strong competition from low-cost manufacturers in Asia. As a result, the firm has looked at ways to reduce its costs.

The firm has recently introduced a just-in-time stock control system. It is the responsibility of operatives such as Jill to identify when stock levels of particular components have reached a low level. The firm has an arrangement with suppliers that orders placed before 5:00 pm will be delivered by 9:00 am the following day. As a result, Noisecraft has reduced its stock holdings by over 80 per cent and saved itself thousands of pounds in the past year.

The system has not always worked smoothly. In fact Jill is so unhappy with the system that she calls it 'just-too-late' not just-in-time!

TASK

1 Identify the possible problems for Noisecraft of using a just-in-time stock control system.

TASK

2 Interview the person responsible for maintaining the computer network in your school or college.

- Which suppliers do they use to help them maintain the network?
- How do they choose the suppliers?
- How can ICT be used to manage the process of purchasing from suppliers?
- How is the level of stock managed?
- How could ICT be used to improve stock control?

Word check

Component – a piece of equipment that is used to form part of a larger piece of equipment. For example a mobile telephone will be made by combining together a number of different electronic components.

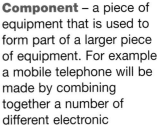

How the purchasing department uses ICT

Computerised stock control – delivery tracking

Once an order has been placed by the purchase department it is important to know when the product is going to be delivered.

Organisations are increasingly using ICT to enable their customers to keep a track on how their products are progressing once the order has been placed.

When an order is processed the supplier's computer system generates a unique reference number (URN). This number is issued to the customer, perhaps by email. The customer can then access the supplier's operations database, usually by using an input form on their supplier's website.

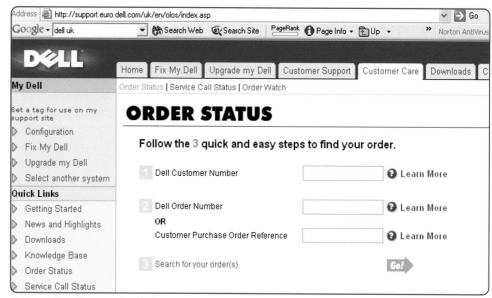

Delivery tracking on the Dell website.

Automatic stock reordering

Most stock control systems will enable the system to keep an accurate record of the quantity currently available in stock. For example, when a supermarket sells a can of baked beans the bar code on the can is read by the bar-code reader at the checkout. This information is then processed by the product database and the quantity of baked beans cans in stock is reduced by one.

Most systems will have an automatic reorder level. When the number of cans falls to this level an output message is generated. The output message could be an entry in a daily printed stock shortage report. This method would be used if the product is to be manually reordered by the purchasing department. More sophisticated systems will send an order automatically directly to the supplier using **electronic data interchange (EDI)**.

e-procurement

This is short for electronic procurement. This is the term used for the process of buying and selling products over the Internet from **business to business (B2B)**. It is particularly useful for buying standard commodity items such as printer paper or light bulbs. Sophisticated systems link e-procurement to automatic stock reordering systems.

How the purchasing department uses ICT

United Distillers is one of the UK's leading suppliers of alcoholic drinks. At its main Coventry distribution centre it carries a stock of up to 8 million bottles of over 400 different products.

United Distillers uses a computerised stock management system to identify, store and locate products within its warehouse.

Products arrive in cases loaded onto pallets. Each pallet is given a URN when it first arrives. The stock management system identifies the best place in the warehouse to store the pallet. This location is then recorded in the system. When an order is received that requires the pallet, the system identifies where the pallet has been stored by using the URN.

This system has a number of benefits for United Distillers and its customers:

- It is paperless, therefore reducing the chances of human error.
- It identifies the most efficient location to store the product; this reduces the chance of wastage.
- It minimises the amount of warehouse space needed, reducing costs for both United Distillers and its customers.

Word check

Business to business (B2B) – a term used to describe when one business deals with another business, rather than with an individual customer.

1 A supermarket would like to have a minimum stock level of 200 cans of baked beans. It sells on average 50 cans per day. It normally takes two days for the cans to arrive after being ordered.

How many cans of baked beans should be in stock when the automatic reorder level is reached?

2 A small sports shop wishes to set up a simple stock control system on its PC. It currently records stock levels for its products on a spreadsheet.

Part of the spreadsheet is displayed below.

Each product has a different reorder quantity. At the moment the owner has to compare the number in stock with the reorder level for each product to identify if any need reordering. The owner wants you to extend the spreadsheet so that when the quantity of a particular item in stock reaches the reorder level an output message is displayed on the spreadsheet.

	A	B	C	D
1	Item	Product code	Number in stock	Reorder level
2	Tennis balls	66926	120	100
3	Golf balls	45380	65	90
4	Cricket balls	41896	40	45
5	Basketballs	12562	10	5
6	Footballs	64814	41	40

The work of the operations department

The operations department is often thought of as the 'nerve centre' of the business. All businesses have a number of 'core activities', these are the activities that generate the sales income that the business needs in order to prosper and grow. It is these core activities that help to define the nature of the business.

For example, the core activity of a supermarket is to purchase, distribute and sell products to shoppers in its stores. In contrast, the core activity of a car manufacturer is the assembly of cars from parts bought in from outside suppliers.

The core activities of the business help to determine exactly what happens in the operations department. In this topic we will look at the typical operations activities of a **manufacturing business** and a **service business**.

TASK

1. What are the core activities of the following businesses:

   - an on-line bookstore?
   - a fast-food restaurant?
   - shoe repair workshop?

Fast-food restaurants have different core activities from a shoe repair workshop or an on-line bookstore.

Main activities of the operations department

All operations departments need to:

- identify and obtain the resources needed for production
- choose the best method for producing the products
- devise a production schedule to make sure that products are produced on time and in accordance with customer requirements
- check the quality of products.

All operations departments need to produce their goods and services using a combination of the following resources:

- buildings and land (for example offices, factories, shops, farmland)
- equipment (for example, vehicles, computers, machinery)
- people (for example, operators, managers, support staff, specialists)
- materials (for example, products for retailing, raw materials for manufacturing goods).

The work of the operations department

CASE STUDY

KP Containers manufactures tin cans for use in the food and drinks industry. Cans are an effective way of storing food products for a long period of time. Most cans made in the world conform to a number of standard sizes and specifications.

KP Containers make thousands of cans each day using a technique called *flow production*. Raw materials enter the factory and are passed along a production line where a number of different processes gradually turn the raw materials into the finished tin cans.

Cans are made from sheets of steel or aluminium which are then shaped and cut into the required size and shape of can. The process is largely automated. During the process a number of different coatings are applied to the cans. These help protect the can and its contents from damage.

At the end of the process the cans are tested to make sure that the can contains no leaks. Otherwise air and other elements will leak into the can, spoiling the contents.

Word check

Manufacturing business – an organisation that produces goods, such as cars, televisions and freezers.

Service business – an organisation that provides services, such as banking, restaurant meals or theme parks.

CASE STUDY

Midshires Bank is a new telephone and Internet based banking service. It does not have any traditional high street branches. At the moment around 60 per cent of the bank's business is conducted over the telephone. Customers call a freephone number which connects them to the bank's main call centre in Leeds. The call centre employs over 300 operators. All operators work with a **dumb terminal** – a computer workstation that is connected to the bank's main computer server but has no processing power of its own.

Staff first check the customer's username and a number of passwords. This gains access to the customer's bank account details which are then displayed on screen. The operator is then able to check the customer's bank balance, answer account queries and process payment requests.

Some of the bank's customers prefer to use their Internet banking service because they do not like the idea that they have no written record of the transactions carried out over the telephone.

TASKS

2 Write a list of the differences between the ways that the two businesses organise their production.

3 How could the two businesses use ICT to help them improve production?

4 If possible, visit at least two different organisations and identify how they organise their production. How do they use ICT?

How the operations department uses ICT

In this topic we will look at how a tin can manufacturer and a telephone banking service can both use ICT to help them carry out their production activities.

Computer aided design (CAD)

CAD software enables manufacturers to design and test new products without having to build full working models or replicas. For example a tin can manufacturer is able to produce a design of a new product. The design helps to make sure that the can will be of the right size, and that the top and bottom of the can will fit together.

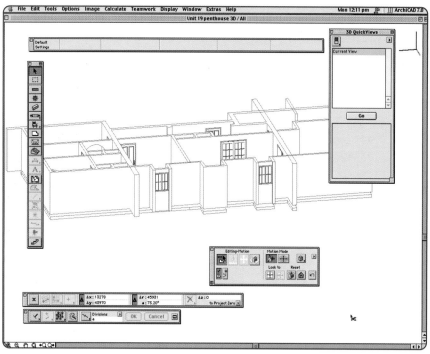

A product being designed in CAD.

Once created on screen the original design can then be modified. For example by increasing the capacity of the can the software can recalculate the size of the can and the amount of materials needed. The design can also be rotated on screen so that a top- and side-projection can be viewed. Software can also be used to test the design to see how it will withstand shocks. For example the tin can may be tested to see how easily it will dent, and whether the dents are likely to create leaks.

Computer aided manufacturing (CAM)

Once the can has been designed, data about its dimensions and materials are used as input into a CAM system. The system will then calculate the most efficient way to manufacture the product. These details can then be fed into robots and computer numeric control (CNC) machines which will then ensure that the product is manufactured exactly as designed.

Some robots and CNC machinery will only operate by carrying out a pre-programmed set of operations: for example a paint sprayer may be programmed to always spray in a particular direction when a signal is given to it. Other systems make use of **feedback** from sensors so that, for example, the paint sprayer may change direction if it detects that the object has moved.

TASK

1 Design a new box for an orange juice manufacturer with an overall volume of 160 cm³. The boxes need to look attractive when stacked on a supermarket shelf. Use the most appropriate software available to you.

How the operations department uses ICT

Quality control

ICT can be used to test the quality of a manufactured product. For example a tin can may be rejected if its weight lies outside a given tolerance (for example + or – 0.5g) or if the protective coating applied is too thin or too thick.

The finished product can be tested using sensors. For example the thickness of the coating can be tested using a laser beam. If the thickness is too great then the can will be rejected. If the coating is too thin the can could be rerouted through the production line to have more coating added.

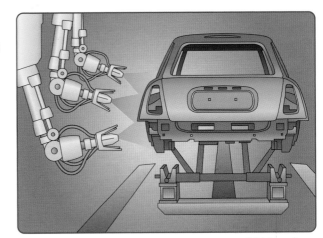

Statistical process control

Manufacturers often check the quality of their products at the end of the process. If the product has any serious defects it may be returned to production to be improved or even rejected. Statistical process control tests the product throughout the production stage and uses the results to provide instant feedback to the manufacturing process. For example, if the thickness of a coating is found to be above the allowed level, the time that the can spends in contact with the coating could be reduced or the properties of the coating changed. This system relies on computer controlled manufacturing processes using feedback from sensors.

The details from CAM, on how to build a car efficiently, are fed into robots, ensuring that the car is built exactly as designed.

Telephone recording, monitoring and analysis

Telephone call centres receive thousands of telephone calls every day. They operate in a very competitive environment and the owners are therefore keen to improve the quality of service and efficiency of the operation. As a result, most call centres record telephone conversations in case of later disputes. The work of staff can also then be monitored.

Computer software is available which can retrieve both a telephone conversation and replay the on-screen commands given to the computer by the operator. The organisation can then check that the commands matched the instructions of the customer.

The organisation is then able to measure the speed at which operators work. Calls can also be analysed, for example data about each call can be collected and entered into a database. The database can then produce reports in the form of charts and graphs which can be analysed to help the call centre improve its performance.

> **Word check**
>
> **Feedback** – a situation where data from a sensor is used to influence the actions of a computer system. For example a temperature sensor can be used to control the operations of an air conditioning system.

TASKS

2 If possible, visit a manufacturer to find out how they ensure that the quality of their finished products is as good as possible.

3 Write a list of the types of information that a call centre might wish to collect and store about each telephone call.

The work of the finance department

All organisations, whether or not they aim to make a profit, need to make sure they account for the money which they receive and spend.

Accounting for income and spending

For most businesses the main source of money is the income received from selling products to customers. Other sources of money include bank **loans** and money invested into the business by the owners. Organisations such as schools and hospitals, which are owned by the government, receive most of their income as **grants** from the government.

Organisations need money to pay suppliers and staff wages as well as other expenses such as taxation and the repayment of bank loans.

One of the jobs of the finance department is to keep records of every item of income and expenditure. This information used to be recorded by hand in large books called ledgers. This required large numbers of clerks to enter the information by hand and so was very labour-intensive. Today, however, the process is largely computerised.

Did you know ...

You can find out more about financial accounts in any GCSE Business Studies or GCSE in Applied Business textbook.

Keeping accurate financial records

As well as making sure that there is enough money to pay the bills, the finance department needs to make sure that an accurate record is kept of all the organisation's income and spending. There are a number of important reasons for this:

- to make sure that the organisation's owners know what has happened to their money
- to reduce the chances of improper use of the money
- to enable the government to calculate the tax that the organisation needs to pay.

Most organisations are required by law to produce accounts which summarise the financial transactions carried out. Two important accounts for a business organisation are the **Profit and Loss Account** and the **Balance Sheet**.

ACME COMMUNICATIONS TRADING PROFIT AND LOSS ACCOUNT for year ended 30th September 2003	£	£
Turnover		115000
COST OF SALES:		
Opening Stock	1500	
Purchases	6000	
Closing Stock	(1100)	6400
GROSS PROFIT		108600
LESS EXPENSES:		
Wages	49000	
Motor Expenses	3000	
Advertising	2350	
Post & Stationery	4200	
Repairs & Renewals	2080	
Heat & Light	3700	
Communications	6500	
Professional Fees	1200	
Depreciation	3000	
Bad Debts	1900	
Sundries	475	77405
		31195
Less Interest Payable:		
Loans payable within 5 years		700
NET PROFIT FOR THE YEAR		30495

A typical profit and loss account

The work of the finance department

Travelglobe is an independent travel agency based in the west of England. It has 20 branches and employs nearly 100 staff. Each branch is run by a manager. One of the responsibilities of each manager is the ordering of office supplies.

All orders must be placed using the firm's official Purchase Order Form. This form contains a unique order number which must be quoted by suppliers on all invoices. The purchase order must be signed by the branch manager.

Items which cost over £200 can only be ordered through the company's Finance Department at head office. The branch manager completes an order form as normal but sends it to the finance department where, if the order is approved, it will be **countersigned** by a senior manager. The finance department will refuse to pay for any item whose value exceeds this amount if it has been ordered by the branch manager.

Word check

Loan – the money given to an organisation that must be repaid.

Grant – the money given to an organisation that does not need to be repaid.

CASE STUDY

John Smedley runs a garden design business. John's customers include private households as well as clubs and businesses.

John usually agrees a fee in advance with each client before starting the work. When the work has been completed John sends the client an invoice. This is a demand for payment for the work John has done. John's invoices give customers 30 days to pay him. When customers have paid John he sends them a **remittance advice note**. This confirms that John has received the payment.

TASKS

1. Find out from your school or college finance officer how the organisation controls the purchase of goods and services. Who has the authority to place orders? How is this monitored?

2. Obtain a copy of an invoice either received by or sent from your school or college. What information does it contain?

3. How could ICT be used to make the production of invoices more efficient?

How the finance department uses ICT

Computerised accounts packages

Every transaction involving money into and out of the business has to be recorded. Modern accounting software makes it easier for an organisation to record income and expenditure, keep a permanent record, locate individual transactions, and produce reports and accounts.

Many software systems also enable the organisation to easily produce the information required by the main government taxation agencies: the **Inland Revenue** and **Customs and Excise**.

Every time the business issues an invoice the system generates a new invoice number. The organisation can use the invoice numbers and the URNs (unique reference numbers) to track all payments and produce reports summarising income and expenditure.

TASKS

1 If possible, try to observe a computerised accounts package in operation. Your school or college finance department might be able to demonstrate it to you.

2 Search the Internet for suppliers of these packages. Sometimes they allow visitors to download sample programs or screen-shots.

Payroll

Many organisations now use ICT to pay their staff. The organisation identifies how much it needs to pay each member of staff. Sometimes the computer system will calculate the total wage from the hours worked by the person multiplied by the person's hourly rate.

Once the amount to be paid has been identified the system sends an instruction to pay the money into the bank account of each employee. This request is sent to the organisation's bank, usually using **electronic data interchange (EDI)**. The bank then transfers the money from the organisation's bank account to the employee's bank account via the computerised **Banks Automated Clearing System (BACS)**.

Most employees have to pay Income Tax and National Insurance to the government. The payroll system will calculate how much has to be paid and deduct this from the money owed to the employee. The employee therefore receives their pay after tax has been deducted. The system finally prints a **payslip** which details how much has been paid to the employee and how much has been deducted.

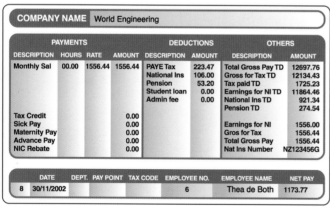

A typical pay slip, showing tax and National Insurance contributions.

How the finance department uses ICT

Using spreadsheets to produce forecasts

Many of the functions of a simple accounting system can be produced using standard spreadsheet software.

A cash flow forecast is an important document which estimates the likely income and spending of an organisation in the future. The organisation can then see if there are any periods when it might be short of cash. If there are it can then take steps (such as obtaining a bank overdraft) to solve the cash flow problem.

To the top right is an example of a spreadsheet cash flow forecast together with the formulas used.

In the example below right **conditional formatting** has been used to turn red any cells where there is a negative number. This makes it easier to identify when there is a potential cash flow problem.

	A	B	C	D	E	F	G
1	Cash Flow Forecast						
2		January	February	March	April	May	June
3	**Money in**						
4	Sales	£25,000	£25,000	£35,000	£45,000	£55,000	£66,000
5	**Total Receipts (A)**	£25,000	£25,000	£35,000	£45,000	£55,000	£66,000
6							
7	**Money out**						
8	Purchase machinery			£25,000			
9	Materials	£9,000	£11,000	£13,000	£18,000	£22,000	£22,000
10	Wages	£10,000	£10,000	£10,000	£10,000	£10,000	£10,000
11	Loan repayments	£200	£200	£200	£200	£200	£200
12	Other payments		£200	£500		£200	£500
13	**Total Payments (B)**	£19,200	£21,400	£48,700	£28,200	£32,400	£32,700
14							
15	**Opening balance (C)**	£800	£6,600	£10,200	-£3,500	£13,300	£35,900
16	**Receipts (A) - Payments (B)**	£5,800	£3,600	-£13,700	£16,800	£22,600	£33,300
17	**Closing balance (C + (A - B))**	**£6,600**	**£10,200**	-£3,500	**£13,300**	**£35,900**	**£69,200**

	A	B	C	D	E	F
1	Cash Flow Forecast					
2		January	February	March	April	May	June
3	Money in					
4	Sales	25000	25000	35000	45000	55000	6600(
5	Total Receipts (A)	=SUM(B4:B4)	=SUM(C4:C4)	=SUM(D4:D4)	=SUM(E4:E4)	=SUM(F4:F4)	=SUM
6						
7	Money out					
8	Purchase machinery			25000		
9	Materials	9000	11000	13000	18000	22000	2200(
10	Wages	10000	10000	10000	10000	10000	1000(
11	Loan repayments	200	200	200	200	200	200
12	Other payments		200	500		200	500
13	Total Payments (B)	=SUM(B8:B12)	=SUM(C8:C12)	=SUM(D8:D12)	=SUM(E8:E12)	=SUM(FE:F12)	=SUM
14						
15	Opening balance (C)	800	=B17	=C17	=D17	=E17	=F17
16	Receipts (A) - Payments (B)	=B5-B13	=C5-C13	=D5-D13	=E5-E13	=F5-F13	=G5-(
17	Closing balance (C + (A - B))	=SUM(B15:B16)	=SUM(C15:C16)	=SUM(D15:D16)	=SUM(E15:E16)	=SUM(F15:F16)	=SUM

CASE STUDY

Travelglobe uses a software package to maintain its financial records. It also uses spreadsheet software to produce its cash flow forecast and has found a number of benefits from using computerised financial systems:

- it is easier to keep track of payments into and out of the organisation
- it has reduced the amount of paper that the organisation needs to store
- there is less chance of important financial information getting lost or filed in the wrong place
- it can carry out 'what-if' analysis, for example by predicting the impact on cash flow of an increase in the number of office staff
- reports can be generated easily.

However a number of problems have occurred:

- the cost of installing and maintaining the computer software has proved more expensive than originally estimated
- new finance staff have to be trained to use the software
- some important data was lost when a back-up disk became corrupted. The organisation now keeps three back-up copies of the data at any one time.

TASKS

3 Use a spreadsheet to reproduce the cash flow forecast. Make sure your formulas and conditional formatting give the same result as the one above.

4 What would be the effect on the business if sales income in January and February were £15 000 not £25 000?

Business communication methods

No organisation can survive unless it can communicate information. The most successful organisations are generally those where the importance of communication is recognised and steps are taken to ensure that communication takes place as effectively as possible.

Communication is a two-way process of **transmitting** and receiving information. Speaking English to a person who only speaks French would enable information to be transmitted but not exchanged, so no communication would take place.

It is also important that the received message is the same as the message that is intended. Messages that are confusing or ambiguous will result in the recipient misunderstanding the communication. Mistakes can happen and sometimes these mistakes can be costly.

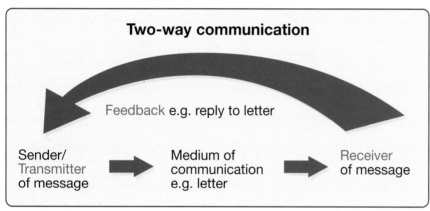

Two-way communication

Feedback e.g. reply to letter

Sender/ Transmitter of message → Medium of communication e.g. letter → Receiver of message

Internal and external communication

Internal and external communication

When communication is between two members of the same organisation it is called **internal communication**. Sometimes the two people may be in the same department, while on other occasions they may be in different departments.

A memorandum (usually shortened to memo) is a written communication device only used for internal communication. It enables written messages to be given from one person to another. Memos are often used to communicate important information from one employee to another. Memos are increasingly being replaced by emails as the main form of formal internal communication.

External communication takes place whenever the organisation exchanges information with someone outside the organisation. This would normally be with customers and suppliers. External communication is important because it is usually the main contact that outside people have with the organisation. How the organisation communicates is an important part of its public image.

Memo

To: All Staff
From: Jayne Smethington, Health and Safety Officer
Date: August 9, 2003
Re: Computer Monitors

Please note that in accordance with the new Health and Safety Policy you may be entitled to use an anti-glare display screen device. To find out if you are eligible please contact me on extension 2523.

Memos are used internally within an organisation.

Business communication methods

Communication methods

There are a number of different methods of communicating information from one person to another.

Some of the important questions that help to decide which communication method to use include the following:

- how quickly does the communication need to happen?
- how complex is the message?
- does a permanent record need to be kept?
- does the information need to be given to more than one person or organisation?
- can the information be made available to anyone who wishes to access it?

Word check

Transmit – the process of sending a message to another person. Communication only takes place once the transmitted message has been received and understood.

Communication method	Examples of when it might be used	Benefits	Drawbacks
Written communication	Letters, memos, reports, brochures	• Complex information can be communicated • A permanent record can be kept • Copies can be circulated to more than one person	• Can take time to deliver the document • Hard to obtain feedback from the recipient that they have understood the message
Verbal communication	Telephone calls, face-to-face meetings, presentations	• Instant feedback can be obtained from the recipient • The message can be repeated and changed if it is not at first understood	• Difficult to communicate with large groups of people • Difficult to keep a permanent record of what was communicated
Graphical communication	Charts and diagrams	• Complex patterns and relationships can be summarised • Some people prefer to receive information visually	• Can sometimes be complex and difficult to understand unless explained

TASKS

1 From your school/college or another organisation obtain a copy of a memo sent internally and a letter sent externally. What are the differences in the design, layout and language of the two documents?

2 You work for Sheriff Public Relations, a company which specialises in providing publicity for celebrities. You have recently gained a new client: Garth Jones, a famous American movie star. You will be helping Garth to raise his public profile in the UK.

- Write two memos. The first is to be sent to all staff and is to tell them the good news that the business has won the job of providing publicity for Garth. The second memo is to inform staff that the business has a vacancy for a new marketing manager.

Business communication documents

Each of the four main business functions uses a number of specific documents to communicate information to other users. A number of business documents were introduced when you studied ICT Tools and Applications.

Sales and marketing

The sales and marketing department is mainly concerned with external communication between the organisation and its customers. The documents produced by this department are very important in helping to persuade customers to purchase products from the organisation.

Brochures and catalogues

Brochures are a way of providing information to the customer about the organisation and its products. Sales brochures are often glossy and expensive to produce. They are designed to make the customer interested in the organisation and its products by providing basic information and include contact details, should the customer wish to receive further information.

Catalogues provide more detailed and specific information about the organisation's products. They are designed to help the customer identify the specific products that are right for them. They will contain more detailed information about each product. They often contain an order form to help the customer place an order for their chosen products.

TASK

1. Obtain a number of sales brochures and catalogues from different organisations.

   Compare them: which ones are designed to be persuasive and which ones provide detailed product information?

Questionnaires

One important way that organisations obtain information from customers is by carrying out **market research**. An important market research document is the questionnaire. This is a document designed to collect information which can then be analysed by the organisation.

Some questionnaires are designed to be completed by an interviewer, others by the customer. If the questionnaire is to be completed by the customer it is important that the questions are carefully worded to avoid any misunderstandings.

TASK

2. Use ICT to design a questionnaire to find out what people in your school or college think about your canteen and how it could be improved. Test your questionnaire by asking five people to complete it and give you feedback on how well the questionnaire has been designed. Use this feedback to make improvements to your questionnaire.

Business communication documents

Purchasing

The main document used by the purchasing department is a purchase order form. This form will contain the name and address of the purchasing organisation, the supplier's name and address, details of the products to be ordered and their agreed price. The document will also contain an order number. This is used to identify the order when the supplier sends an invoice requesting payment.

Operations

One of the most important documents produced by the operations department is a job card. This contains details of the work to be done in order to fulfil a particular order.

An order form

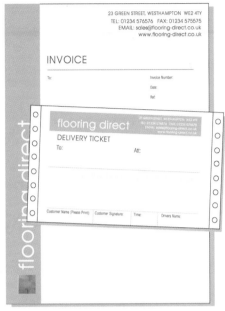

An invoice and a delivery note

Finance

The finance department produces a number of important business documents. They are all designed to make sure that both customers and suppliers are aware of the terms on which they have agreed to work together. Some of the more important documents are summarised below.

Document	Purpose
Purchase order	To inform the supplier which goods or services are being ordered
Delivery note	To identify the products delivered to a customer by a supplier
Invoice	To request payment for goods provided or work done for a customer
Statement	To summarise the invoices sent to and payments received from a customer

Word check

Market research – the term for the different ways to obtain information from existing and potential customers.

TASKS

3 Design a template that could be used by an organisation for the production of its invoices.

4 Find out how your school or college produces its invoices.

• How could the system make greater use of ICT?

Business communication technologies

Over the past few years there has been a revolution in the way that communication takes place within and between organisations. There has been an increase in the use of ICT to improve communication.

In this topic you will learn about some of the most important technologies. Some of these technologies will already be familiar to you.

Electronic mail

Electronic mail is fast replacing letters and memos as the main way to communicate information from one person to another. Today there are well over one billion email accounts in the world! There are a number of benefits of using email:

• a permanent record can be kept of the communication
• messages can be copied to large groups of people. This makes it an ideal medium for circulating memos
• documents can be attached to the email message. This makes it an ideal medium for circulating copies of reports
• messages can be sent more quickly than using postal services (but the speed at which the message is received does depend on the frequency with which the receiver checks their email!)
• some email accounts can be accessed via the Internet from any computer. This makes it an ideal medium to send messages to people who are travelling.

There are, however, a number of problems:

• viruses can be deliberately or accidentally carried in an attachment
• the ability to send multiple copies of messages has created the problem of **SPAM** mail – unwanted advertisements that can flood an email account
• the sender needs to know the exact email address of the recipient, otherwise the email will not be delivered.

CASE STUDY

Fastbooks.co.uk uses email as an important tool in providing support to its customers. Customers place their orders online, having to supply an email address. Fastbooks' computer system then sends an automatic email reply to the customer. The email is a confirmation of the order placed by the customer. A further email is then sent to the customer at the time that the goods are dispatched.

If there is a problem with the goods Fastbooks' customer service department can be contacted by the customer, again by email.

Fastbooks occasionally sends emails to its customers informing them of special offers and new releases. It builds up a **customer profile** based on the products the customer has searched for and bought when using the site. It uses this profile to target specific products in its emails. This, it believes, reduces the negative effects on the customer of too much unwanted SPAM mail.

Business communication technologies

Intranets and extranets

You will be familiar with the **Internet** and will probably know that it is a technology that enables data to be shared from one computer to another. Information posted onto the **world wide web** by one computer can be accessed by any other computer also connected to the web.

An **intranet** works in exactly the same way as the Internet except that the extent of the network is limited. Intranets are mainly used inside organisations. They make it possible to exchange data and files across a controlled group of people within an organisation.

An **extranet** is simply an intranet that is also made available to specified users outside the organisation. This makes it possible, for example, to allow suppliers and customers direct access to parts of the organisation's product database. This enables faster and more accurate data transfer between the two organisations.

The wave is the name of intranet for Brighton and Hove City Council. This is a typical page from it.

CASE STUDY

Sanders-Goodman is one of the world's largest pharmaceutical companies. Its Global Research Division employs around 3000 researchers in different locations around the world. The organisation uses an intranet to enable researchers to share and exchange information. This has reduced the time taken to share new research throughout the organisation. It has also reduced wasteful duplication of research: when two teams unknowingly work on the same problem.

Mobile phone

Mobile phones have become an almost essential business tool over the past few years. The main advantage to organisations of using mobile phones is that staff can be contacted when they are not at their usual place of work.

Personal Digital Assistant (PDA)

PDAs are small portable devices that contain enough processing power to run applications software such as spreadsheets, word processors and databases. More sophisticated PDAs allow the user to download data from the organisation's computer system, edit it and then upload the amended data.

The main benefit of PDAs is that they are smaller and lighter than laptop computers but share the ability to work while away from the organisation. Some PDAs can be connected to the Internet, usually via a mobile phone, to allow access to an intranet or extranet.

Mobile phones ensure that you can be contacted when not at the office. No matter where you may be!

TASKS

Visit the websites of some mobile phone manufacturers and retailers.

1. Investigate the range of communication products available.

2. What benefits are claimed for these products?

Word check

Customer profile – a collection of data about a customer and their buying habits. It can be used to help recommend new products to the customer.

Overview of an ICT system

By the end of this topic you will be able to:

- identify the main parts of an ICT system
- understand how the parts of the system work together

If you have ever used a personal computer (PC) then you have used one of the most common types of **computer system**.

A computer system is simply a collection of hardware and software that enable information to be entered, processed and communicated to a person or device.

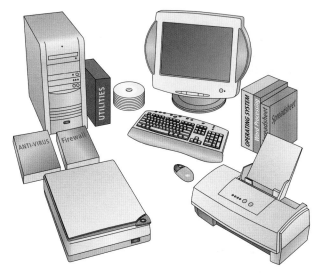

A computer system is a collection of software and hardware.

TASK

① Look at a standard personal computer system.

In what ways can information be entered onto the computer?
In what ways can information be transmitted from the computer?

Main stages in a computer system

There are three main stages in any system: input, process and **output**.

Input

At the input stage information is entered onto the computer system. Before the information can be entered it has to be turned into data, in other words a format that the computer can recognise.

Data is defined as information which has no meaning. For data to have meaning it must be analysed and have a context for the user. For example, the data 22.50 could represent £22.50 or 22.50 kilograms.

Data is stored in a computer as a sequence of binary digits (numbers that can only contain a sequence of 1s or 0s). When information is entered into a computer it is converted into binary code by the computer. Most computers use the ASCII code system. For example, when you press letter F on a keyboard the code 01000110 is entered into the computer system.

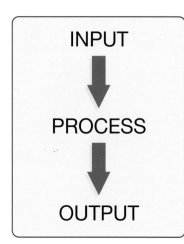

INPUT

PROCESS

OUTPUT

TASKS

② What different types of information could the item of data 251202 represent?

③ Some databases ask you to enter a date of birth using the format dd/mm/yy. What would happen if someone born on the 10th of June 1980 entered their date of birth as 06/10/80?

Overview of an ICT system

Process

At the process stage data is changed or edited so that new data is created. In order to process the data a sequence of commands or instructions must be given to the system. A **computer program** is normally used to do this.

TASK

4 Enter the following data onto a spreadsheet:

Name	Hours worked	Wage rate per hour (£)
Sarah Jenkins	33	4.50
Brian Johnson	24	4.50
Emile Lauren	42	5.50
Fabian Mendez	12	5.50

How must the data be processed to calculate the total amount to be paid to each worker?

Extend the spreadsheet so that it can perform the calculation.

Output

At the output stage the data is communicated from the system to a human user, another computer system or a piece of equipment. It is therefore important that the data which leaves the computer system is in a format that can be understood by the recipient. In the wage rates task above, it would be helpful to change the format of the output data so that the results are clearly displayed as currency values.

Feedback

Most computer systems use feedback. This means that the output of the computer system is used as input into the system. An example would be if you sent a document to be printed but the printer was out of paper. The printer would send a message (output) back to the computer (input) telling it that it needs to display an error message to the user.

Storage devices

All computer systems require storage devices where data that has been saved can be stored. All the separate parts of the computer system need to be connected to each item of equipment by a cable via a port. For more information on cables and ports see pages 138–139.

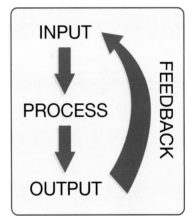

TASK

5 Which types of output would be most suitable for the following tasks:

• Checking a word-processed document while it is being created?
• Reading through a completed document to check for spelling errors and layout improvements?
• A letter to be sent to 500 customers on a mailing list?

Requirements of a computer system

- identify the main requirements of a computer system

You have learned that there are three stages to any computer system. However, a computer system cannot operate without hardware and software.

Hardware

This is the term for all of the physical equipment that makes up the computer system. This includes **input devices** and **output devices** as well as the equipment that will be needed to carry out the process of changing the data. Over the next few pages you will learn about the main hardware used in computer systems. This hardware can be summarised in the following groups:

- **Input devices:** the hardware that enables data to be entered onto the computer system.
- **Processors:** the hardware that carries out the main processes of the computer system.
- **Output devices:** the hardware that enables data to leave the computer system.
- **Ports and cables:** the hardware that enables the various parts of the computer system to connect together.
- **Storage devices:** the hardware that enables the data used and created by the computer system to be stored.

Software

Computer hardware can only operate if it is given **commands** to perform. Computer software is the term for the **programs** that enable the computer system to operate.

Computer software can be divided into the following main types:

- **Systems software** (also called operating systems software): this is the software that enables the computer system to work. It allows the various parts of the computer system to perform tasks and exchange data. Over 90 per cent of the world's computers use the *Windows* operating systems produced by Microsoft®.
- **Applications software:** this is the software that carries out the specific tasks that the user requires a computer system for. The main types of applications software include word processing, spreadsheet, database and desk top publishing software.
- **Utility software:** this is software that carries out a specific task that the user of a computer system might find useful. Examples include anti-virus software and file-compression programs such as *Winzip*.

Each computer system is likely to feature a different combination of hardware and software. The particular combination used is called the **configuration** of the system.

TASK

1. Write a list of all the different software that is used by the computer that you normally work on. Group the software under the following three headings:

   - systems software
   - applications software
   - utility software.

Requirements of a computer system

Main types of computer system

Organisations use a range of different computers to carry out their operations. These vary from large mainframe computers down to small personal digital assistants (PDAs).

Mainframe computers

This is the name reserved for the largest computers, which will typically be large enough to fill an entire room. The heat given off by the hardware will require the room to have its own air-conditioning system. Mainframe computers have a very large processing capacity, and are used to operate some of the largest computer systems in the world. Examples include the computers used to operate the government's National Insurance offices in Newcastle and the Driver's Vehicle Licensing Centre (DVLC) in Swansea.

Personal computers

Personal computers (PCs) are so called because they are designed to be used by an individual user and are most often found in offices. They are also known as micro-computers because when introduced they were considered to be the smallest type of computer in operation.

PCs can be operated either as self-contained **standalone** computers or as part of a **network**. Some network computers do not contain all the hardware needed to operate as standalone computers. They can only operate when they are connected to the network and are known as dumb terminals.

Portable computers

An increasingly broad term for all computing devices which are designed to be carried by an individual and used while 'on the move'. This includes laptop and **notebook** computers which have a similar processing capacity to PCs and contain all the input and output devices within a single unit. Portable computers are often used by people who need to spend time working away from their normal place of work.

Smaller devices include **palmtop computers** and **Personal Digital Assistants (PDAs)**. These devices are powerful enough to run applications software but are usually so small that the input and output devices are less user-friendly than laptops. These devices are useful for working in confined spaces such as while travelling on a train.

Embedded computers

Embedded computers are devices found inside larger machines. They receive input data from the machine and use this to send output signals back to the machine. Examples include embedded computers in microwave ovens, weighing machines, and fridges and freezers. Embedded computers are perhaps the smallest type of computer.

Laptops can be used anywhere.

TASK

 Visit a large supermarket. Write a list of the different types of computer systems in use.

Input devices: keyboard and mouse

Input devices enable the user to enter data and commands into the computer system.

Keyboard

QWERTY keyboard

The standard computer keyboard is the input device that most people are familiar with. It gets its name from the way that the keys are arranged. When a key is depressed a signal is sent from the keyboard to the computer's processor.

QWERTY keyboards have become the **industry standard** design. However there are two main problems with the standard design:

- the position of each key is not designed to make the keyboard easy to use by an untrained typist
- the keys are usually arranged in a rectangular grid. To reach some keys the user has to stretch their hands and fingers. This can put a lot of strain on the user's joints.

An ergonomic keyboard

To try to overcome these problems a number of **ergonomically designed** keyboards have been developed. These have layouts which are designed to reduce the stress to the body caused by continuous data entry.

Concept keyboards

Concept keyboards do not use the standard QWERTY design of keys representing individual characters. Instead, each key on the **keypad** represents a command to the computer. Concept keyboards are used in places such as restaurants and theatre booking systems where the operator is required to perform a limited number of specific operations quickly. Concept keyboards are often used as part of a bigger **electronic point of sale (EPOS)** system.

Touch screen devices

Touch screen devices are very similar to concept keyboards. The main difference is that the commands are entered by pressing the system's display unit. This can help to reduce the size of the unit.

Touch screen devices give instructions that are easy to follow.

TASK

1 Over the next week whenever you visit a shop, sports club or restaurant keep a log of the type of input devices used. Which type of device seems to be the most popular?

Input devices: keyboard and mouse

Mouse

A mouse is the other input device that most computer users are familiar with. There are a number of different designs but they all share the same basic principles.

All mice contain a device which monitors how far and in which direction the mouse has travelled. This device sends a signal to the processor which sends a command which alters the position of the **cursor** or other selected object on the screen.

The mouse also contains a number of buttons which are used to input commands into the computer system. A common mouse arrangement is to have a left and right button, each of which performs different operations. Some mice also have a small wheel which can be rotated to scroll the screen up and down.

Standard mouse

A standard mouse uses a ball which is underneath the mouse. When the ball is moved across a flat surface it rolls across four sensing rollers. The ball will affect each roller differently depending on the direction of movement. The mouse is connected to the processor by an electrical cable. A problem with a conventional mouse is that a mouse pad is usually needed. Another problem is that the ball can pick up dirt which eventually will reduce the performance of the mouse unless it is cleaned.

Cordless mouse

A cordless mouse works in a similar way to a standard mouse except that the signal is sent via radio waves. This makes a cordless mouse easier to use as there are no wires getting in the way.

Infra-red mouse

This is the latest version of mouse. Instead of rollers the mouse contains a digital camera which takes over a thousand pictures every second and uses this data to analyse the movement of the mouse. The major benefit of this technology is that the mouse does not need to be used on a flat surface such as a mouse mat.

Tracker ball

A tracker ball works like an upside-down mouse. The user moves their hand or finger over the ball and this then controls the cursor on the screen. An advantage of this is that the device can be used in a smaller space. This is why they are found on portable computers.

Touchpad

Touchpads are found on laptop computers – they are designed to control the cursor without using a mouse. The user moves his or her finger across the surface of the touchpad and this moves the cursor on the screen. When the user taps the touchpad it has the same effect as clicking a mouse button.

Word check ✓

Ergonomic – the process of designing an object that takes into account the way in which the object is likely to be used.

Did you know ...

In 1998 four employees at Midland Bank's processing centre in Surrey won compensation of £60 000 for disabilities suffered after being trained to use a computer keyboard at high speed. Many organisations now use ergonomic keyboards in an attempt to reduce the problems caused by **repetitive strain injury (RSI)**.

A tracker ball

TASK

2 Find out more about the different types of mouse and the latest products by visiting the websites of some computer retailers.

Input devices: scanners and card readers

The input devices in this topic are all examples of devices that 'read' data in some way.

Scanners

A scanner is a device which 'reads' information on a printed page or other object and converts this information into digital data. This data can then be stored and used by a computer system. Most scanners store the data in a picture format so that the image can be viewed using graphics software.

A scanner

Some scanners use 'text recognition software'. The scanner is then able to convert a page of written text into text data which can be edited using word processing software.

CASE STUDY

Family Life is a large insurance business. The organisation sells life insurance policies throughout the UK. Each policy document can run to many tens of pages.

Recently the organisation has begun to run out of space to store all of the paper-based policies. It has therefore decided to introduce a paperless system where all policies over 25-years old will be the first to be scanned and stored in digital format. The organisation believes that the space savings brought by the reduction in storage space will more than compensate for the cost of the computer equipment needed.

TASK

1 Apart from space saving what other benefits might result from storing these documents digitally?

Bar code readers

Bar codes are now found on almost every product you can think of. There is even one on the back of this book. A standard bar code consists of a 12-digit number which is then represented by a series of black and white lines. The bar code is passed across a bar-code reader which reads the code and inputs the number into the computer system. Most bar code readers use a light beam to read the data. Some readers take a digital image of the bar code which is then analysed by the computer. Bar code readers can be built into devices such as supermarket checkouts or be used in small hand-held devices such as light-pens.

Some uses for bar code readers include:

- entering a unique reference number such as a person's club membership or library card number
- entering a product's details at a supermarket checkout. The system will then extract the price of the product and use this to calculate the total amount spent.
- use in a stock control system. Every time a product is taken from a warehouse it will be scanned and the number in stock on the database will be reduced by one.

The bar code number is the key data in a product database which can be used to extract information such as the price of the product. The computer will match the bar code number with a number in a product database and then extract other data from the same record. Bar codes on the back of club membership cards work in the same way for a members' database.

A bar code reader passes a light beam over a bar code number, matching it with that held in a database.

Input devices: scanners and card readers

Magnetic swipe-card readers

A magnetic swipe-card reader meets the same purpose as the bar-code reader. Data that is stored on a separate object can be entered onto the computer system. The differences come in the technology used to store and read the data.

The data is stored on a magnetic strip, usually on the back of a plastic card. The card reader works like a cassette player in that it reads the data stored on the magnetic tape. This data is then input into the computer system.

This system has the benefit that more data can be stored on a magnetic strip than on a bar code. Also, it is possible to identify the code on a bar code by reading the numbers. It is only possible to read the data on a magnetic strip if you pass it through a reader. Swipe cards are therefore used to store confidential information.

The most common use of swipe cards is as bank cards such as credit cards and cards for use in **automated telling machines (ATMs)**.

Using an ATM saves having to queue at the bank.

Portable data entry terminals (PDETs)

These are not separate devices to the others in this topic. Instead, PDET is the name given to hand-held input devices.

PDETs are used to count stock in a warehouse or shop.

PDETs are used in some supermarkets for shoppers to scan their own products as they go. At the check-out the PDET's contents are downloaded to the check-out system. Many shoppers believe the system is faster.

PDETs are also being introduced in restaurants. Customers who pay by credit card can have their card read at the table by the restaurant staff.

> **Word check**
>
> **Automated telling machines (ATMs)** – machines used to dispense cash to bank customers. Customers are required to insert a credit or debit card and to follow the ATM's on-screen instructions.

CASE STUDY

Marshall's Leisure Centre is an exclusive members only sports club in central London. Members pay over £1200 a year to enjoy the club's facilities. To enter the premises members show their membership card to the receptionist. The receptionist has to check that the card is valid and, if it is, the membership number is written into the day-book. The receptionist then releases the entry barrier. At busy times, particularly weekday lunchtimes, this process can result in long queues for members.

TASK

2 How could the sports club use ICT to make this process more efficient?

Input devices: sensors and other input devices

The third main category of input devices are those used to collect data from the environment. Input sensors are often used in manufacturing processes to help control equipment.

You need to be aware of the different types of sensor and what data they are designed to collect. This is because you need to be aware of how organisations, both manufacturing and non-manufacturing, can make use of sensors in their ICT systems.

There are several different types of sensor, each with its own uses.

Type of sensor	What it can measure	Typical uses within organisations
Light	Levels of light and reflection	To monitor light levels in a greenhouse
Humidity	The proportion of water vapour in the atmosphere	To monitor humidity levels in swimming pools and greenhouses
Heat	Temperature	To monitor the temperature of ovens and food on display in a restaurant
Infra-red	Infra-red radiation	In a burglar alarm system, to help detect the presence of intruders
Pressure	Air pressure, pressure applied to another by an object	To weigh the materials being put into a container, for example a ton bag of cement
Sound	Noise levels	To monitor noise levels in a factory
Tilt	Angle of movement of an object	To monitor the angle of rotation of a robotic paint spray arm
Touch	Contact between two objects	To identify when a robot has come into contact with another object

A typical sensor that would control the humidity in a greenhouse or conservatory.

CASE STUDY

Trafficmaster is an organisation providing road traffic information to motorists. Infra-red sensors positioned on motorway bridges send two infra-red beams onto the road surface. Traffic passing through the beams breaks the signal and the processor can calculate the speed of traffic flow. Traffic speeds of below 30mph cause the system to contact Trafficmaster's control centre warning of traffic delays.

TASK

1. Sue Grant is the catering manager in the canteen at a busy London hospital. The hospital sells a range of sandwiches and salads that are displayed on a cold-food counter. Current food regulations state that chilled food on display must be kept at a temperature of below 8 degrees centigrade.

   How could Sue use ICT to help her comply with this temperature regulation?

Input devices: sensors and other input devices

Other input devices

Graphics tablets

Graphics tablets are also known as digitising tablets, graphics pads or drawing tablets.

A graphics tablet

They consist of two parts; a flat surface and a pen, stylus or **puck** for drawing with. The user draws an image in the same way they would use a pen or pencil. Most users find this easier than drawing an object with a mouse!

Graphics tablets are useful for graphic designers, architects and others who wish to create high quality drawings and input them directly onto a computer. Some users also prefer them because they believe that these devices can reduce the likelihood of repetitive strain injury.

Digital cameras

Digital cameras use an image sensor to convert light into electrical signals. The data is stored as a **bitmap** file. The individual items of light data are called pixels. Basically, the more pixels a camera uses the greater will be the clarity or resolution of the saved image. Basic cameras have a resolution of 640 × 480 pixels (307 000 in total) but more recent cameras have a resolution of around 3 million pixels.

> **Word check**
>
> **Bitmap** – a picture formed from an array of dots.

Digital cameras are used in many different organisations. Their main advantages over conventional film cameras are that images can be edited using **photo-editing** software and can be distributed quickly via email attachments and posted onto web pages.

Web-cams

Web-cams work rather like digital cameras except that images are collected at predetermined intervals. They can then be viewed in sequence. The only practical limit that prevents web-cams working like digital movie cameras is the memory capacity needed to store and play images. Web-cams are often used to display images on a web page.

Video-conferencing

Video-conferencing is the name for the process of communicating both orally and visually with others across the Internet. The technology currently used most uses a CODEC to **co**mpress the image and sound data so that it can be transferred across the Internet before being **dec**ompressed into a format that can be played.

Video-conferencing is used in many different organisations when face-to-face meetings are difficult, time-consuming and expensive to set up.

TASK

 Explain how ICT could be used to meet the following needs:

- A botanist wishes to make sure that a tropical plant greenhouse is kept at 95 per cent humidity.
- A worker at an organisation's Head Office in London wishes to hold a face-to-face meeting with a colleague in New York and one in Tokyo.
- A property developer has found an interesting looking building to buy while in France and wishes to show it to her colleague in London.

Computer processors

In the previous topics we have looked at the hardware needed to input data onto a computer system. In this topic we will look at the hardware needed to process this data and convert it into new data.

The main processor that is used in computer systems is called the **central processing unit (CPU)**. The CPU can be thought of as the 'brain' of the computer system. Most personal computers combine the functions of the CPU inside a single **microprocessor** computer chip.

Main functions of the CPU

The main tasks performed by the CPU include the following:

- storage of data
- carrying out instructions such as the opening and closing of programs
- performing arithmetic and logic operations
- control the flow of input and output signals within the computer system.

There are three main parts to the CPU: the **control unit**, the **arithmetic** and **logic** unit and the immediate access store.

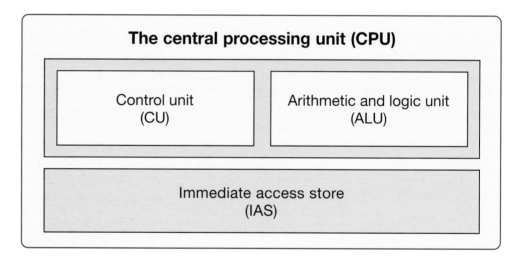

The central processing unit (CPU)

Control unit (CU)	Arithmetic and logic unit (ALU)

Immediate access store (IAS)

Control unit (CU)

The control unit co-ordinates the work of the entire computer system. Its main functions are to control the flows of data through the system and to control the operations of the hardware and software.

Arithmetic and logic unit (ALU)

The ALU is the main part of the CPU that actually processes data and makes decisions based upon the data. For example it can add two items of data together to create a new item of data.

Immediate access store (IAS)

This is the part of the CPU where the data and programs currently in use are stored.

In most modern personal computers the ALU and the CU are stored on a single microprocessor chip and the IAS is stored elsewhere on the computer **motherboard**.

Computer processors

Modern computer microprocessors

Modern personal and portable computers operate using a microprocessor chip. The first microprocessor chip was produced by Intel in 1971.

There are many different types of microprocessor. Each one is generally designed for a specific purpose, for example there are microprocessors specifically designed for use in laptop computers. There are two main ways that microprocessors can be compared:

Clock speed: the number of commands that the microprocessor can execute per second.

Bandwidth: the number of bits of data that the microprocessor can process at one time.

For example, 32-bit microprocessors with a speed of 800 megahertz will be more powerful than a 16-bit microprocessor with a speed of 400 megahertz.

The following graph shows how the power of microprocessors has grown since 1974.

MIPS refers to the number of operations the microprocessor can perform, it is short for millions of instructions per second!

A microprocessor is very complex.

Word check ✓

Arithmetic – performing calculations on one or more items of computer data.

Logic – taking decisions based on whether or not a particular item of data meets a specified condition.

Motherboard – carries all the main items of hardware inside a computer. Other boards, for example extra memory cards, are attached to the motherboard.

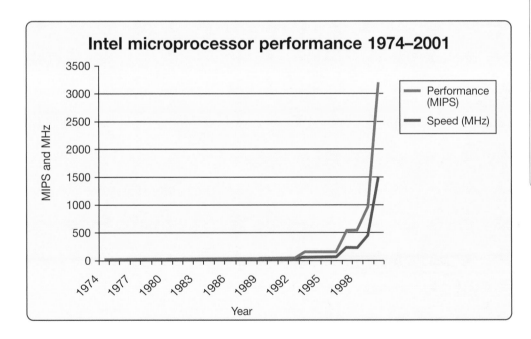

Intel microprocessor performance 1974–2001

Legend:
Performance (MIPS)
Speed (MHz)

Y-axis: MIPS and MHz (0, 500, 1000, 1500, 2000, 2500, 3000, 3500)
X-axis: Year (1974, 1977, 1980, 1983, 1986, 1989, 1992, 1995, 1998)

TASK

1 Different microprocessors have been developed that are best suited for different uses. Use the Internet to find out about the different microprocessors that have been developed for PCs, laptops and graphics software such as CAD and computer games.

Computer memory

All computers need to work with data, which has to be stored and made available for use. The way that computer data is stored is called memory. There are two main types of computer memory: temporary and permanent memory.

Temporary memory (also known as volatile memory)

As we have seen, the CPU operates at very high speeds. To work effectively it needs to have fast access to the data that it needs. This data is stored in an area called the immediate access store (IAS).

RAM (random access memory)

The IAS uses random access memory (RAM) to store the data. The problem with RAM is that it is **volatile**, in other words it needs an electric current to operate. This means that data stored in RAM will be lost when the electrical power is switched off.

The amount of RAM available to a computer system sets a limit to the number of processes that the system can perform at any one time. Systems with relatively small amounts of RAM can only run a few programs at one time.

A modern personal computer will use between 128 megabytes and 1 gigabyte or more of RAM.

A RAM memory chip

Permanent memory (non-volatile memory)

The data held in permanent storage is non-volatile, in other words it will not be lost when not in use.

ROM (read only memory)

ROM stands for read only memory. It is stored inside the computer system and is used to store the programs needed by the CPU to load the computer's **operating system**. These include the **BIOS (basic input–output system)**. ROM data cannot be deleted by the user. This is important because without the ROM data the computer system cannot work.

Computer memory

BIOS (basic input – output system)

BIOS is the program that enables the computer and the operating system to function. When you switch on a computer the BIOS is the program you see running before the operating system becomes active.

> **Word check** ✔
>
> **Volatile** – data which will be lost if the computer loses electrical power.

TASK

1 Switch on a computer and try to observe what the BIOS does before the operating system is loaded. Do not enter any commands onto the computer at this stage!

The five different types of ROM

There are five different types of ROM:

- ROM
- PROM
- EPROM
- EEPROM
- Flash memory.

ROM is the most basic type of non-volatile memory. All the data is stored in fixed positions on a computer chip. Once made, the chip cannot be reprogrammed. If the chip contains any errors it is useless and so must be destroyed and a new one made.

PROM chips are programmable ROM chips. They are cheap to buy and can have data written to them only once. However they are very fragile and a small surge of electric current is enough to damage the chip.

EPROM chips are erasable programmable read only memory devices; that is they can have data written to them many times. The data on an EPROM chip can only be altered if the chip is removed from the motherboard and an EPROM eraser used to remove all the data from the chip.

EEPROM (electrically erasable programmable read only memory) chips are better than EPROM chips in that they do not have to be removed from the motherboard before being rewritten to. Their biggest drawback is that writing new data on them takes a very long time because data is added 1 byte at a time.

Flash memory solves the biggest problem with EEPROM by writing data much more quickly, typically 512 bytes at a time.

TASKS

2 Find out how much RAM data is available on the computers that you use at school or college. Does the amount of RAM affect the performance of these machines?

3 Investigate a range of devices such as digital cameras and personal digital assistants. What use do they make of flash memory?

Data storage

Secondary storage devices

The data held in permanent storage is non-volatile, so it will not be lost when not in use.

Hard disk

The hard disk is a high capacity storage device. In personal and portable computer systems it is located inside the main computer unit. The hard drive usually consists of a number of circular magnetic disks which are stored on top of each other. A number of read/write heads are able to write data onto the disk and read data from it. The data transfer takes place when the disks are rotating. Because the hard disk drive operates inside the computer unit it is always rotating when the computer is active. This helps to increase the speed at which data can be transferred.

The capacity of hard disk drives can be very large; some modern desktop PCs can store up to 80 gigabytes of data or more.

Floppy disk

Most personal computers come with floppy disk drives as standard. A floppy disk works using the same principles as a hard disk. The main differences are that it is much smaller and the disk can be removed from the floppy disk drive and used in another computer. This makes a floppy disk a useful medium to store files when on the move. The main weakness is that they can only hold 1.44 megabytes of data. This is often too small for many files, particularly if they contain graphics.

> **Did you know ...**
>
> 120 megabyte floppy disks were developed but very few were sold. This was largely because of the increasing availability and popularity of CD-RW which allowed even larger amounts of data to be stored and transferred.

Magnetic tape

Magnetic tape is sometimes used to store **back-up** data in large computer systems. The main advantage of magnetic tape is its large storage capacity. The main weakness has been the speed at which data could be read from the tape. However, modern tape drives have overcome this problem.

Optical storage

Optical discs use a different technology to store data than magnetic media. Rather than storing it as magnetic particles on a magnetic tape it is stored as a series of small pits on a disc which are read by a laser beam. Because a laser beam can be made very narrow, much larger volumes of data can be stored on an optical disc.

It is important to make back-ups of your data and store them in a safe place.

Data storage

The main optical media are as follows:

CD-ROM
A disc which can store up to 650 megabytes of data. Data cannot be written onto the disc by the user. As a result they are used by commercial organisations to contain music, multimedia products such as encyclopaedias and to distribute software.

CD-R (CD-Recordable)
Optical discs which can have data written to them only once.

CD-RW
A disc which can have data written to it by the user. They have the same storage capacity as CD-ROMs. They can be used to make back-up copies of data and can be used to transfer relatively large files and programs from one user to another. Blank CD-RW discs are more expensive to buy than CD-R discs.

DVD
A disc which looks the same as a CD but can store much more data, typically 4.7 gigabytes. As a result they are currently used to store entire movie programs which can be viewed using a **DVD player**. Most DVDs are read-only, but recordable DVD players are becoming more common. It is possible that the DVD player will replace the CD player as the main medium to play multimedia optical discs.

Other storage devices
There are many other different types of storage device. Many of them are specific to particular products, for example memory cards for digital cameras. Some products, such as the **memory stick**, are designed to be able to transfer data between many different types of computer devices.

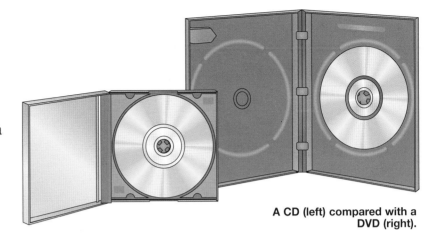

A CD (left) compared with a DVD (right).

> **Word check**
>
> **Memory stick** – a small device designed to transfer data quickly between different items of hardware.

TASK

1 Identify the most suitable storage media for the following needs:

- An estate agent wishes to make a regular weekly back-up copy of the files on her desktop PC. The total file size is approximately 320 megabytes.
- A training company wishes to provide all delegates to a conference with an electronic copy of the paper handouts used. They assume every delegate has a computer but do not know what storage media they can use. The total file size is 1.2 megabytes.
- A garden centre has a computer program it wishes to distribute to its customers. The program helps customers design their new garden. The total file size is 4.5 megabytes.

2 A sales representative uses a laptop computer when away from the office. He wishes to be able to use a copy of all the files on his hard drive for use on his laptop. His desktop PC has a CD-RW drive but his laptop only has a CD-ROM drive. How can he exchange files between the two computers?

Output devices: printers

Printers are used to create paper copies of output data. There are three main types of printer. Each printer type is suited to particular purposes. Each of the three types of printer can come in many different forms. It is important to be able to select the right kind of printer for the particular needs of the user.

Laser printers

These printers offer the fastest printing and the best quality resolution of any printer. As a result they are also the most expensive. Laser printers offer both black and white, and colour printing.

The printer works by the original image being transferred into the printer's memory. The printer uses this data to move a laser beam across the surface of a magnetic drum. The drum then becomes electrically charged with an image of the document to be printed.

Magnetic ink contained in a **toner cartridge** is then passed over the drum. The magnetic ink is attracted onto the surface of the drum. A sheet of paper is then passed over the surface of the drum and the ink is transferred onto the paper. The ink is fused onto the paper by the heat generated by a **fuser unit**.

Laser printers can print very high quality documents at very high speeds of over 10 pages per minute. They are also very quiet. They are particularly suitable for the production of high quality documents.

Dot-matrix printers

Dot-matrix printers are the oldest and most basic form of printer technology.

The main part of the device is called the **print head**. This consists of a **matrix** of either 9 or 24 pins. The pins are moved to form individual characters. Between the print head and the paper is a ribbon with ink on one side. The print head pushes the pins against the ribbon which is then pressed against the paper to leave ink in the shape of the character on the page.

An artist's impression of the Community Centre, East Grinstead, which has been drawn in CAD.

CASE STUDY

Michael Barron is an architect who specialises in designing new office developments. Michael produces designs for new developments which include artists' impressions of the finished buildings. Michael prints these documents using a laser printer because it gives him the high quality resolution that his clients demand.

Output devices: printers

Benefits of dot-matrix printers

Dot-matrix printers can be used to print multi-part documents, where the printer prints more than one copy at the same time. An example would be a sales invoice where the organisation sends one copy to the supplier and keeps a copy for its own records. Also they can use continuous paper. This is paper that is in a long roll or series of folded sheets. An example would be the mass printing of several hundred different invoices at the same time.

Drawbacks of dot-matrix printers

They are slow; print speed can be less than 100 characters per minute. They are also noisy. The noise of the pins striking the ribbon can mean that it is too noisy to have a number of the printers in the same room. Also the print resolution is very low. Each character can only be formed by a combination of 9 or 24 pins. This makes a dot matrix unsuitable for any application that requires more than simple 'plain text' characters.

Ink-jet printers

Ink-jet printers are also known as desk-jet printers. For most users, especially in small businesses, they offer good quality printing at an affordable cost. Ink-jet printers offer both black and white, and colour printing.

The print head on an ink-jet printer is a miniature spray gun that contains tiny holes or nozzles. The nozzles are computer controlled so that they form a different shape for each character. Ink is then sprayed through the nozzles onto the paper.

The resolution of ink-jet printers is improving, as is the speed. They are now the most technologically advanced pieces of equipment that most users of computers have beside their desktop computers.

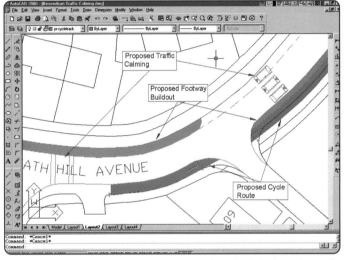

A typical design, drawn in CAD, for a cycle lane, which would be included within a proposal to a council.

TASK

1 Identify the printer most appropriate for the following needs:

- An electrical goods manufacturer has to print 600 invoices to send to its customers. It needs to keep a copy of each invoice. Its customers are not too concerned about the quality of the invoice, only that the details are readable.
- A transport consultancy business has a proposal for a new cycle lane which it needs to send to its local council. The proposal is 30 pages long and contains images taken using a digital camera, as well as graphs and diagrams. The organisation needs to send four copies of the document.
- A marketing manager has been asked to produce a report summarising the results of a recent advertising campaign. The manager wants to proof-read a copy of the report before printing the final version.

The report contains images taken from the organisation's website, as well as text and graphs.

Output devices: other devices

Monitor

Other names for a computer monitor include **visual display unit (VDU)** and **computer screen**. The monitor is the output device used most often because it is used while the operator is using the computer.

Most personal computer systems have a monitor as a separate output device which has to be attached to the main processor unit. Devices such as laptop computers, hand-held scanners and touch-screen checkout systems integrate the monitor into a single unit along with the rest of the system.

The resolution of a screen is important. Resolution is measured by pixels. Each pixel represents a dot on the screen. The more pixels there are the greater the resolution will be. Standard monitors have a resolution of 1024 × 768 pixels. High resolution monitors have 1600 × 1200 pixels.

There are two main types of monitor: those based on a **cathode-ray tube (CRT monitors)** and those based on a **liquid crystal display (LCD monitors)**.

CRT monitors

CRT monitors are based on the same technology as television screens. They are the oldest type of monitor in use today. As a result they are the cheapest form of monitor. Their main disadvantage is their bulk; they can take up a large surface area and can be very heavy.

Screens are measured from corner to corner.

Computer monitors are rated by their size. The monitor on a standard desktop PC can be anything from 15 to 19 inches in diameter (inside corner to inside corner). Some users, especially designers who work with graphics and desktop publishing files, will use a larger monitor of over 20 inches.

CRT monitors are bulky, take up a large area of space and are heavy.

LCD monitors

LCD monitors display the image by manipulating a liquid crystal display board. As a result they are not as bulky as a CRT monitor and are also much lighter. The technology to make them is much more recent. Their screen resolution is not yet as good as the best CRT monitors and they tend to be smaller and more expensive. They are suited to users who do not have much space and do not need to work with very high resolution images. Portable computers use LCD screens because CRT screens are impractical to carry around.

LCD monitors are lighter, but give poorer resolution.

TASK

1. Who would need the higher resolution: a secretary who mainly uses his computer to word process letters or a graphic designer who uses her computer to design greetings cards?

Output devices: other devices

Loudspeaker

Sound, like other forms of data, can be stored electronically in a computer system. The technology used to transmit music through the system is called musical instrument digital interface (MIDI). The user will need a **sound card** installed on their computer system in order to be able to play music which has been stored digitally. The electrical signals are converted into sound by loudspeakers.

Buzzers, bells and lights

Computer signals can be used to control the actions of a wide variety of output devices. These can include standard electrical devices such as buzzers, bells and lights. These devices are often used in intruder alarm systems.

Some alarm systems also use output signals to start a digital camera which can then record images. Software can analyse the images so that the camera only records when the image captured by the camera changes. This system makes use of feedback from the data captured by the computer to control the output signals. Because this type of system requires no human intervention it is called **closed-loop** feedback.

Motors

Output signals can also be used to control the actions of electric motors. The electric motors can themselves be used to drive larger equipment such as lifts machinery, cranes and robotic manufacturing equipment.

Electric motors operate at different electrical currents from computers; their ability to transmit and receive data is also limited. Therefore all data passing between a computer and a motor must pass through an **interface**, an electric device that acts as a buffer between the two pieces of equipment.

A motor is a device controlled by an electrical signal. **Stepper-motors** move a device in a number of small but accurate steps. They are used to control devices like the print head on an ink-jet printer. **Servo-motors** move a device with more force and at higher speed. They are used to control devices such as fork-lift trucks and drills.

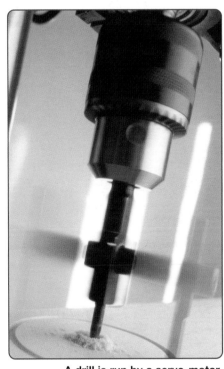

A drill is run by a servo-motor.

TASKS

2️⃣ A telesales office wishes to replace all of its computer monitors which are currently over eight years old. Computer operators use a monitor for up to seven hours a day (excluding breaks). The programs used by the operators do not use graphics. The organisation wants the monitors to take up as little space as possible. The organisation wants to spend around £300 per monitor but would be happy to pay less!

Conduct some research into the types of monitor currently available. Recommend to the organisation two monitors that they could use.

3️⃣ Write a list of the different ways that a supermarket organisation could make use of computer controlled motors. Divide your list into stepper- and servo-motors.

Ports and cables

Often neglected, but very important parts of any computer system, are the cables and connectors that enable the various hardware devices to communicate. Input and output devices that do not form part of the main computer system are called **peripherals**.

There are a number of different technologies that enable peripherals to connect to the main system. You need to be aware of them and how they differ.

Parallel ports

Until recently the parallel port was one of the main devices for transferring data between the CPU and peripherals. Many peripherals still use this type of connection, particularly printers, scanners and network adapters.

A parallel port

The industry standard parallel port provides a 25-pin socket on the back of the computer. The cable has a 25-pin connector at one end to connect to the computer and a 36-pin connector at the other end to connect to the peripheral device.

The device is called a parallel interface because different parts of the signal are passed through the pins and along separate wires at the same time.

One of the weaknesses with this system is that the pins are very fragile. Most connectors contain clips or screws which are used to hold the pins in place. There is a risk that the pins will be damaged when the connector is moved. Another problem is that the signals may become distorted if they have to travel along a lengthy piece of cable.

Serial ports

Serial ports also use pins to pass data between hardware devices. They are sometimes used to connect communications devices such as modems. One way to tell them apart from parallel ports is that they are usually smaller, containing either 9 or 25 pins.

A serial port transmits data in a single stream along a single wire. The stream is broken up into sequences of small chunks or **bytes**.

An advantage of serial ports over parallel ports is that they need less cable to transmit the data. As a result they are cheaper than parallel ports.

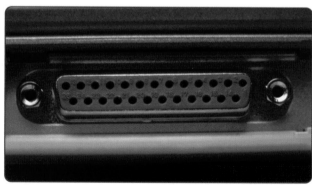

A serial port

Ports and cables

Universal serial bus (USB) ports

USB ports are a more recent invention. As a result many older computers do not have them installed. They are expected to replace serial and parallel ports as the main way to exchange data.

USBs transmit data in a similar way to the telephone or cable network. As a result they can transmit large volumes of data very quickly. A computer can communicate with up to 127 USB devices at any one time.

The main constraint on the transmission of data and the number of devices in use is the maximum **bandwidth** of 12mbps (a standard 56k modem on a normal telephone line will transmit data at a rate of around 40kbps).

Most personal computers only contain one or two USB ports. If you need to attach more devices than this it is possible to connect them to a USB hub. This is an interface that contains a number of USB sockets.

A USB port

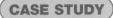 **CASE STUDY**

Michael Martin operates his architects business from a four-storey eighteenth century townhouse in the centre of Bath. The building is listed which means that all alterations to the building must leave it looking as authentic as possible.

Michael's business is expanding and he now has ten PCs on all four floors. He wishes to connect them in a network. Michael would like to use cable to connect them but in an old building this would prove to be very expensive. He is considering the use of a wireless network to connect all his equipment together.

How could an expanding business like Michael's benefit from using a wireless network?

Word check

Bandwidth – the speed at which data can be transmitted. Measured in bits per second (bps).

Wireless connections

Another more recent development is that of using wireless technology to transmit data between two hardware devices. This could help solve one of the biggest computer hazards; the large amounts of cable found at the back of the computer!

One example is **bluetooth** technology. This technology is designed for use inside a single room. Data is transmitted at a rate of 64kbps. The technology contains security codes that only allow authorised hardware to use the data.

At the moment wireless technology is in its early stages but it is likely to become more widely available in the future.

One of the benefits of wireless communication is that it can be used to link hardware together in a network where installing cables between rooms would be difficult.

You will find out more about these and other newer technologies later in this book.

TASK

❶ Find out how all the hardware devices on your computer system are connected together.

Operating systems

- identify the main purposes of an operating system

- understand the main types of operating system

- identify some of the operating systems used in large organisations

An operating system is the software used to control the workings of a computer system.

Functions of an operating system

The main purposes of any operating system are to:

- run the applications software (word processor, spreadsheet, and so on) required by the user
- enable the applications software to communicate with input and output devices
- manage systems resources, for example dividing microprocessor time between different software applications
- monitor the performance of the system, for example to detect if a sound card or printer are operating properly and sending **error messages** to the user if they are not.

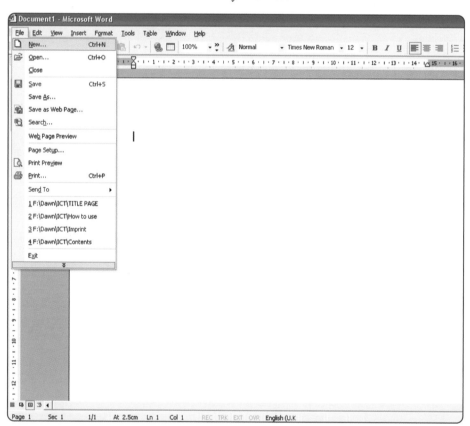

A screen showing the drop-down list of commands.

The main operating systems used by personal computers are called **graphical user interface (GUI)** systems. The user communicates with the operating system via a screen display containing menus (drop-down lists of commands found at the top of the screen). Commands can either be given by using a mouse to control a cursor or by the use of keyboard shortcuts.

These operating systems are also known as WIMPs because they make use of Windows, **Icons**, Menus and Pointers.

Most personal computers use the *Windows'* family of operating systems, first introduced by Microsoft® in 1985. At the time of writing the most recent version is called *Windows XP* and comes in two versions, one for the home user and one for the small business user.

TASKS

1. Compare two different types of operating system, for example *Windows XP Home* and *Windows XP Professional*.

2. Which operating system would you recommend for use by a self-employed consultant who works from home and uses a computer to write reports and contact clients via the Internet?

Operating systems

Network operating systems

A network is a group of computers which are connected together for the purpose of sharing and exchanging data.

Networks where all the computers are located within one building or site (for example several buildings close together like a school or hospital) are called **local area networks (LANs)**. Networks that connect computers in different towns, cities or countries and that need long distance communication technologies to connect them are called **wide area networks (WANs)**.

> **Word check** ✓
>
> **Icon** – an image which has been designed to represent a standard computer command. For example a printer icon represents the command 'print'.

Functions of a network operating system

As well as the functions common to personal computer operating systems, network operating systems have the following additional functions:

- to maintain a log of users and the tasks performed
- to maintain network security by assigning user identification (ID) and **access rights** to different users
- to manage access to the CPU when the network is used by more than one user
- to manage access to output devices such as shared printers.

Types of operating systems

In large organisations in late 2002 you might have expected to see the following operating systems in use:

Windows NT or *Windows 2000*: produced by Microsoft® for business users.

UNIX: a system designed for large mainframe computer systems. It is better than some other systems for **multi-tasking** (handling the demands of many different users simultaneously).

OS/2 Warp: a system designed by the computer manufacturer IBM for use in electronic point of sale (EPOS) devices at the checkout in shops. Some users believe that it is a very stable system, reducing the amount of downtime when the system is inoperable. This makes it popular with retailers and the financial services industry.

> **CASE STUDY**
>
> Select Country Cottages rent holiday cottages to holidaymakers. It has three offices throughout the UK. Each office operates a separate local area network. The LANs can each connect with each other using the telephone network when required.
>
> Mainland Insurance Services operates 30 separate offices throughout the UK. Customer records are stored on the organisation's main computer at its Head Office in Swindon. Staff in each regional office access the records using a dumb terminal attached to the head office system by a high-speed data cable. This is a permanent connection.

> **TASKS**
>
> **3** What type of network does your school or college operate? Is it a single network or a group of separate networks?
>
> **4** Which operating system does your network use? Why was this system chosen? What are its main features?

Network technologies (1)

Most organisations, apart from the very smallest, have more than one computer. These computers are usually arranged into a network.

In the previous topic you learned that there are two types of network, local area networks (LANs) and wide area networks (WANs). In this topic you will learn how networks are built.

A computer network is an arrangement where a group of computers are connected together so that they can share access to data as well as exchange data. A network is therefore an arrangement that enables computers to pass information from one to another. Computers usually pass data between themselves along lengths of computer cable. Networks can be arranged in different ways, according to how the cables connect up all the computers.

Computer networks need a computer to act as a focal point for the network. The job of the central computer is to run the operating system that controls the workings of the network. This computer is called the **network file server**.

Computer networks are vital to the success of many business organisations. Networks require a separate set of technology from **standalone** computers to make them operate. Much of this technology is based on the problem of how to enable the various parts of the network to exchange data with each other.

Network hardware

File servers
A file server is a computer whose job is to act as the focal point of the network. The file server co-ordinates the flow of data between the various parts of the network. It may also store the programs and files that are used on the network.

Workstations
This is the name for the computers attached to the network. Workstations that do not have the ability to act independently of the network are called **dumb terminals**.

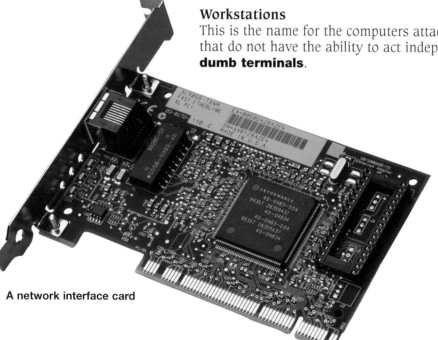

A network interface card

Network interface cards (NIC)
A network interface card is required to enable a computer workstation to transmit and receive data from the network.

An NIC slots into the back of a computer and is used to connect the network cables to the computer.

NICs vary widely in specification and performance. They can be a major constraint on the performance of the entire network.

Network technologies (1)

Routers

A router is used to enable two different networks to be connected together. They can also be used to add a new extension to an existing network. They are able to monitor traffic on the network and direct data along paths that have the most spare capacity.

Modems

Modems are required to make a connection to a wide area network (WAN). A modem enables two computer systems to transfer data between themselves using a telephone line. The modem converts the streams of data into a form that can be transmitted as a noise signal along a telephone line. The signal is then 'heard' by the modem at the other end of the line which then converts the signal back into strings of **binary data**.

Most modems will transmit data at a rate somewhere between 28 and 56 thousand bytes per second (kbps).

ISDN

ISDN is short for integrated services digital network. It is a technology that uses the same telephone lines as a conventional modem, but it is able to transfer data at much faster rates. ISDN is capable of transmitting 128kbps: up to five times faster than a modem.

ADSL

ADSL is short for asymmetric digital subscriber line. Like ISDN it uses existing telephone lines but is capable of much faster data transfer. ADSL has the capacity to transfer data ten times faster than ISDN. However, it is also much more expensive.

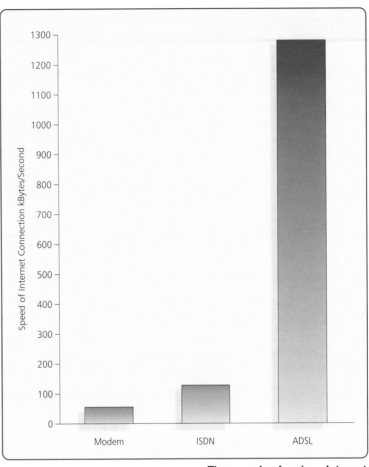

The speeds of various Internet connections

TASK

Alison Eaves is a freelance computer graphic artist. She works from her home in Birmingham and communicates with her clients via the Internet and telephone. She has asked you to recommend how she should connect to the Internet.

1 Find out about the different ways that Alison can connect to the Internet. Produce a report outlining the benefits and drawbacks of using a modem, ISDN, ADSL and any other available technologies. Recommend a system for Alison to use.

Word check

Binary data – the system of numbers using combinations of the digits 1 and 0. All information entered onto a computer system is converted into binary codes.

Network technologies (2)

By the end of this topic you will be able to:

- understand the protocols needed to transfer data within and between networks

Network protocols

One of the problems with computers is that they were not designed to communicate directly with each other. The differences between computers include the language of the operating system and the speed of data transfer. A **protocol** is the agreed standard used to enable different computers to talk with each other.

The situation is similar to the problem caused by having different human languages. Three hundred years ago most contact between governments was conducted in French, which was the language that was the agreed protocol in use by diplomats.

Some of the main protocols used to exchange data between different computers include:

Ethernet
One of the problems with networks is that two computers transmitting data at the same time can 'drown out' each other's signal. Ethernet uses a technology that prevents one computer from interrupting another. It is one of the most common protocols in use in networks.

Asynchronous transfer mode (ATM)
This is a technology used by **internet service providers (ISPs)** to transmit data across the Internet. Data is sent in 'packets', each one a fixed size. It is also used to connect two or more local area networks together.

File transfer protocol (FTP)
One problem of having different operating systems is that the computer transmitting the data may not know where or how to store it on the computer receiving the data. FTP enables the data to be sent to a location not determined by the operating system. The operating system will then transfer the data once it has been downloaded using FTP. This means that the data is transmitted twice, once by FTP and once by the recipient's operating system.

Cuteftp is one FTP program that is used for transmitting data.

Transport control protocol/Internet protocol (TCP/IP)
This is the main technology used to transfer documents across the Internet. This group of related protocols uses a unique 'address' for each computer attached to the Internet. This address is used to correctly route data transferred across the Internet.

TASK

1 What protocols are used to transfer data across your school or college network?

Network technologies (2)

Network services

A number of different services are available for users of a network to share information with each other. Some of the more useful ones for those who work inside organisations include:

Internal and external mail

Electronic mail is designed to operate just like the traditional postal service. Each user has a specific address and messages sent to that address are stored in a mailbox which only the person who has access to the email account can open.

Internal mail is the name for communications which are sent to a user on the same network and external mail is the name for communication between users who are not on the same network.

Bulletin boards

A bulletin board works just like a traditional notice board found on the wall of an office or classroom. It is a facility where the user can deposit a message which other users can then access and read. Most bulletin boards will only allow text messages to be deposited. Some allow the user to use a search engine to locate messages of a specific type. Some bulletin boards arrange messages by thread. The thread of a message is the subject, usually written into a subject line at the top of the message.

Discussion groups

Discussion groups use email technology to enable people who have a common interest to communicate information with each other. Users can **sign-up** to a discussion group and send and receive messages. Messages sent to the group can be read by all members of the group. Sending a message directly to the email account of a group member, rather than to the whole group, is called communicating **off-list**.

Most discussion groups have a set of rules that members are expected to follow with at least one **moderator** who has the job of making sure that members follow the rules. The moderator usually has the power to ban from the group any person who breaks the group's rules.

WORLDWIDE Camaro ASSOCIATION
HOME

A National Voice Uniting Car Clubs & Enthusiasts World

Worldwide Camaro Association Discussion Board
login | register | search | faq | forum home

» Today's Active Topics «

» You are not logged in. Login or register | Welcome to our newest member: safus1979

Forum	Topics	Posts	Last Post
Worldwide Camaro Association Discussion Board Recent Visitors: 5			
87IROC, John Payne, MyTMous, and 2 guest(s)			
General Discussions			
Camaro's If it has to do with Camaro's ... this is the place!	297	1148	Re: 89 Camaro~ Fixin to kick... (smn10) 01-28-2003 15:36
Save The Camaro Keep the tradition alive!	6	69	Re: 5th gen camaro... (SmcDwnlItel) 01-27-2003 22:26
WCA Classifieds Buy/Sell/Trade (No commercial Vendors Please)	131	237	82-92 v6 t5 setup (patgizz) 01-27-2003 22:17
Tech Support			
1st Gen (1967-69) 1st Gen tech tips, questions, and answers.	93	445	Re: Question for the EXPERTS... (supv26) 01-28-2003 20:08
2nd Gen (1970-81) 2nd Gen tech tips, questions, and answers.	43	179	Re: Seatbelts (69X11SS) 01-28-2003 07:29
3rd Gen (1982-92) 3rd Gen tech tips, questions, and answers.	140	935	Re: APE 3rd Gen Performance (385LT1) 01-28-2003 22:16

Page from a discussion group, where people with a common interest can discuss their ideas.

Word check ✓

Protocol – an agreed set of standards that enable data from one computer system to be exchanged with another computer system.

TASKS

2 What network services are available to users of your school or college network?

3 Produce a list of rules that members of a discussion group should follow.

Matching software to users' needs: configuring software

Throughout this section you have learned about the main hardware and software components of information systems. In this topic you will learn how the application software programs used can be adapted to meet user needs. This book covers the main Microsoft® *Office* packages because they are the ones used in the majority of business organisations.

Microsoft® *Windows* programs such as *Word, Excel, Access* and *PowerPoint* all share a number of common design features. They are designed to operate in very similar ways. This helps the user to become familiar with the way that the programs work and to make it easier to transfer data between the different applications. Configuring these common features can result in a customised system that is more suited to an organisation's particular needs than the original software.

Configuration

Configuring software means making changes to the way that the software looks and works. These changes will remain in place until the software is reconfigured.

There are a number of different ways that a standard Microsoft® *Office* program can be configured.

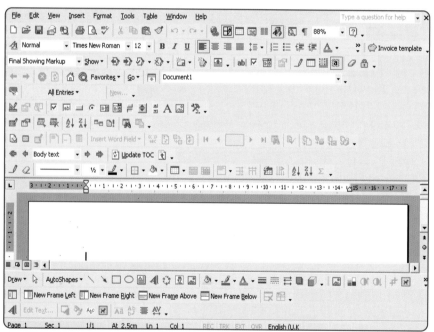

If all the toolbars were displayed at the same time your screen would look like this.

Toolbar display

A toolbar is a list of icons displayed on screen. Each icon represents a particular command. Icons are grouped into toolbars based on standard categories. For example the commands used when working with images are contained on the drawing toolbar. Most toolbars are not displayed all the time. The picture opposite shows what would happen if all the toolbars were displayed at the same time!

The software can be configured to display particular toolbars whenever the program is loaded. Someone who works with graphics, for example, could have the picture toolbar and someone who writes reports could use the reviewing toolbar.

Customised toolbars

Customised toolbars can also be created. These contain the icons most frequently used by the user. Icons can be taken from any existing toolbar.

New icons can be created by putting a new icon onto the toolbar which, when selected, will run a **macro** which the user or system designer has created.

A customised icon could look like this.

Matching software to users' needs: configuring software

Macros

A macro is a sequence of commands given to the software that have been recorded and stored by the computer. The macro recording can then be played back and the commands repeated.

An example would be a macro which always inserted the user's name into a document. The user would set the macro to record and then enter their name using the keyboard. They would then tell the macro to stop recording. When the macro is replayed the person's name is entered automatically by the computer.

A macro can be linked to an icon on a toolbar. When the user clicks on the icon the macro is played. An example would be an icon which automatically loaded a template onto a word processor.

Customised templates

A customised template is a file which cannot have new changes made to it by a user. Any changes that are to be saved must be saved as a new document. Many organisations use templates to create standard letters. These are letters which already contain a number of common features (heading, space for date, greeting, closing text, and so on). The user opens a template and adds their new information; this can then be saved into a new file.

A template ensures that everybody's documents look the same.

TASK

1. Sally Bradshaw is an administrative assistant at The Franklin Hotel in York. The hotel has recently installed new word processing software. Sally would like the software to be able to do the following tasks:

   1. Display a toolbar that will allow her to edit pictures she has entered onto a word processed document.
   2. Display a new icon on the toolbar which, when clicked on will enter her name into a document.
   3. Create a letter template which she can use to send letters to customers who have made a reservation. All letters will contain the following information:
      - "Thank you for your recent reservation. We will hold your accommodation until 7:00 pm on your day of arrival. If you expect to arrive later than this we would be grateful if you could telephone the hotel on the above number."
      - All letters will end: "Yours sincerely".
   4. Create a macro to automatically open the template. Display an icon on the toolbar which, when selected, will run the macro.

   Configure your own computer's word processing software so that it is able to perform these tasks.

Matching software to users' needs: processing

By the end of this topic you will be able to:

- recognise that different users require a computer system to perform different tasks
- match applications software to the processing needs of particular users

For most of this section we have been looking at how organisations use their ICT systems and what those systems contain. In the next section we will look at how those systems are designed and created.

One of the tasks of the people who design ICT systems is to identify the needs of computer users and then find the most appropriate software that will meet those needs.

We covered the main types of applications software earlier in the book. The software we covered included the range of software found on most personal computers, as well as some of the software used to monitor and control events. You may wish to go back and revise the different types of software in more detail before you progress with the rest of this topic and move on to the next section.

The main types of applications software we have covered are:

- word processing software
- desktop publishing
- presentation software
- spreadsheet software
- database software
- multimedia software
- control and monitoring software.

You should by now be familiar with the different types of software and have become reasonably adept in their use, be aware of their advantages and disadvantages and be able to compare the features of different types of software.

Integrated software suites

Many large organisations do not use the standard applications software packages produced by companies such as Microsoft®. They are large enough to have their own personalised computer programs, or **software suites**, written for them. However, these programs usually contain elements of the standard software applications. This is because all organisations will usually require staff to edit text, perform calculations and retrieve data stored in a database.

These packages often combine the features of different applications software. You can get an idea of this when you use a program such as Microsoft® *Word*. Recent versions of *Word* allow you to create a spreadsheet in it without having to open the associated spreadsheet package, *Excel*.

Matching software to particular processing needs

Some processing needs can be met by more than one type of software. It is therefore important to consider carefully the different options available and select the most appropriate software.

Matching software to users' needs: processing

TASKS

Word check ✔

Software suite – a group of related software programs that are designed to make it easy to transfer data between them.

Read the following case studies of different computer users. For each user you should:

a. identify their particular processing needs
b. consider a range of software that could meet those needs
c. select the most appropriate software to meet those needs
d. explain how the chosen software meets those needs.

You could produce your work as a series of written answers or as a presentation to the rest of your class.

1 Jenny Sanderson is the Deputy Headteacher at a secondary school in Nottingham. One of Jenny's tasks is to produce the newsletter to parents which is distributed at the end of every term. To produce the newsletter Jenny needs to:

- receive brief summaries of various school activities from the staff who supervised them
- add photographs taken during the term
- produce summaries of any examination results, including graphs
- combine all this information into a single document
- check and correct spelling, punctuation and grammar, and the layout of the document.

2 Brian Walsden works for a well-known holiday company. The company sells package holidays which customers can book over the telephone. Brian's job involves:

- locating the details of the holiday that the customer wishes to book
- checking availability of the holiday
- obtaining the customer's personal details from them
- sending the customer a record of the holiday they have booked together with a request for payment.

3 George Helios is a graphic designer working for an advertising agency. George's job involves producing designs for the packaging of new products based on sketches produced at brainstorming meetings with clients. George is sometimes asked to edit images produced by other designers.

4 Sandra Makeba is a finance manager at a hospital in Manchester. Sandra is responsible for producing next year's annual hospital budget. To do this Sandra needs to be able to take last year's budget and make changes to the figures. In this way Sandra can see the consequences of her decisions on the overall finances of the hospital.

The systems life cycle

Creating a new information system

From time to time an organisation will need to develop a new information system. There are a number of reasons for this:

- the organisation wishes to **computerise** a part of its operations that was previously done manually
- the capacity of an existing computer system is too small to carry out the work now demanded of it
- an existing system is outdated and no longer suited to the organisation's needs
- an existing system has come to the end of its life and needs to be replaced.

In this section we look at how ICT systems are developed. This is an important section as one of your main **portfolio** tasks is to design and produce a working information system.

There are a number of stages to the creation of a new information system. Together these stages are called the systems life cycle. The reason it is called a cycle will become clear once we have had a look at the life cycle in outline. Later topics will look at each part of the cycle in more detail. It is important that as you look at each part of the cycle you are aware of its wider place in the whole process. Use the diagram on the next page as an important reference point.

The people whose job it is to develop new ICT systems and so move the organisation through the systems life cycle are called **systems analysts**.

The stages of the systems life cycle

Identify user requirements
The first stage of the process is to identify user requirements. In other words, find out from them the tasks that they need the system to perform and the way in which they would like the system to perform them. The main aim of the systems analyst is to produce a computer system which meets these needs.

Produce a design specification
The name of this part of the process is often shortened to just the design stage. At this stage the systems analyst specifies the hardware and software that will make up the system, together with how the system will enable data to be input, processed and output to the end user. The design will also explain how the systems analyst will test the system and the data that it will use to make sure that the system works properly.

Test the system
At this stage the systems analyst will need to build a first version of the system. This working model will then need to be tested to make sure that the full system will work properly. The system will need to have data input into it in order to see whether it processes the data in the ways that were designed.

Implement the system
This stage is often called the **implementation** stage. In this part of the process the final system is built and installed.

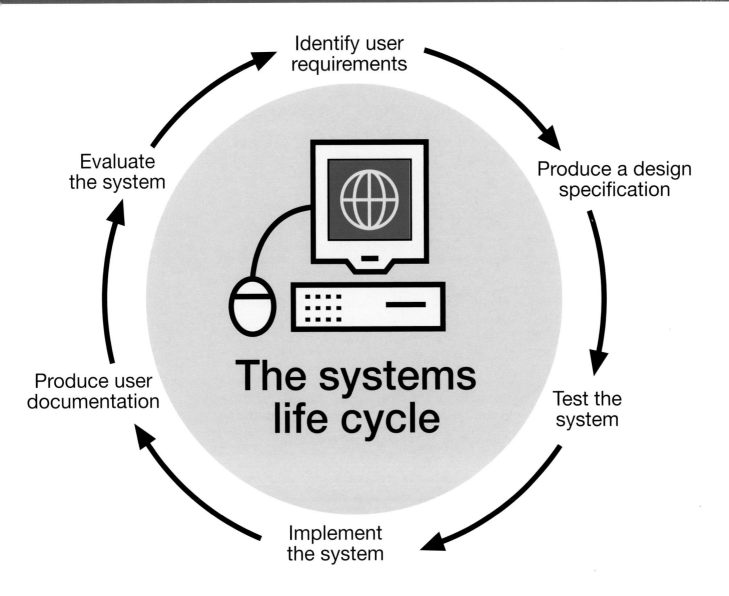

Produce user documentation

This stage can happen at the same time as the system is being implemented. It certainly needs to happen before the users are introduced to the system. The systems analyst will not be available to every user of the system. Therefore a range of guides need to be written that fully explain how the system works and how it can be maintained.

Evaluate the system

This stage brings the process to a close but also allows the cycle to begin again. Once the system is in use it needs to be constantly monitored to see how well it meets the aims originally set for it at the start of the cycle. There may come a time when the system no longer meets the aims set for it and so a new system needs to be developed. The systems life cycle starts all over again.

Word check

Computerise – use a computer system to perform tasks that were previously done by hand.

Systems analysis: identifying user requirements

The aim of the systems analyst at this first stage is to find out why a new system is needed, what is wrong with the existing system and how a new system would work.

What information is needed?

Why is a new system needed?

The systems analyst needs to identify why the existing system is not meeting the needs of the organisation. In the previous topic we looked at four reasons why a new system might be needed. The systems analyst should identify which of these reasons apply.

What are the terms of reference?

The systems analyst is working for a client, the organisation. The terms of reference is a document which sets out what the client expects the systems analyst to produce. One important area often included in the terms of reference is how much the organisation might expect the new system to cost.

What are the key questions to be asked?

The analyst should at this stage draw up a list of the important information that their research should find answers to. This research will help them to identify the most suitable way of developing a new system.

Key questions to ask include:

● What does the organisation want the existing system to be able to do?
● What hardware and software does the current system use (if any)?
● How is the data needed by the system collected?
● How is it entered onto the system?
● Where is it stored?
● How is the data processed?
● What types of output are used?
● Who uses the output from the system? How useful do they find this output?
● What are the strengths and weaknesses of the current system?

How can we find out answers to the key questions?

Observation of processes

If possible the analyst should observe the system in action. This might enable the analyst to identify how long it takes to perform a particular task and what hardware, software and people are involved.

The analyst needs to be aware that, although they are only interested in the system, they will inevitably have to observe people. The consultant should always ask permission of those involved and not refer to them by name in any reports.

Interviewing users

The analyst can find out much useful information from the people who use the system. This can include the people who **operate** and **maintain** the system as well as the people who use the output generated by it.

Some information can be found by using a questionnaire. A questionnaire is a good way of finding out basic facts about the system from a large group of people. A weakness of questionnaires is that they only find out what the researcher asks.

Systems analysis: identifying user requirements

Sometimes the user of the system may have useful information that the researcher has not identified as being relevant. An **interview** or a less formal **discussion** may therefore enable the researcher to find out more in-depth information about the system.

Studying documents
The analyst should also study the documents produced by the system. There will be two types of document produced:

- output documents: printed output from the system
- system logs: records maintained by the **operating system**. They can include records of error messages and how much of the system's memory and processing capacity has been used.

An interview will obtain specific information.

Objectives of the system
Once the analyst has studied the existing system a list of key **objectives** for the new system can be produced. These objectives should state how the new system is going to meet the original needs of the user and how the new system will be better than the old system.

Examples of suitable objectives include:

- a reduction in the number of printed pages in each report from 5 to 3
- a reduction in the processing time of 30 per cent
- an increase in the memory capacity of 50 per cent
- a 50 per cent reduction in the number of system crashes.

The objectives are important because they are the way that the system will be judged once it is up and running. They should all be capable of being measured in some way.

> **Word check**
>
> **Objectives** – the tests that will be used to help decide whether or not the computer system is successful.

Feasibility study
The final stage is to produce a feasibility study. This document reports back to the organisation the key information found out by the analyst. It will also state whether a new system can be produced which both meets the objectives set and be within the terms of reference set at the start. It will end by identifying a number of possible ideas for a new system. The client will then work with the analyst to choose the idea that will be turned into a full design.

TASKS

1 Find out how your school or college produces your school report.

2 Work through the steps outlined in this topic to produce a feasibility study into a new ICT system for producing school reports.

Describing an information system: data-flow diagrams

One of the most important tasks when designing a new ICT system is to think about how data will move between the different parts of the system. Showing the flows of information in a diagram can help you do this.

Context diagrams

Context diagrams are also known as high level data-flow diagrams. They give a summary of the information system. A context diagram shows the main **external entities** and the information that flows through the system. Context diagrams do not show the process that happens to the data in the system.

An example of a simple context diagram for a DVD hire system is shown below:

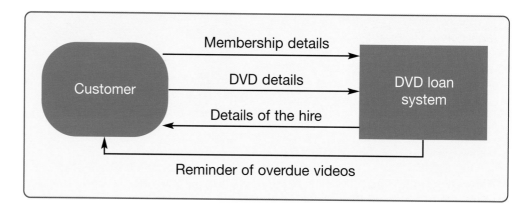

The system

In this system, information is taken from the customer's membership card and also from the DVD. This information is used to update the data on the system. The data is then used to calculate the return-by date and to produce reminder letters to customers whose DVD is overdue.

Data-flow diagrams

A data-flow diagram shows how data moves around an information system. It shows what data is needed, where it comes from and where it ends up.

Data-flow diagrams do not show the hardware and software required to operate the system.

A data-flow diagram uses the following three symbols:

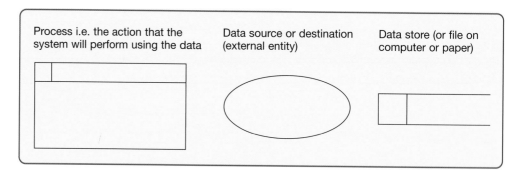

Each process contains a number in the top-left corner. The process labelled 1, in the following diagram, is performed first.

Describing an information system: data-flow diagrams

The following is an example of a data-flow diagram showing the flows of data needed to process the hire of a DVD to a customer.

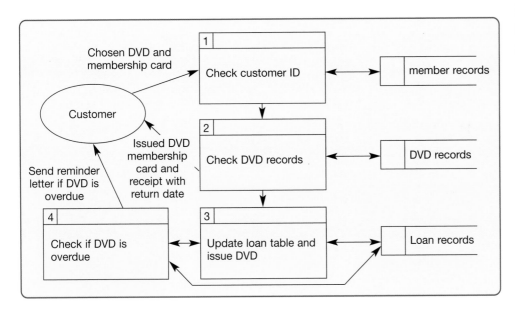

Data-flow tables

Another way to present the flow of data through the system is to use a table. The following table shows one way of representing the flow of data through the process of hiring a DVD.

Process	Process description	Input	Processing	Output	Data store
1	Check customer ID	Customer membership card	Match number on membership card to an entry in the member records datafile	Screen display	Member records datafile
2	Check DVD records	Stock number on DVD box	Match stock number on DVD box to an entry in the DVD records datafile	Screen display	DVD records datafile
3	Update loan table and issue DVD	Membership number, DVD stock number	Update loan table with details of membership number and DVD stock number. Calculate return-by date	Loan information. Printed receipt for customer	Loan datafile
4	Check if DVD is overdue	Data in loan records datafile	Compare return-by date with current date	Reminder to customer	Loan datafile

Designing an information system (1)

- identify the main items included in the design of an information system
- produce a system design to meet a particular user's needs

The design stage is very important. This is the stage where most of the hard thinking about the system is done. By the end of this stage all those involved in the development of the system should know exactly what type of system is going to be developed.

The key test in looking at a system design is to ask the question, "Would someone other than the person who wrote the design be able to implement it?". The process of producing the design should consist of the stages as shown in the diagram below.

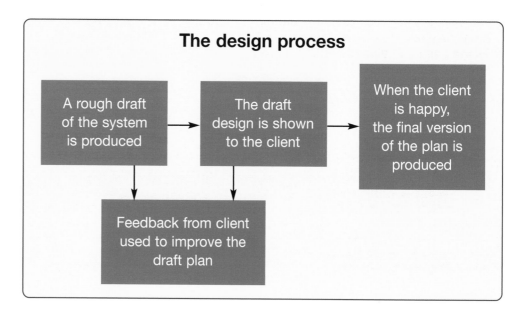

At the first stage a system diagram should be produced together with a rough plan of the system. This should include sketches of important documents such as printouts. These can be shown to the client before the full design is written.

The rest of this topic and the next one explain the features which should be included within the system design.

Details of the hardware and software required

The design should describe the hardware needed. This could include:

- the number and type of computers needed, for example desktop, dumb terminal, and so on
- the input devices, for example mouse, scanner
- the type of processor required, for example speed of microprocessor and quantity of RAM needed
- the output devices, for example type of monitor and printer
- data storage devices, for example hard disk capacity, back-up data storage types
- any external data transfer devices, for example modem, CD-RW drive.

The applications software should be chosen and the reasons for choosing this software should be explained.

The operating system to be used should also be identified and justified.

Designing an information system (1)

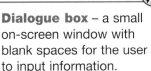

The information to be used and how it will be captured

A description of the information will need to be obtained before it can be entered onto the system.

- A description of where the data is currently stored. For example the data could be stored on another computer system or it might need to be collected from new customers.
- How the data is to be captured. For example the data may need to be extracted from an existing computer and saved to a floppy disk. Alternatively the data may need to be downloaded from the Internet.
- There should be sketches of any data capture forms: either paper-based forms or screen-based forms. Paper-based forms include items like **order forms** and new customer information forms. Who will use the forms should also be specified.

A typical data input screen.

A hand-drawn sketch of a spreadsheet showing where a graph will be created.

Details of any files that need creating and their properties

This is particularly important in the case of database files where the **fieldnames** and field **data types** should be specified.

How the information needs to be prepared before it is input onto the system

The information which is to be collected may need to be modified into a format that the computer can work with. For example a list of customer records in a paper-based system might display a customer's date of birth as 26th September 1964. This will need to be changed to a format such as 26/09/1964 before it can be entered onto a database.

Details of input screens

The design should explain what the users of the system will see as they work with the system. For example it should include the layout of any spreadsheets or **dialogue boxes** that will give prompts to the user.

Data storage

The design should describe how and where data is to be stored including any procedures to produce back-up copies of the data.

ACME COMMUNICATIONS
Customer Survey

1. How important are these factors to you?
   Please mark with a cross between 1 (unimportant) and 10 (very important)

   a. Value for money   1..10
   b. Quality of work   1..10
   c. Speed of work   1..10

2. How do you rate Acme Communications against each of these factors?
   Please mark with a cross between 1 (poor) and 10 (excellent)

   a. Value for money   1..10
   b. Quality of work   1..10
   c. Speed of work   1..10

3. How do you think Acme Communications could do better? ....

4. Do you have any other comments?
   ....
   ....

   Many thanks for your help

Answers from a data collection sheet can be input into a computer.

TASK

1 A bookshop wishes to set up a database stock control system. Produce a design for this system.

Designing an information system (2)

The processes to be carried out using the data

We now come to the processes which will be carried out by the computer system. This section will vary depending on the type of applications software to be used.

Word processing and desktop publishing

Most of the processing here will be concerned with how visual information such as text and images will be formatted. The formatting will be done to try to improve the way that the document communicates its message to the reader.

The processes will include:

• the ways in which plain text will be **formatted**, for example font styles and sizes
• the ways in which images will be **edited**
• any use of **automatic processes** such as spell-checking and mail merge.

Spreadsheets

The main processes will involve the use of formulae to perform calculations and take decisions based on the data and include:

• the **formulae** which will be used
• any formatting of data to improve its appearance, for example currency formats, as well as the rules for any conditional formatting
• details of any **sorts** to be carried out
• details of any **data validation** formulae to be used.

Databases

The main processes will involve the extraction of selected records and the manipulation of data to produce reports and include:

• any **searches** and/or sorts to be carried out, with the search criteria identified
• any reports which will be produced and how they will be generated
• details of any **data validation** formulae to be used.

Multimedia (including web pages)

The main processes will include those covered under word processing and desktop publishing that relate to the way that the text and images are edited to improve their appearance.

The other main processes involve the hyperlinks that take the user from one page to another, including to locations outside the immediate system, for example external web-links.

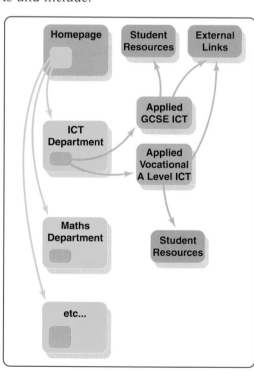

Links between web pages

Designing an information system (2)

Control and monitoring systems

The main processes relate to the way that the system makes decisions based on the information it analyses.

In other words the **algorithms** which describe the rules that will govern the decisions to be made should be identified. How the system will monitor the environment (for example the sampling rate at which data is measured) should be identified.

The different types of output that are needed

The design should include hand-drawn sketches of the output data. There should be sketches for both screen-based output and printed output.

Some forms of output, such as database reports and multimedia pages, may look different when viewed on screen and when printed out. Different users may prefer different types of output. A design should take account of these differences and try to produce output which will look good both on screen and on paper.

A test plan

We will look at testing in more detail in the next topic. However it is worth noting here that the design should show how the following things can be tested:

- a plan to test whether the system will accept or reject any data that is unsuitable
- a plan to test whether the processes which have been designed will produce the expected results.

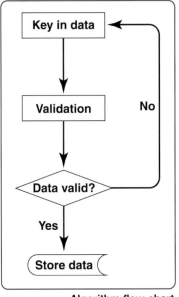

Algorithm flow chart

Marion Jones operates a library service at a hospital in Lancashire. Patients at the hospital are able to borrow up to two books for a period of one week. At the moment Marion operates a manual system. Patients wishing to use the system are given a card listing their name and membership number.

Marion keeps details of each book in the library on a card which is stored in a filing cabinet. When a patient takes out a book, the card is removed from the cabinet and the patient's name, hospital number (a six figure number) and ward are written onto the card together with the date the book was taken. The card is put into the 'on-loan' file until the patient returns the book. At the end of each week Marion checks the file by hand to see if patients have overdue books. If they do she writes them a hand-written note requesting that they return the book.

Marion is concerned that this system is slow and cumbersome. She is worried that cards may become lost, resulting in books not being returned. She wants a system that will:

- store details of all the books
- identify which books are on loan to which patients
- produce a list of overdue books and the patients who have them
- automatically send reminder notes to patients with overdue books.

Word check

Algorithm – the sequence of decisions to be made and operations to be performed by a program. Algorithms are usually shown as a flow diagram.

TASK

1. Produce a design for a computer-based system that will meet Marion's needs.

Validation and testing

ICT systems can sometimes produce results which are unexpected. There are usually two main reasons for this:

1. there are problems with the data that has been input into the system
2. there are problems in the way that the system operates; either the hardware is at fault or there are problems with the way that data is processed.

In this topic we will look at how the system designer can limit the chances of the system failing to produce the required output.

Data validation

Data validation is an automatic process that the system can use to check if the data that has been input into the system is appropriate.

For example a spreadsheet might be set up to convert examination results into percentages. The test is marked out of 60. The teacher inputs the score out of 60 and the spreadsheet converts this into a percentage. It would be impossible to have a test score of 66 out of 60 but it would be possible to enter this onto the spreadsheet and produce a 'result' of 110 per cent!

A data validation procedure can be written to make sure that the spreadsheet only accepts data that is between 0 and 60. Data outside these limits will be rejected and an error message displayed to the user. The error message can tell them why the data has been rejected.

This is an example of a data validation method called a range check. There are other validation checks that can also be used:

Name	What is checked	Example
Presence check	A check that data has been entered into the specified place	An online order form on a website requires customers to enter their email address. The order form is not complete until the data has been entered
Data type check	A check that the right type of data has been entered	A database field containing the price of products will not accept data that is in text or date format
Check digit	A check that a string of numbers has been entered accurately	The final (check) digit of a product bar code is based on a mathematical formula that uses all the other numbers in the bar code. The check digit will only be correct if all the other numbers are correct

Testing data validation rules

A validation rule can be tested by using test data. There are three types of test data:

- **Normal data:** data which the user knows should be accepted. For example an examination score of 50 out of 60.
- **Extreme data:** data which lies on the boundary of the acceptable data. For example examination scores of 0 and 60 out of 60.
- **Abnormal data:** data which lies outside the acceptable range. For example examination scores of −10 and 70 out of 60.

Validation and testing

Producing a test plan

A test plan sets out how the system will be tested to make sure that it performs its tasks accurately. It should contain headings to enable the following information to be included:

- the things that need to be tested
- how they will be tested, for example the test data to be used
- what the expected results will be
- whether or not the actual result was the same as that expected
- what the result was if it was unexpected
- any action that needs to be taken as a result of the test.

An extract from a test plan for a spreadsheet is shown below.

Item to be tested	Data to be used	Expected result	Actual result	Action
Validation rule: allow data greater than 50 and less than 100	50	Data rejected	Data rejected	None
Validation rule: allow data greater than 50 and less than 100	75	Data accepted	Data accepted	None
Test the formula D5=C5*3	50	150	150	None
Test the formula H10=E3+E4*2	E3=5 E4=6	22	17	Change formula to H10=(E3+E4)*2

The plan should also include details of a plan to test the system with the intended users. This would then help the designer to test whether or not the system is **user friendly**.

Word check

User friendly – the extent to which a computer program is easily used by an operator. User friendly programs will have clear instructions written in straightforward language.

TASKS

1. Explain how the following could all be validated and tested.

   a. A library database stores information about its customers. One of the fields is called Town. It is the town where each customer lives. All records must have data entered into this field.
   b. The database stores the date of birth of each customer in the format dd/mm/yy.
   c. The database stores a unique number for each item in the library. This is a six figure number between 000001 and 999999.
   d. The library has multiple copies of some very popular books. This quantity is recorded in the database. The maximum number of copies of any one book is nine.

2. A system is required to produce a personalised letter to 300 people in a database. Explain how you could test the system without having to print all 300 letters.

Implementing the system

- understand the different ways that an ICT system can be implemented

- identify how a given system should be implemented

The implementation stage is where the design is turned into a reality.

In this topic we look at two areas:

- the different ways that ICT systems can be implemented in an organisation
- the tasks that need to be performed at the implementation stage.

Implementation methods

It is unlikely that you will be asked to install the systems you build into real organisations. However you need to be aware of the different ways that systems can be installed as well as their benefits and drawbacks.

CASE STUDY

Not all new ICT systems work perfectly.

In April 2002 it was reported that the new computer system operating the UK's air traffic control system was causing problems for its operators.

Operators claimed that the size of fonts and characters on their control screens were too small. They argued that this made it difficult for them to read data accurately. They said that they had difficulty distinguishing between the numbers 8, 6 and 0.

The computer system opened in January 2002, six years behind schedule.

Direct implementation

Direct implementation is used when the old system is closed down and the new system is introduced at the same time. For example, staff might end the working day on a Friday using the old system and begin work on the following Monday using the new system.

Parallel implementation

This is where, for a period of time, the old system and the new system work side-by-side. For example there might be a period of one week where the organisation uses both the old system and the new system.

Phased implementation

Phased implementation occurs when the new system is gradually introduced alongside the old system. Staff continue to work on the old system while beginning to work on the new system one section at a time.

There are benefits and drawbacks of using each method as shown in the table below.

Method	Benefits	Drawbacks
Direct implementation	The benefits of the new system are gained as quickly as possible	Any problems not identified during testing will affect the operations of the organisation
Parallel implementation	The new system can be tested in a real environment without harming the operations of the organisation	Both the old and new systems are in use, so all tasks need to be performed twice. This reduces the **efficiency** of the organisation
Phased implementation	Parts of the system can be tested in a real environment without harming the operations of the organisation	Hard to test whether the different parts of the system work together

Implementing the system

Marshall's Bakery makes bread and cakes for use in hotels and restaurants. In April 2001 it introduced a new computer system. The old system was shut down at 6:00pm on Friday. Staff were paid overtime to come into work on the Sunday to practise using the new system. On the Monday morning the new system crashed. Staff had to revert to using the old system until the problem was fixed.

TASKS

1. Which implementation method was used in Marshall's Bakery?

2. Explain how a different method of implementation might have prevented this problem from happening.

Word check

Efficiency – an efficient organisation will carry out its operations using as few raw materials and people as possible, thereby saving on time and money.

Implementation tasks

A number of records need to be kept by the system builder at the implementation stage:

- a log of the activities carried out by the builder
- a completed test log based on the test plan
- a log of unexpected errors (bugs) and how they were overcome
- a series of screen prints to show how the system has been built. These screen prints should be **annotated**, in other words notes should be written onto the screen prints to explain what they show
- an explanation as to how the system that has been built is different from the one that was planned.

It is important that the records tell the story of how the system was built from beginning to end. This means that the records must be in the correct order. There are two ways to do this:

- Import all the documents and screen prints into a single document at the time that they happen. Use automatic page numbers in the header or footer.
- Attach a footer to all screen prints detailing the date and time that the screen print was printed. The individual print-outs can then be assembled into the correct sequence.

The records produced by the builder should be detailed enough for someone else to be able to recreate the system. This is important if, for some reason, the system needs to be completely rebuilt, which may happen as the result of a natural disaster.

TASKS

3. Make sure you know how to produce a screen print and how to attach a header or footer displaying the date and time of printing.

4. Find out if your computer system at school or college has been upgraded. How was the upgrade implemented?

5. Speak with the ICT manager at a local business. Find out how they have implemented any changes to their computer systems.

User documentation

By the end of this topic you will be able to:

- describe the main types of user documentation
- produce user documentation that meets a particular need

One of the most important parts of the systems design process is the production of the documents that will be read by the system's users.

There are three main types of documentation, because there are three different types of people who will work with the system:

1. Installation engineers are the people responsible for installing the system.
2. Users are the people who will perform tasks using the computer system and its software.
3. Engineers are responsible for finding and repairing any faults with the system.

The three main types of documentation are:

Installation documentation
This will contain information that will help the engineer to install the system. This information can include:

- details of hardware requirements such as RAM, processor speed, operating system and monitor specification
- instructions on how to load programs, such as names of set-up files.

User documentation
This will enable ordinary users of the computer system to carry out operations and commands using the system. This information should include:

- how to open and close the system and its software
- lists of menu items, icons and what commands they perform
- how to carry out simple and more complex operations
- how to add and delete data, save and print work
- screenshots showing typical screen layouts and dialogue boxes
- a list of common error messages and what they mean (also known as a **troubleshooting** guide).

Maintenance documentation
This will enable ICT systems managers and technicians to carry out tasks such as system back-ups, fault finding and repair, as well as upgrades to the system itself.

Did you know ...

The following are all quotations from real user documentation. They have all been badly written.

- Type the field name Name in the Field Name field.
- If you wish to save any unsaved work make sure that the unsaved work is saved by first using Save.
- To undo undo please choose to redo the done work.

Try to rewrite them so they make more sense.

Did you know ...

It is important to think carefully about the needs of the person who will use the guide. Users of installation and maintenance guides tend to be computer experts, so the documents can use technical language. User guides tend to be used by non-computer experts, so they should contain less technical language. However, a user guide should be able to explain how to perform all the tasks required by users of the system. The guide should be written in clear English and refer to specific parts of the system (such as menu commands) by name.

User documentation

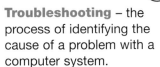

User documentation should always be tested on a sample of the target audience before being published. The authors will then be able to correct any errors and badly worded passages before issuing the final version.

For many years user documentation was only published in paper format. Technical guides were bulky books that took up a lot of space on bookshelves. This made them impractical to use if a large number of users shared the same system as part of a network.

More recently, there has been substantial growth of online help. This has typically been in the form of help files embedded into the system's software. In a Windows environment users can access the information they require by selecting the help function on the menu bar. More sophisticated help menus use a database to enable users to query the help files by keying-in questions and problems. Some systems use animated help characters to make the process more user-friendly.

> **Word check** ✓
>
> **Troubleshooting** – the process of identifying the cause of a problem with a computer system.

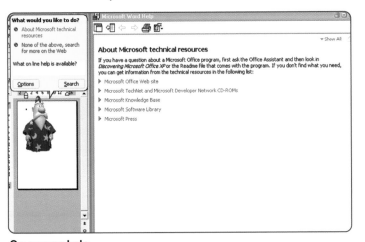

On-screen help

Help files can also be stored on CD-ROMs, rather than bulky manuals, and more recently there has been a growth in web-based help and support where software manufacturers require users to access help files via the Internet.

> **CASE STUDY**
>
> Tariq Aziz is a systems engineer for an education software business. Content authors work from home writing learning materials which they upload onto the company's computer system using the Internet.
>
> Tariq has been responsible for the production of all the user and technical documentation for this system.
>
> The main version of the user guide is a 230-page manual which has been issued to all managers within the business. However, it was decided that it would be too expensive to issue the manual to all 70 of the firm's authors who work from home.
>
> Instead, the firm decided to issue all authors with a copy of the manual on CD-ROM together with online help which can be accessed when the user is connected to the system.

> **TASKS**
>
> **1** Make a list of the documentation available to you when you use a computer at school or college.
>
> Describe where this information is stored and in what form.
>
> **2** Evaluate the online help available on your computer at school or college.
>
> Describe how user friendly it is and how it could be improved.
>
> **3** Write a short user guide describing how to carry out ONE of the following operations: producing a mail-merge document; producing a database report; using a look-up table in a spreadsheet. Include: how to open and close the software applications; use of menus and icons; how to print any final documents; a troubleshooting guide. Include any relevant screenshots in your guide.
>
> **4** Test your user documentation by asking a friend to use it. Obtain their feedback on your guide. Use this feedback to make improvements to your guide.

Evaluating and maintaining the system

Once the system has been installed it is important to obtain information on how well the system is performing. There are two reasons for this:

1. to identify any problem that needs fixing. Examples could include problems with printers and cables, or **corrupted** program files that need replacing
2. to examine the extent to which the system meets the needs of its users. For example the organisation might change the way that it would like to perform its operations and finds that the computer system will have to be modified.

Monitoring and maintenance

Maintenance is the process of checking the system to make sure that all of its parts are operating properly. The aim of the maintenance engineer is to make sure that the system is working as intended. In other words the system meets the objectives that were set for it.

The system needs to be monitored to ensure that it is performing to everyone's requirements.

The system is maintained by having its performance **monitored**. Computer users, systems engineers and computer managers will all be involved in monitoring the performance of the equipment.

The main concern of the users will be that the system performs the tasks that they require. They may be able to perform some of the routine maintenance themselves. This includes things like checking printer paper levels and ink cartridges and replacing them when necessary.

The systems engineers will be more concerned with the overall performance of the system. They will monitor aspects such as processing speed, memory capacity and the ability of the system to perform scheduled tasks such as system back-ups and virus checking.

Evaluation

Evaluation is a much broader task than monitoring, as it involves judging the extent to which the system is able to meet the objectives set for it. The objectives for the system are:

● the original objectives that were set for the system when it was designed
● the current objectives based on what the organisation now wants the system to do.

Evaluating and maintaining the system

Most systems eventually cease to meet the needs of their users. This is for two reasons:

1. The age of the system and the volume of work to be done might mean that the system no longer meets its original objectives.
2. The activities of the organisation itself change, so that the original aims set for the system are no longer relevant.

The information sources used to evaluate the computer system should ideally be the same as those used to research the original system.

It is particularly important to obtain feedback from users. They should be asked to comment on the ease-of-use of the system, in other words whether or not it is user friendly. They may also have comments and suggestions about the tasks that they would like the system to perform. All of these comments can be used to try to improve the system in the future.

Word check

Corrupt – the existence of errors in a set of data, or in a computer program. Corrupted programs or data may not work and might have to be deleted and reinstalled.

CASE STUDY

In 1999 Atish Mehta installed a new computer system to handle the sales operations at his Edinburgh-based travel agency telephone call centre. The system was designed to have a capacity of 20 000 customers and be used by 20 operators at the same time. All data was entered by hand by telephone sales operatives. There was no facility for customer records to be extracted and used when booking a second holiday.

By 2002 the system no longer met the needs of the business. Atish wanted to introduce a website where customers could make bookings online. He had been surprised by the number of customers who had made repeat bookings and he wanted to make it easier for them to do so. Also, the growth of the organisation meant that the system was close to capacity. Atish now employs 18 telephone sales operators.

In what ways does this computer system fail to meet its original objectives? Why is this?

TASKS

Read the following comments from users. For each comment suggest what could be done to overcome the problem.

1. "The system is fine, but I find it difficult to read the characters on screen."

2. "I like the database but at the moment I have to copy and paste information from it into the letters that I write to customers. Is there any way that the system can be changed to do this?"

3. "The system now seems to be running out of memory capacity."

4. "I'd like the spreadsheet to be able to enter the data itself rather than me having to type it in manually."

3 ICT and society

Contents

This section of the book will explore the role of Information and Communication Technology (ICT) and the impact it can have on society.

In recent years the use of computers in all walks of life has increased. In section 2, you will have looked at how organisations have utilised ICT and computers in general to improve their efficiency. Now you will investigate how members of society have been affected by the increased use of ICT.

This section is based upon the ICT and Society section of the Applied ICT GCSE specification. The section is designed to help you to understand how far ICT systems affect everyday life, by exploring how individuals, families, clubs and societies, work teams and community groups use ICT, in their personal, social and professional lives.

Not all sectors of society have access to ICT, yet it still affects their lives.

You can check your emails, or look things up on the Internet, at cybercafés.

A constant development of ICT, both in terms of hardware and software, can have negative as well as positive effects. Over the following pages you will be introduced to a range of scenarios where ICT has, or could have, been implemented. You will be set a number of tasks to help you to understand the information contained in the text, or to carry out further investigations of your own. For many of these there will be no correct answer, it is up to you to form an opinion and, in some cases, argue a position. This can only be done with knowledge – so read the text carefully, and follow the instructions in the tasks.

You will be asked to consider how developments have influenced and may continue to influence areas such as:

- business
- working styles
- **legislation**
- entertainment and leisure
- personal communications.

You will need access to the Internet for a number of the tasks, as you will be asked to gather information. Over the past two sections of the book, you should have developed a method of searching and collecting information. Be sure to record all sources and only use what is relevant.

Many of the tasks will ask you to describe or explain a particular concept. You may wish, with agreement from your teacher, to compile these into a website or multimedia presentation to be delivered at a later date.

Other tasks will require you to make notes about different technologies or carry out investigations of your own. These should be kept safe to be used for revision or support during the compilation of your portfolio.

If you decide to follow this subject beyond GCSE, the notes you make here may prove useful in your further studies.

Maintenance engineers use their mobile phones to keep in touch with their head office, for instance to inform them of potential problems, or to report on progress.

Word check

Legislation – the framework of laws and regulations put in place by the Government. These are updated when situations change, or technology brings about a new problem, such as email confidentiality.

Internet technologies (1)

By the end of this topic you will be able to:

- describe the structure of a website address
- explain the term URL

The Internet is an enormous resource; unfortunately it is also a very confusing one, as the areas of information, the websites, are sometimes named in a logical manner, but are more often named in a peculiar way!

When people talk about the Internet, they usually mean the world wide web, although these are two different things. The Internet is the network of networks; millions of computers exchanging information around the world. It consists of billions of pages of information. The public side of this system is known as the world wide web, often referred to simply as the web.

The address of a particular page can be found using a web address or Universal Resource Locator (URL) – this is made up from a number of elements:

http://www.matereality.co.uk/links.htm

http:// (HyperText Transfer Protocol) – the system used to transmit and receive all data over the world wide web. When you type a URL into your Internet browser, you're actually sending an HTTP request to a web server, which is another computer, for a page of information.

www (world wide web) – this tells the web server to look for any files that are available to be seen by anyone with an Internet connection. Some websites do not have www as the second part of the URL, this means that they are not available to everyone; it may be that you need a password, or other form of permission to see these pages.

. (full stop, or dot) – this tells the computer to look for a file within the area of www files.

matereality – the name of the page or group of pages, in this case it is a group of pages.

.co.uk – this shows that a company that is based in the UK owns the website. The most common domain is .com.

/ – this shows that there are other pages within the site.

links.htm – this is the name of a particular page's 'links' that is written in a language the computer can convert to be seen in the browser, HTML or HyperText Markup Language.

The slightest mistake in typing the URL will mean that your browser cannot request the correct page from the web server, so you will not get to see the page you expected to see.

Nearly half of all websites are hosted in the US, although this number is falling as companies and individuals move their sites to other countries where labour costs and hosting the site costs are cheaper. However the top ten websites visited in Autumn 2001 were all American, as shown in the table opposite.

Did you know ...

- January 2002 – 550 million emails sent and received in the UK.
- Winter 2001 – 33 million UK residents use the Internet regularly – approximately 60 per cent.
- It is expected that games consoles will be the largest growth area of Internet access up to 2005.
- Some 17 per cent of users do so through 'freeserve', the largest ISP in the UK. 'AoL' (America on Line) has 12 per cent of the market.
- Over 16 000 people join the Internet each month in the UK.

Internet technologies (1)

Using a laptop computer and a **satellite telephone** allows access to the world wide web and email from any point on earth.

Site	Visits (in millions) (Sept. – Dec. 2001)
AoL Time Warner Network	83.87
MSN – Microsoft sites	70.72
Yahoo	68.36
Terra Lycos	39.51
X10.COM	39.33
Vivendi-Universal sites	36.46
About/Primedia	33.22
Ebay	25.95
Walt Disney Internet Group	25.39
Euniverse Network	25.16

TASK

1 Visit some of these URLs: http://www.aqa.org.uk, http://www.edexcel.org.uk, http://www.ocr.org.uk, http://www.icaag.com these are the examination boards that offer qualifications in ICT.

Alternatively take a look at: http://www.bbc.co.uk, http://www.itv.co.uk and other TV-based sites.

Experiment with URLs, try typing **www.YOURNAME.com** (replace YOURNAME with your name) or **www.YOURFAVOURITEFOOD.com**; if you don't get anything try altering the .com to .co.uk.

Internet technologies (2)

Electronic mail (email) is a system that uses the same hardware as the Internet.

Email is a method of sending messages from one terminal or computer to another via a communications link.

As with all other applications, it requires the appropriate software. You also need to have an **email account**, which is usually supplied by the Internet service provider (ISP) that you use. You can then have an email address, which must be different from anyone else's address. To send an email message, you also need to know the email address of the person you are sending it to.

Email addresses are similar to URLs, in that they are also made up from some of the elements used in web addresses:

dave@matereality.co.uk

dave – the name of the person. This is sometimes a department, or section of a company, such as enquiry or sales.

@ – this symbol means 'at'. It tells the email software to look for the person dave 'at' the address which follows.

matereality.co.uk – this is the address of the mailbox, a storage area where the email is saved until the recipient, or their software, asks for it.

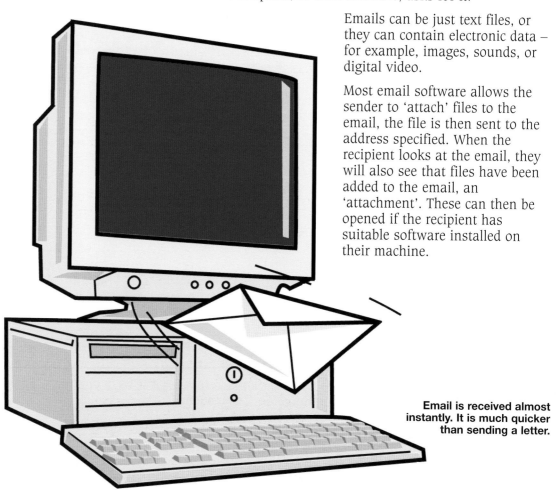

Emails can be just text files, or they can contain electronic data – for example, images, sounds, or digital video.

Most email software allows the sender to 'attach' files to the email, the file is then sent to the address specified. When the recipient looks at the email, they will also see that files have been added to the email, an 'attachment'. These can then be opened if the recipient has suitable software installed on their machine.

Email is received almost instantly. It is much quicker than sending a letter.

Internet technologies (2)

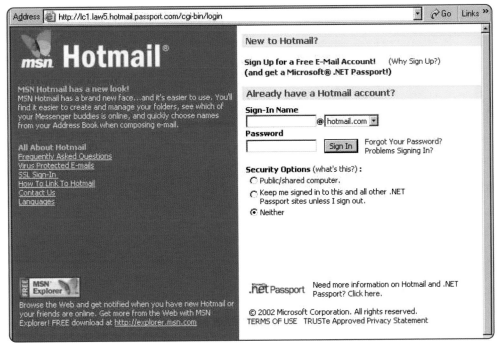

Hotmail is one of the free email accounts available.

Attachments are sometimes the method for transferring viruses around the Internet. This will be covered in more detail later.

Depending on your Internet connection, receiving emails can be an automatic operation – if your computer is permanently connected to the Internet the software used to manage your email account can be set to check your mailbox every few minutes. If you have a dial-up connection the software will usually check immediately after your connection is made.

The Internet and email are open to abuse if security measures are not taken. All web pages are protected on web servers by software called a **firewall**; this stops people getting access to the files without permission. In theory this stops hacking – the process of defacing web pages or vandalising and stealing information from sites.

Email must also be protected by some security measures; this usually involves some form of encryption. The email text is scrambled using a numerical formula, so that the only person who can read it is the person with the code breaker.

TASKS

1. Set up an online email account at one of the following sites:
   - **www.hotmail.com**
   - **www.yahoo.co.uk**

2. Record each stage and produce a guide for others to use when they set up their email accounts.

3. Explain why email accounts are protected by a password system.

Internet connections (1)

For devices to be able to communicate there are a number of factors that need to be considered:

- the distance between devices
- the type of connection
- the speed of data transfer
- the type of data to be transmitted
- the language common to both devices.

The device used to enable transfer of data over long distances is called a modem. Until recently this was an external device, with a cable coming out of one end attached to the computer and a second cable joined to a telephone line. Many computers now have internal modems with a cable joining the computer to the telephone system.

Advances in telephone technology have meant that the lines can now be used in different ways; a number of lines can be linked together to increase transfer rates, the capacity of single lines can be increased by sending chunks of data at a time, or other systems can be used, such as **microwaves** and radio waves.

The most common connection in the UK is via a normal telephone line and a 'dial-up connection' using a 56k modem (maximum transfer speed). This means the computer works in a similar way to a normal telephone. It is connected to the telephone line, and dials a special number. This is usually the number of another computer, run by an Internet service provider (ISP). Once the connection is made the ISP computer starts to send information back to the user's computer, which is converted into data that can be viewed with a piece of software called a **browser**. The first page shown in a browser is called the **homepage**.

The browser enables the computer to convert the signal from the modem into a structure with which the user can interact. It can show text, images as well as play movies and sounds. The user can use their mouse, or other input device to navigate around the page and follow links, press buttons or otherwise interact with the display.

Netscape's homepage

Internet connections (1)

Historical information

The speed of the Internet has always been the same; data can be transferred along cable, or via radio waves and microwaves, at almost the speed of light, 299 792 458 metres per second. But the problem has always been the translation of the signals from a computer into a form that can be transmitted and then converted back at the other end. Early modems (they get their name from the job they do – **mod**ulating the signal, then **dem**odulating it) were able to process 14 000 bits per second, modern broadband systems can process over 500 000 bits per second.

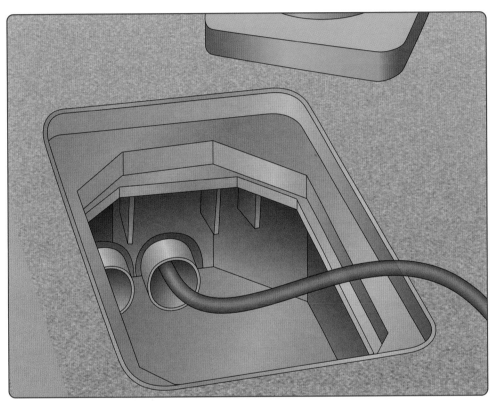

Data is transferred along cables under the ground.

TASKS

1. Produce a timeline, charting the development of Internet connections from the 1970s to the present.

2. Use the data in the table opposite to produce a graph, showing the relative speeds of the systems.

Modem speeds

Method	Speed (kilobytes per second)
56k modem	6
128k ISDN	16
ADSL	125
Cable modem	150
T1	188

Most modern computers use one of the modems listed in the table above.

Internet connections (2)

By the end of this topic you will be able to:

- understand how computers deal with numbers

As the telephone system and dial-up connections develop, the ability to transfer data improves. Private homes can now get linked to the Internet through high-speed Broadband connections. This allows data transfer speeds of over 200 times faster than a standard 56k modem.

Mobile telephone technology has also recently developed, allowing access to a limited Internet and email service with standard equipment. With the introduction of 3rd generation (3G) technology, multimedia and interactive sites are becoming more available.

Computers deal only with numbers. They store letters and other characters by assigning a number for each one. Before the system called Unicode was invented, there were hundreds of different encoding systems for assigning these numbers.

With the development of these systems it has been important to regulate the language used to code and transmit data. Unicode is a system, which allows computers to decode a list of digits into a meaningful display, using base 16 (hexadecimal – a system that uses the figures 0, 1, 2, 3, 4, 5, 6, 7, 8, 9, A, B, C, D, E, F to represent the numbers 0 to 15, 16 is shown as 10 – one 16 are zero units).

Although computers work in binary 1s and 0s, the hexadecimal data is converted into a continuous stream of 1s and 0s. 'Plate 1' – would be coded as shown in the table below. Making the code sent to the computer:
0101000001101100010100010111101 0001100101001000000110001

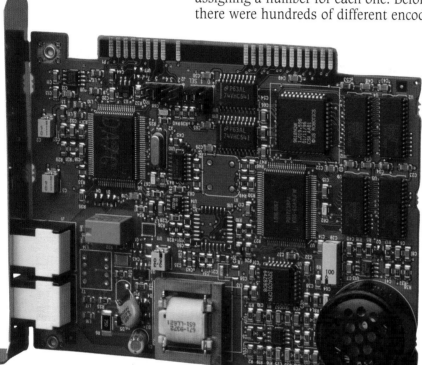

A modem circuit board

Letter	Hexadecimal	Decimal	Binary
P	50	80	01010000
l	6	108	01101100
a	61	81	01010001
t	74	116	01110100
e	65	101	01100101
space	20	32	00100000
1	31	55	00110001

Internet connections (2)

Although the language used by computers has had to be regulated, so that there is an international standard, the language used by computer users still varies. In 2001 the top seven languages used over the Internet were as shown in the table opposite.

Out of the total of Internet users over a third use English as their main language online, although that also means that almost two thirds don't!

Language	Number of users
English	217 800 000
Japanese	47 300 000
Chinese	40 700 000
German	30 000 000
Korean	22 700 000
Spanish	20 400 000
Italian	17 500 000

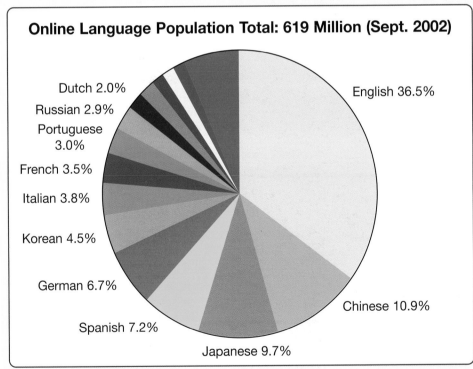

Online Language Population Total: 619 Million (Sept. 2002)

Dutch 2.0%
Russian 2.9%
Portuguese 3.0%
French 3.5%
Italian 3.8%
Korean 4.5%
German 6.7%
Spanish 7.2%
Japanese 9.7%
Chinese 10.9%
English 36.5%

Source: www.global-reach.biz/globalstats

Pre-paid connection is technically the same as a dial-up, except the user pays a flat rate per month instead of telephone bills.

ISDN uses a special modem that links two telephone lines, doubling the capacity. The user pays a subscription and phone call charges – because it uses two lines the bills are for two calls!

With ADSL (DSL) the modem allows the user to make phone calls while online, charges are through subscription.

A cable modem is a separate cable connection to the phone line, using the digital television network cabling. Subscription service charges are levied.

T1 is 24 lines linked together to give very high speeds, paid for by subscription.

T3 is 672 lines! Used as the backbone of the Internet – 30 times faster than T1. The modem converts the electrical pulses into a digital sequence, the zeros and ones; the browser then converts the digital sequence into the letters to be displayed on the screen.

1. Write a short essay, outlining how these developments in technology have influenced the design of websites.

2. Describe how the traditional methods of long distance communication – telephone and letters – have been affected by the Internet.

Mobile telephone technologies (1)

Mobile telephones are a relatively new technology.

We take it for granted that communication is available more or less everywhere. This section will look at the significant steps in mobile telephone development.

The telephone system is probably the biggest and most complicated machine on earth.

The first stage in its development was the telegraph, invented in 1837; Alexander Graham Bell went on to patent the telephone in 1876. Since then there have been a number of developments, although most of them have happened behind the scenes; for example, automated exchanges, fibre optic cable, and so on, making the use of the telephone easier, more reliable and efficient.

The first mobile phones were very large.

Mobile technologies have also been around for a lot longer than many people think! In 1894 Marconi patented radio in the UK (this was originally digital, **analogue** radio came along much later!).

In the 1920s the first two-way radios were developed; in the 1950s these became available for use by the public, although because of the frequencies used there could only be a few thousand in the whole country.

1980 saw the introduction of the analogue mobile telephone, using the TACS system (total access control system).

In 1991 the first digital system, GSM (Groupe Spécial Mobile) went live.

Satellite systems have been in existence for over 20 years, but at present are still extremely expensive and really only for use in extreme conditions.

So although the use of mobile telephones is a recent phenomenon, the evolution has been taking place for over 150 years! It would be interesting to imagine what Alexander Graham Bell would think of the latest developments of the telephone!

Mobile telephone technologies (1)

What is SMS?

Short message service (SMS) is a system that allows 160-character text messages to be passed to and from GSM mobile phones using the control channels. This means that a text message can get through even when a call is in progress. SMS doesn't go direct to the destination, but you send it to a message centre, which sends it on to the destination as soon as there is capacity available. You can send cards, pictures and customised ring tones as well as text, if you have the correct mobile handset and use a suitable SMC (short message client).

In the message settings menu, you may find the option of sending messages as fax or email, as well as text and other formats. Although these options are not available on all UK networks. These systems allow the user to send and receive email by SMS.

Modern mobile phones get smaller and smaller.

CASE STUDY

A telecommunications company offers installation of DSL broadband systems. A customer requests an installation via the Internet. This request instantaneously generates a work item in a service technician's work list, who receives it on his WAP-enabled mobile phone (see the following section for more on WAP). This enables him to go to the customer's property. He performs the installation and along with the job completion message, he sends the customer's phone number. The service centre then activates the system.

The engineer has not had to go to the service centre, or speak to anyone in the office; all the information has been transmitted electronically, and instantly.

Word check

Analogue – a system which continuously changes between extremes. In computing terms this means that voltage or frequency can be variable, whereas a digital system only has two states, on or off, high or low, 1 or 0.

TASKS

1 Carry out an investigation into the history of the telephone system.

2 Use the information from this investigation to develop a presentation to be delivered to your classmates.

Mobile telephone technologies (2)

By the end of this topic you will be able to:

- explain the difference between SMS and WAP

- discuss the developments in mobile telephone technology

Receiving email by SMS

Some networks will provide you with an email address associated with the mobile telephone, and you can then send and receive messages using this email address. It tends to be expensive, and some companies charge for the SMS used to deliver each incoming email: potentially a very high expense if you get a lot of mail.

You can receive email by SMS for free by registering with an email delivery system. Customers of all mobile telephone networks can use these services. You choose a name, and get an address. The service can only send the first 160 characters of each email, due to the limitations of SMS, but as most emails are relatively short this is usually adequate.

Sending email by SMS

You can't send an email by SMS directly: you have to send it to a **gateway** that will convert the SMS to email format. There are several services that do this for free; these often offer a fax service as well. The gateway provider will convert the text into an email format and send it on to the recipient. They can then read the email through their computer software and reply. The reply is then converted into a format that the mobile telephone can display and is sent to the telephone.

WAP

Wireless application protocol (WAP) is a way of sending information to and from mobile devices, particularly mobile telephones. It provides a way to minimise the amount of data sent, keeping the data size small, as download speeds are slow compared with computers on normal telephone connections. There are limited interactive scripting facilities, meaning that the pages have simple hyperlinks, rather than the full interactivity of an HTML web page.

There are three components in a typical WAP setup: the **WAP server** providing the information, the **WAP gateway** and the **WAP browser**.

Only 160 characters can be sent by SMS to an email address.

Mobile telephone technologies (2)

A WAP site

Word check

WAP server – is simply an http: (web) server set up to understand the content types used by WAP – the language is slightly different from normal HTML.

WAP gateway – translates the http: used across the Internet to the WAP: used for the link to mobile devices.

WAP browser – some models of mobile phones have built-in WAP browsers. There are also versions that can be used on a computer, so that WAP pages can be seen over a normal Internet connection.

TASKS

1. Describe the weather using the restriction of 160 characters (including spaces).

2. Describe in detail the difference between SMS and WAP. Design a home page that could be shown on a WAP browser.

3. Make a list of abbreviations used in text messaging, for example: hi m8 r u ok?

CASE STUDY

There are various systems for receiving emails via a mobile phone. One of these is when the recipient is sent a short text message containing the sender's email address and the subject line of the email. The recipient is then given the options of either downloading the whole email, deleting it, replying to it and so on, as with a normal email program.

Unfortunately this can be a nuisance if you receive hundreds of emails every day, as it means that your mobile phone is continually vibrating or ringing to inform you that you have a new message.

To overcome this there are a number of filtering programs being developed that will allow a user to set up filters to allow only emails from certain senders, or with particular words in the subject line, to be sent on to the mobile network. This could mean that important messages are missed when the sender uses a different account or misspells a word in the subject line.

Digital broadcasting (1)

By the end of this topic you will be able to:

- describe the elements of digital broadcasting
- explain the concept of convergent technology

Digital broadcasting is a way of transmitting more TV and radio channels and other extra features on fewer frequencies. It has consistent quality widescreen pictures and crystal clear stereo sound.

As the signal is digital, it must be decoded to be shown on a normal television. This is done in one of two ways: a set-top box, which is a separate device similar in size to a VCR or DVD player, usually rented from a service provider; or an integrated digital television (iDTV), which is a TV with the necessary components contained within.

A home entertainment system

Other digital devices, digital radio, computers, and so on, can also pick up the digital signal. However, the developments in this area are leading to **convergent technology** where all of these devices are built into one home entertainment system. This allows the user to watch TV, browse the Internet, play video games, listen to radio and send emails all through one piece of equipment.

Digital broadcasting (1)

The digital fridge is a device which allows the user to access the Internet while working in the kitchen. The idea is that if, while cooking a meal certain ingredients are required, they can be ordered online.

The emergence of online gaming with powerful games consoles and broadband Internet connections is believed by many developers to be the driving force behind digital broadcasting. More people are spending more time in front of their televisions, but are now aware that the device in front of them is capable of doing more than just showing moving pictures, with limited sound.

Full **surround sound** systems, with large flat-screen TVs mean that the viewer becomes more immersed in the experience of watching. Add to this the ability to interact with the programmes, choosing camera angles and requesting information, means that the viewer can have a much more rewarding experience.

All of this costs money, but as there are a number of companies competing in this market, the potential customer has a wide choice of packages and prices available from which to choose.

Word check

Surround sound – an audio system that has been developed to deliver sound that seems to be coming from all around the user, much like being at the cinema. It usually requires at least five speakers, each one positioned carefully within a room. The audio equipment then decodes the signal from the stereo and causes it to be played through the appropriate speaker or speakers. This system is supposed to make the user feel much more involved, or immersed, in the experience. It is particularly effective when watching films or playing video games.

CASE STUDY

'Interactive TV standards will be the broadcasting industry's worst nightmare. By incorporating Internet and the web, iTV creates a trojan horse for deregulated digital broadcasting. This may be good for consumers, but creates major problems for business and for government regulators.' *T. Worthington* Tomw Communications Pty Ltd.

The development of digital broadcasting and interactive TV has opened up a much wider level of choice for the viewer. But it has also meant that the regulating bodies are finding it more difficult to control the standards of what is broadcast.

TASKS

1 Produce an onscreen advertisement for a home entertainment system – include the equipment required and the potential costs.

2 Produce a table of the functions available on the following devices:
- VHS video recorder
- DVD player
- Video game machine
- Sky satellite system
- Cable TV package.

Digital broadcasting (2)

By the end of this topic you will be able to:

● understand how ICT will change our lives

Digital broadcasting is a different way of transmitting TV and radio signals. It turns them into computerised signals (streamed bits of data). These have to be decoded into signals to reproduce sound or pictures. There are over 200 TV channels available to be viewed in the UK, with hundreds of radio stations broadcasting through the digital system.

Broadcasting companies are developing a range of new technologies to make their systems more appetising for the consumer. They are developing links with a number of ICT companies, including Microsoft®, to bring together broadcasting and computing technology. It is already possible to play some video games through digital television, but in the very near future it is expected that the majority of households will have access to a full interactive gaming environment.

A number of digital companies offer the ability to send and receive email and browse the Internet through the television.

With the advent of **digital video cameras**, everyone has the ability to produce TV programmes. In America there are a number of 'public' broadcasting stations where individuals or groups can produce their own programmes and transmit them over the digital network. There are also a growing number of 'reality' TV programmes appearing – *Big Brother*, *Castaway*, and so on. This is leading to the call for greater controls over what is permitted to be broadcast. The control of quality, decency and legality of programmes transmitted over a digital system is becoming more difficult to enforce. However, this freedom has also had some benefits; people from minority sections of a community can now broadcast or view programmes made specifically for their needs, enabling them to promote their beliefs or culture in a way that major TV channels would not be able to.

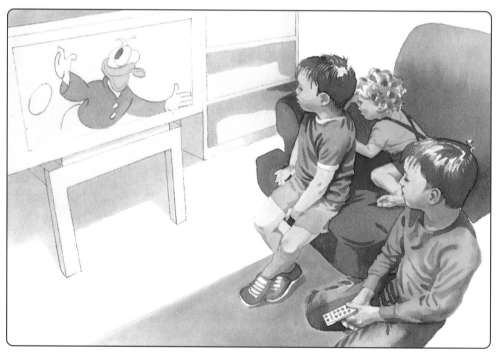

Digital television allows parents to monitor their children's TV viewing, so that they only watch appropriate content, such as cartoons.

Digital broadcasting (2)

A day in the life of a digital household ...

7:30 awoken by radio alarm playing digital radio station.

8:30 use digital fridge to order shopping and catch up on up-to-date news via the Internet.

9:30 start work at home, accessing email via the television.

12:30 break for lunch, catch up on stocks and shares on the digital fridge while cooking.

13:30 return to work, updating the personal website through the television.

15:30 finish work; watch an interesting documentary on the digital television channel.

18:00 back to the kitchen, watch the news while cooking supper.

19:30 settle down for the evening watching a football match, choosing camera angles, listening to the commentary over digital radio.

21:30 go online to play a three-dimensional interactive driving game.

22:00 bedtime, set digital radio alarm.

A remote control

CASE STUDY

In 1955 the first independent television channel in the UK started to broadcast.

There are now over 2000 independent channels available to be viewed over the digital TV system. Though not many of them have an opening ceremony quite like ITV's!

Broadcasting is the term used to describe the transmission of information to the public. It covers TV, radio and general information systems. There is also a term – narrowcast – which is where information is transmitted to a selected group, such as people who live in a certain postcode district.

The first evening of independent television programmes, in 1955, were:

7:15 The Ceremony at Guildhall with the Halle Orchestra playing The National Anthem

7:45 Inaugural Speeches: The Lord Mayor of London, Sir Seymour Howard, The Postmaster-General, Charles Hill. Chairman of the ITA, Sir Kenneth Clark

8:00 Channel 9 – A sparkling variety show from television theatre

8:40 Drama – The Importance of Being Earnest (excerpt)

9:10 Professional Boxing

10:00 News and Newsreel

10:15 Gala Night at the Mayfair

10:30 Star Cabaret

10:50 Preview – a glimpse of some of the programmes to come on Independent Television during the coming months

11:00 Epilogue

The National Anthem and close-down.

TASKS

1 Make a list of TV channels available in your area; divide the list into terrestrial, analogue and digital.

2 Keep a diary of your TV and radio use over a week; make notes of when you use the Internet. Would you use the Internet more if it was available through your television?

3 Carry out an investigation into the cost plans of digital broadcasting services available in your area.

4 Draw up a table describing the advantages and disadvantages of digital broadcasting.

Personal Digital Assistants (PDAs)

By the end of this topic you will be able to:

- describe the advantages and disadvantages of PDAs

- describe the main components and software used on PDAs

Over recent years electronic technology has enabled the miniaturisation of components, to the point where a relatively powerful computer can now be manufactured small enough to fit into a pocket.

Developments in software have meant that operating systems and applications have been written which require little memory, while still being useful.

Many PDAs use a *Windows*-based operating system with familiar Microsoft® applications, such as *Word*, *Excel* and *Outlook*. Some have developed their own operating systems with variations on these applications.

Most PDAs can be synchronised with a desktop computer. This means that diary functions, email and documents can be worked on while away from the desk.

Hand-held computers have an advantage over desktop PCs or laptops in that they are small enough to be carried anywhere and relatively inexpensive. However due to the relatively small memory capacity, some of the claims made by companies have been disputed.

The PDA usually comes with a stylus, a tool that is used to 'write' on the touch sensitive screen, the software converts the patterns described on the screen into digital data that can then be used by the applications software. This, however, can be time consuming and inaccurate, and to overcome this a number of accessories have been developed, including; keyboards, voice activated software, digital cameras and so on. Although these enhance the practicality of the devices, they also make the device less portable!

The main use of PDAs has been to store **diary entries**. They have taken the place of the paper-based diary or **personal organiser**, used by many people. With accessories such as removable and upgradeable memory, software companies are developing ever more useful applications.

The manufacturers are also keen to integrate the PDA technology with mobile communication technology, such as 'bluetooth', to enable the user to transmit data, wirelessly to computers, printers and mobile phones.

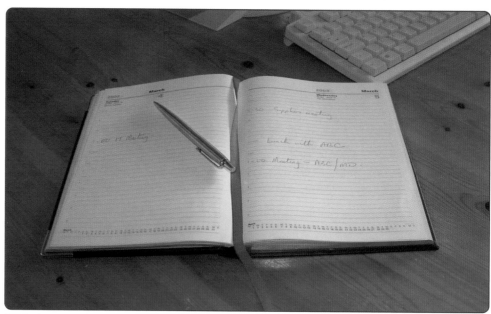

PDAs have taken the place of the traditional paper-based diary.

Personal Digital Assistants (PDAs)

A PDA with stylus in use.

CASE STUDY

While a number of schools are banning mobile phones and pagers, some schools are embracing mobile ICT.

'23 per cent of teenagers aged 13 to 19 say their schools forbid them from bringing in PDAs, 60 per cent of schools ban pagers and 55 per cent of schools prohibit the use of mobile phones.'

In some schools pupils are encouraged to use **portable** devices to help them with their school work; dictionaries, graphing calculators, e-books and thermometers can be downloaded onto the PDAs and used to simplify studying and classroom participation.

TASKS

1. Collect information describing three different PDAs and draw up a table describing the advantages and disadvantages of each one.

2. Collect pricing information on a PDA and the accessories needed to enable it to function as a portable computer in order to carry out word processing and spreadsheet tasks, save and print documents, send and receive emails and access the Internet. Comment upon your findings.

3. Discuss whether you think PDAs should be banned in school, or whether their use should be encouraged.

Floppy disks, CDs, optical media and minidiscs

By the end of this topic you will be able to:

- recognise and describe the differences between storage media

The storage and retrieval of information drives research, business, education and entertainment. The quantity of information continues to grow, while market forces drive the quest for smaller and more efficient storage media.

Historically, storage of information has been a significant challenge. Magnetic tapes, once thought to be permanent have turned out to be short-lived. Heat and humidity cause binding material in tapes to **deteriorate**. The magnetised layer that contains data separates from the plastic tape, rendering it unreadable.

As a result, historians can find more information from the 1860 US census, which was recorded on paper, than from the 1960 census, which was recorded on magnetic tape.

Storage media have evolved from simple, low capacity media that were difficult to duplicate and distribute, to today's digital environment with huge storage capacities and simple distribution.

A floppy disk

A recent internet survey of information storage estimated that 1 per cent is stored in recordable media such as disk drives and CD-ROM, 4 per cent in photographic microfilm and fiche, and 95 per cent on paper.

Floppy disks are the most common portable storage device, although the capacity is limited compared to other systems.

The disk is a thin layer of plastic coated with a magnetic film. Data is stored by converting the polarity of the magnetic material. The disk is protected by a hard plastic case.

Standard floppy disks can store up to 1.44 megabytes of data, around 1.5 million bits of information, or approximately 500 pages of text. However, with many software applications needing to save a variety of control aspects, such as fonts, with the file, the capacity of a floppy disk is starting to become too small to store some files, particularly anything containing graphics.

As a floppy disk costs about the same as a CD, many computer users are moving to using CDs to store data, as they can hold more information and tend to have faster access times. They also tend to be more robust, although, properly looked after, a floppy disk can hold its data for many years.

Great Parndon	Northbrooks	STEELE	Eleanor	Wife	M	38	F	Solicitor Wife	YKS	Hemsley	1739	19	10	1341419
Great Parndon	Northbrooks	STEELE	Eleanor N.	Daur	–	5	F	Scholar	MID	Potters Bar	1739	19	10	1341419
Great Parndon	Northbrooks	STEELE	Adams R.	Son	–	4	M	Scholar	MID	Potters Bar	1739	19	10	1341419
Great Parndon	Northbrooks	STEELE	Camillia	Daur	–	2	F	---	MID	Potters Bar	1739	19	10	1341419
Great Parndon	Northbrooks	STEELE	Mary	Daur	–	11m	F	---	ESS	Parndon Gt	1739	19	10	1341419
Great Parndon	Northbrooks	GILLMAN	Elizabeth W.	Serv	U	38	F	Nurse	IRE	Kinsale C Cork	1739	19	10	1341419
Great Parndon	Northbrooks	BARRAK	Mary A.	Serv	U	16	F	Nursemaid	MID	Sudbury	1739	19	10	1341419
Great Parndon	Northbrooks	LEE	Harriett	Serv	U	24	F	Cook	HUN	Brampton	1739	19	10	1341419
Great Parndon	Northbrooks	BANNISTER	Sarah	Serv	U	23	F	Parlourmaid	HEF	Hereford City O1	1739	19	10	1341419
Great Parndon	Northbrooks	LEO	Grace	Serv	U	13	F	House Maid	HUN	Buckworth	1739	19	10	1341419

An extract from a census record.

Floppy disks, CDs, optical media and minidiscs

Compact discs, read-only memory (CD-ROM), digital video discs (DVD), and holograms are optical storage systems.

Optical media encode data by altering reflectivity, transmission, or other optical characteristics of the material. This is like arranging a set of mirrors or prisms to reflect a particular pattern which can then be decoded at a later date by another device.

Optical media use a variety of methods to change the reflection or transmission of light to represent the data. CD-ROMs use the presence or absence of a pit to indicate a binary 0 or 1. Recordable optical media use techniques such as burning holes into the media, or creation of crystal structures with different reflecting properties to encode the 0s and 1s.

Minidiscs are smaller than CDs and have the ability to be re-recorded up to 1 million times [claimed by Sony]. Although very few people would have the chance to prove Sony's claim, it is widely accepted that the minidisc is highly reliable. Unlike magnetic tape, which records a much poorer quality, and CD, that can be scratched, the minidisc is very useful for recording audio. As the disc is protected inside a carriage sleeve, you could accidentally drop it on the floor and then step on it, yet still listen to the music without a problem!

A CD

A minidisc (right) compared with a CD (left).

Recording a minidisc

The process involves a laser head heating up the recording spot to a temperature of 1800C/4000F while the recording head uses positive and negative magnetic signals to write audio data patterns. As the disc moves away, the magnetic recording head records new spots, while the already recorded spots cool down retaining the magnetic signals. This requires no physical contact between the laser/recording heads and the disc itself. Hence, the disc does not wear out even with repeated writings.

> **Word check** ✔
>
> **Deteriorate** – to lose quality, as things are stored they can lose their ability to work – fresh fruit and vegetables go bad, printed documents fade, magnetic tape breaks-down. This is a natural process that can be slowed through careful preservation. For all of these items, the removal of air, as well as storage in a cool, dry and dark place, will prolong their useful life.

TASKS

1. Produce a table showing the relation between the percentages of data stored in recordable media, photographic media and paper.

2. Produce an annotated diagram describing how data is stored on a minidisc.

DVDs

CDs and minidiscs are useful for storing audio data, such as music, but video files are much larger. A CD can hold approximately 15 minutes of video, with the average length of a film being 100 minutes, this would mean changing the CD 6 or 7 times to watch a film!

DVD technology has enabled much more data to be stored on a disc the same size as a CD. However, although there are various different formats of DVD, no particular format has been adopted for recording DVDs, but there are two basic playing formats:

● DVD-ROM is the base format that holds data, such as software and games.
● DVD-Video (often simply called DVD) defines how video programs such as movies are stored on disc and played in a DVD-Video player or a DVD computer.

A single-layer disc can easily hold 150 minutes at the typical average video data rate if there's only one audio track. Lowering the data rate slightly can accommodate over three hours on a single layer. Dual-layer discs can hold over four hours on one side. Discs can be double-sided, making up to eight hours of playable storage.

With the advent of home DVD recorders there is now a call for standardising the recording format – at present there are DVD-R, DVD-RW and DVDRom systems with different capacities and media. This means that a DVD recorded on one machine may not play on another.

Many home recording systems also contain a computer hard disk, with 40Gb of space, which can be used to record the TV programme before transferring it to DVD. This means that the system can be programmed to record a programme, or a number of programmes in the user's absence. In digital quality, this can then be transferred to DVD to be kept permanently, while the original recording is erased. Although this capability has been around for some years with tape, the quality is much higher and, in theory, the DVD will not degrade as a tape does over time.

DVDs hold a lot of data.

DVDs

When Senate historians finished recording Senate workers' accounts of the **impeachment** of President Clinton, the CDs containing those oral histories were locked away, not to be heard for 20 years. They will then be made available to the public.

However the historians were told by document storage experts to lock up a CD player, an instruction book and some spare parts with the CDs, because it is likely that CD players will be ancient, obsolete technology in two decades.

Word check

Impeachment – is a term used in America to describe legal action taken against the US President and some other officials. So far there have been only two Presidents impeached and removed from office, Bill Clinton was nearly the third.

The impeachment of President Clinton.

TASKS

1. Produce a graphical representation of the capacity of the three storage systems – CD, minidisc and DVD.

2. Describe why DVD is so popular with film-making companies.

3. Detail the advantages and disadvantages of using CD or minidisc for recording audio files.

4. Describe why minidiscs are not generally used to store computer data.

Technologies

A touch screen gets rid of the need for a mouse with a computer. You move your finger across the screen and the mouse pointer moves with it. Instead of a mouse click, you tap on the screen.

Keyboards can be replaced with many systems, as a software keyboard can be displayed on screen when a user needs to type in information. Many touch screens also come with hand-writing recognition software, so that writing on the screen with a **stylus** or pen can be converted to text.

A computer mouse needs regular cleaning and is easily damaged or stolen. Touch screen computers can easily be built into custom cases, so that only the screen can be seen, which makes them ideal for public places.

A touch screen VDU

There are several different technologies available that create touch screens for a variety of different uses:

- **Cathode ray tube (CRT)** – are similar to standard computer monitors, but are often used where the operator is unable to use a mouse or a keyboard.

- **LCD monitor touch screens** – are flat screen monitors that generally range in size from 300mm to 450mm and either come with a stand or wall-mount brackets.

- **Plasma screens** – are generally larger than LCD screens, ranging from 500mm to 1200mm. Many plasma screens can be supplied with optional touch screen fronts and software.

- **Interactive whiteboards** – these are used alongside an LCD projector replacing the usual projector screen. Generally used for training as the teacher/trainer can touch the screen to control the computer while at the front of a class. These screens are generally 1200mm to 1800mm in size.

- **Rear projection touch screens** – are effectively another kind of interactive whiteboard which are used with an LCD projector. Generally the whiteboard is mounted in a false wall with the projector behind it to display the image. When people are in front of the whiteboard, they see what appears to be a huge monitor or television screen. The mouse is again controlled by touching the screen. Flight and other training simulators use this technology, to give the trainees a realistic image out of the windows.

Technologies

At a special school for children with physical or medical difficulties, students explored the theme 'Ourselves'. One part of the project involved children using an interactive whiteboard to create electronic images. The children first took a self-portrait using a digital camera, then loaded the image on to a computer, and finally 'painted' it on to a whiteboard using their fingers. This technique opened up huge possibilities for students, particularly for Joe. Joe has virtually no gross motor control and very limited fine motor skills, meaning that he has great difficulty manipulating a pen or pencil to be able to draw on paper, but using the interactive whiteboard he was able to produce some stunning images.

Word check

Stylus – a device used to point at or to write something on a screen. Most PDAs use a special stylus made in the form of a pen. Although anything really can be used; a normal pen will do, except that it may mark the screen.

Rules

Display systems can be used effectively, but only if certain rules are followed:

- Backlit systems should use light backgrounds with dark text: yellow and blue are often clearest.

- Reflective displays such as interactive whiteboards can have darker backgrounds with light text.

- Touch zones must be clearly defined if untrained users will be accessing the machine.

Touch screen technology is used for many varied purposes.

TASKS

1. Write a report detailing where you might find touch screen technology being used.

2. Design a project that could be used with disabled children, using touch screen technology.

3. Produce a report describing the advantages of using touch screen technology over keyboard/keypad and mouse control systems.

Accessibility (1)

The Disability Discrimination Act 1996 has made a great impact on the world of ICT, as well as helping to prevent and address RSI-type symptoms and **musculo-skeletal** conditions, such as arthritis, from excessive use of ICT equipment.

A number of companies have developed hardware accessories for computers. Software applications have to contain facilities for making the programs suitable for disabled users.

There are many ways that *Windows* and some of the more popular programs can be altered to improve visibility for people with a visual impairment or simply for personal preference. *MS Windows* has a variety of settings, allowing for colour, font size and window size.

Other applications allow the user to adjust display properties and therefore improve the visibility of items on the screen. The mouse pointer can be changed, font size increased, background altered and so on.

Many websites are visually complex and confusing with multiple columns and text in strange combinations of colours. All of the most common browsers, including Microsoft® *Internet Explorer* and Netscape *Navigator*, can force the text background and foreground colours of the page to be of the size and colour the user prefers.

There are also a variety of programs available that allow the user to speak to input commands, rather than using a mouse or a keyboard, although these tend to need rather high specification machines.

The ability to speak to the computer has been covered elsewhere in this book, and it has its limitations. One of the more useful applications of speech technology is in the field of 'screen readers'.

Software has been developed to help poor-sighted people to use computers.

Accessibility (1)

A screen reader is a piece of software that converts the text and images on the screen into a verbal description, thus allowing users with poor eyesight to understand what is on the screen.

Screen readers can read out text from documents to save having them printed into Braille, they can read text from websites and if the site complies with the **World Wide Web Consortium** (**W3C** – a group of experts from all over the world, working to improve the quality of the Internet) guidelines, they can read a description of the images on the site as the mouse passes over them.

They can also read out icon names as the mouse moves around the desktop.

Some of these systems also produce feedback through a specialist mouse. To help a user stay within a window for instance, the mouse will vibrate as the pointer moves over a boundary.

Much of this software technology can also be incorporated into digital broadcasting media, allowing people with disabilities to have access to a whole range of systems.

Word check

Musculo-skeletal – is a term used to describe a range of conditions which affect the muscles and skeleton. For example arthritis is a condition which causes pain and inflammation of the joints. This can be very painful and can prevent people being able to use a traditional mouse and keyboard.

CASE STUDY

The RNID (Royal National Institute in Aid of the Deaf) have worked with software developers to produce a program which can be used with deaf students called 'speedtext'. It utilises the ability of laptop computers to share information via the serial port.

One laptop is set up for the student and a second is set up for a hearing support worker. The hearing support worker can then type on their laptop anything that they hear, such as a lecture or discussion. The student sees this in a window on their machine. They can then enter queries which will appear on the support worker's screen. The support worker can then ask a question for the student and type the response.

This system requires that both users are trained in its use, but once it has been set up on the machines it can prove useful for various types of users. It has obvious benefits in education, but it can also be useful in the business world as a translation tool.

TASKS

1. Investigate how to adjust the monitor settings of a computer, to enable a user with visual impairment to read the information shown on the screen.

2. Produce an instruction leaflet to be distributed to visually impaired students, telling them how to alter the settings as described above (remember that the instructions should be in a format that they will be able to access).

Accessibility (2)

There are a wide range of devices that can be used instead of the traditional mouse and keyboard:

- **ergonomic keyboards** – have a specialist key layout
- **one-handed keyboards**
- **joy sticks** – allowing a pointer to move around the screen, with buttons to carry out commands
- **trackerballs** – these are, in effect, a mouse turned upside down; the user moves the ball with their fingers, this moves the on-screen pointer
- **head pointers** – a device worn on the head, that allows control of the on-screen pointer, either through radio, infrared or light emission
- **light pens** – used directly on the screen, having a similar effect to touch screens.

Of course there are many other issues connected with the adaptation of ICT equipment. Access to the room, furniture design and general room design, all play an important part in enabling disabled people to have full access to ICT.

Many colleges and workplaces are also addressing the issue of age. A wide section of society are now starting to use ICT, this has implications on training needs for both work and recreation.

Courses such as 'silver surfers' are offered to enable over-50s to learn how to use the Internet and email.

Internet users in the 35 to 49 age range are the biggest web audience in the UK. They represent 25 per cent of the online population, closely followed by those over age 50 (20 per cent) and 25 to 34-year-olds (18.6 per cent).

A number of colleges also have an outreach programme, where they run courses in village halls, community centres, prisons and hospitals, ensuring that everyone in society is given the opportunity to learn how to use ICT.

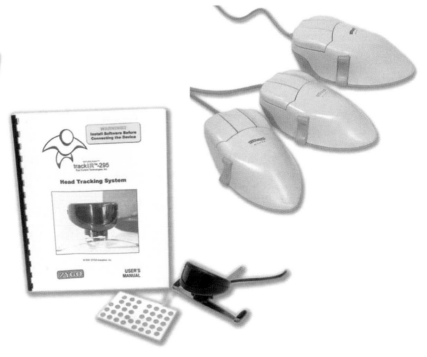

An ergonomic keyboard (left), a head controlled mouse (centre) and right-handed contour mice (right) have all been developed to assist people, especially the disabled, in using their PC.

Accessibility (2)

Legal information

The Disability Discrimination Act 1996 makes it illegal to unreasonably discriminate against existing and potential employees on the basis of their 'disability', and employers are charged with a duty to make reasonable accommodations in the employment of people with disabilities.

Computers are, of course, an increasingly important tool in a number of jobs. Adaptive and alternative technologies, from simple and free to sophisticated and more expensive, can make a computer accessible to people with disabling conditions of all kinds, temporary and permanent, physical and sensory. The computer systems in use must be set up so that the most common adaptations can be used.

A trackerball

CASE STUDY

Specialist ICT facilities were installed in a college, designed to cater for students with a variety of disabilities. However the room was also to be used by able-bodied students, so a compromise was sought. The equipment included: a hearing loop, adjustable height tables, large-screen monitors, rollerball mice and ergonomic keyboards. The room has been used extensively and all students find the equipment a worthwhile investment. Voice recognition software has also been installed, but this has proven problematic, for all! On the whole the college has been pleased with its investment, and so have the students.

TASKS

1. Design a computer workstation for use by someone who uses a wheelchair.

2. Produce a web page displaying a range of equipment developed for increasing the accessibility of ICT to disabled users. Your page must be suitable for viewing with a screen reader.

Buying from home (1)

The Internet has developed from a network of computers used to share educational files around the world, into the biggest shopping centre imaginable.

All major high street shops now have websites; most of them allow customers to view and purchase items online.

This aspect of their sales is expected to grow: American online sales in the fourth quarter of 2001 increased 34.4 per cent over the previous quarter. By comparison, all retail sales (both online and off-line) grew by a significantly smaller margin in the quarter, only 9.5 per cent.

The UK Government are continually monitoring social trends. The results of surveys, questionnaires and interviews are presented on the Internet at http://www.statistics.gov.uk The following table shows Internet use in the UK from July 2000 to October 2001.

	Jul. 2000	Oct. 2000	Jan. 2001	Apr. 2001	Jul. 2001	Oct. 2001
Finding information about goods / services	70	66	67	73	74	74
Using email	69	73	65	71	71	73
General browsing or surfing	64	64	54	61	57	56
Finding information related to education	34	34	28	38	35	33
Buying or ordering tickets / goods / services	28	33	30	35	35	36
Personal banking / financial / investment activities	21	22	23	25	27	26
Looking for work	18	20	18	18	21	21
Downloading software, including games	17	21	20	25	23	19
Using chat rooms or sites	17	18	13	17	18	15
Playing or downloading music	16	17	15	20	19	16
Using or accessing government / official services	15	18	18	20	19	16
Other things	11	5	5	4	4	2

Note: All results are a percentage of the user's time online.

Buying from home (1)

Online auctions

One of the most popular ways of buying or selling over the Internet has proven to be online auctions. The following is an extract from eBay, showing how popular it actually is "eBay is the world's largest online marketplace. With over 10 million items for sale at any one time and 42 million registered users, eBay is your place to find the things you want, to sell the items you have, and to make friends while you're at it.

eBay UK offers you the best of both worlds: a site tailored to the needs of British traders combined with the largest and most advanced online trading community in the world." http://pages.ebay.co.uk/help/basics/n-index.html

These auctions allow members of the public to offer items for sale, other Internet users then bid for the goods online over a period of days. At the end of the bidding period the highest offer can be accepted by the seller, or turned down and the item remains the property of the seller.

The increase in online auctions has led to many similar web-based companies competing for the largest market share, at the moment held by eBay.com.

TASK

1 Produce a report on the use of online auctions. Include details on how the seller advertises their goods and how the prospective buyer bids, and, if successful, purchases the goods.

Books can be bought from the Amazon website.

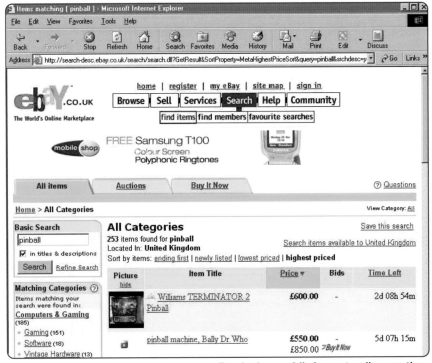

eBay is the world's largest online auction.

Buying from home (2)

Many UK consumers use the Internet to investigate flight prices, as there are often savings to be made over the high street prices. There are a number of websites set up specifically to help users quickly search vast databases: www.deckchair.com for example searches for cheap flights from a wide range of operators, over any date and time requested by the user. The results are ranked and the user then chooses the one closest to their requirements.

Online banking has been developed over the past few years; in many cases this is responsible for the closing of high street branches! People lead busy lives and the opportunity to visit the bank branch during opening hours has become more difficult. The technology available via the Internet allows users to log on to secure websites, where they can access their account information, pay bills and carry out other essential transactions.

For instance, in the US the amount of money spent in the e-commerce sector (electronic commerce – buying and selling over the Internet) is expected to increase from US$38 billion in 2002 to US$122.6 billion. This is almost a quadrupling of the amount of online transactions.

This growth in the use of the Internet to buy, sell and manage your money is still a concern to many. The greatest worry being credit card fraud. The companies managing the development of online shopping are making a concerted effort to win over potential users, through the development of secure systems.

Deckchair.com searches large databases to find the cheapest flight.

All of these facilities are made possible because of Internet security provided by secure server technology. This is a system of **encryption** and decryption used by computers on the Internet, which stops anyone getting personal details, such as credit card numbers, without the user's permission.

When entering a secure website a small padlock appears in the browser border. Although even the most secure website can still be 'hacked' it is actually more likely that a credit card will be counterfeited and used, rather than the details taken from a website.

Buying from home (2)

A number of high street shops and banks are developing online systems that can be accessed from PDAs and mobile telephones. This is having an impact on the website design, because of the limited graphical capability of these devices, but the freedom to shop, access bank accounts, take part in an online auction or book a flight, from anywhere, at any time is thought to be a great advertising ploy.

Word check

Encryption – to alter a file using a secret code so that it is unintelligible to anyone without the software needed to decrypt (or unscramble) it.

Ryanair offer cheap flights on their own website.

TASKS

1. Collect the web addresses for ten online shops, and produce a report comparing the online service with the high street service.

2. Investigate the security in place to make shopping online attractive to the public.

3. Compare flight prices between the online operators and the high street brochure prices.

Technical services

Gathering business information can be a difficult and challenging task. Businesses need information to help in their market research or for marketing purposes. This task is often contracted out to a separate company which specialises in this area.

These data specialists use the vast data stores of governments, the Internet and other sources to gather relevant information. This is then developed into a customised database according to the customers' requirements.

The information contained in this database may include:

- registered name of company
- key executive names
- business addresses/registered addresses
- nature of business activities
- number of employees
- financial figures such as sales turnover, net profit and other key indicators
- industry trends
- market outlook
- competitor analysis
- overseas information.

Market researchers obtain information by asking people questions.

The customer can then use this information to make decisions about new products or services. They may also use it as a basis for carrying out further research.

Because the information is being used to influence major decisions, it is important that the information is correct and verified. This may involve a third company who will independently scrutinise the data. This company may also advise on how best to secure the data so that competitors don't get to use it.

The area of data security has grown enormously over recent years, as more companies are storing important information on computers. Companies that do not use high levels of security can leave themselves open to 'hackers' who can steal, destroy or alter data.

To prevent such damage, software such as firewalls – barriers that stop access to areas of a computer or network – and monitoring programs that check who has been using a computer and for what reasons, can be installed.

Technical services

A Government survey revealed over 41 per cent of companies did not have adequate data protection in place through 2001. There have been a number of high-profile data leaks: A sales engineer from Hertfordshire noticed the loophole when using a bank website to search for some information. The engineer, who has requested not to be named, said that he was 'amazed' at the simplicity of the loophole and he has alerted the company on three occasions to the problem but they have never acknowledged his messages!

Having a secure system means that it must be continually monitored and updated. It is not good enough to merely install some security software and then hope that everything will be alright!

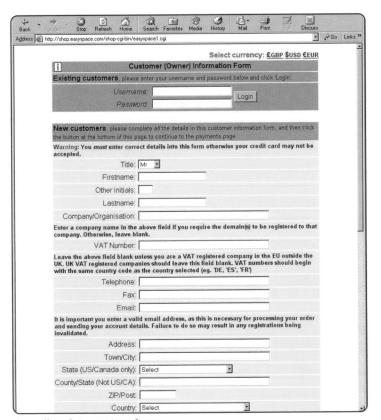

An online data capture form

CASE STUDY

MORI (Market & Opinion Research International) is the largest independently owned market research company in the United Kingdom.

Since its foundation in 1969 MORI has been one of Britain's fastest growing research agencies.

MORI provides a full range of quantitative and qualitative research services and has a reputation for creative research. They specialise in both private and public sector research and are particularly strong in the areas of corporate communications, business to business, consumer, e-MORI, employee opinion and social research.

To carry out the market research required to compile their data, a variety of systems are used. However whichever system is used to collect the data, it always ends up being manipulated on a computer. The results can then be presented in a variety of ways to suit the client, whether it be the Government or a manufacturing company.

Recent polls have included:

- Age discrimination at work – looking into how people may be disadvantaged because of their age.

- Technological Christmas – a survey to investigate the use of computers to help with Christmas shopping.

- Waste charges – a study of what people feel about spending more of the National Income on managing waste.

TASK

1 Develop a questionnaire that you could use to determine a range of statistical information about favourite foods/bands/teams/hobbies/ animals. Carry out your survey with a sample of people. Enter the data gathered into a suitable ICT application and produce a graphical representation of your results.

Call centres

By the end of this topic you will be able to:

- describe the role of a call centre in business

- discuss the advantages and disadvantages of automated customer enquiry systems

A number of large companies have their own **call centres** – offices with a team of staff answering telephone queries. But many are now starting to 'outsource' this to other companies. Smaller businesses cannot always afford to employ staff to carry out this duty, so they also have to outsource if they want to deal with a high volume of calls.

One police constabulary received over 110 000, 999 calls in the year 2000. This is one call every 5 minutes, 24 hours a day, every day of the year. To deal with this amount of calls, they are answered by staff at a call centre.

Staff in the call centre are well trained often working from a script, and all calls are monitored. This service is also used by other businesses to handle any overflow call traffic during peak periods.

Staff are fully briefed on the company's products and services, so that they can answer queries from the public. The staff answer the call, collect information and deal with incoming enquiries, whether it is an emergency 999 call, or a request for a kitchen unit brochure. The caller will rarely know when they are dealing with the company they are calling or with a separate company who will pass on the information.

Call centres have a high level of automation now due to the improvements in technology. Telephone systems can hold messages, redirect callers, take information in the form of numbers 'dialled' from the caller's telephone and allow voice recognition. These developments mean that callers are often given a range of options before they get to talk to an operator.

Employing staff in a call centre is often cheaper than employing shop assistants and renting shop premises. This means that with an online catalogue and telephone ordering system a company can sell their goods to the public, without incurring many of the traditional costs involved.

The average transaction cost in America using traditional methods is approximately $90. Through using the Internet and telephone ordering this drops to approximately $5, a saving to the company of around $85. This difference in cost is being seen in the UK, although not as dramatically as in the US.

CASE STUDY

Pauline works in a telesales call centre. Her job is to call small shops and other outlets that sell a particular brand of sweet. The majority of the information she uses is a script displayed on a computer screen. It takes her through an interview with the manager of the shop, and she types the responses straight into the computer.

Her calls are recorded and sometimes monitored by her manager. As she types in the information from her conversation this is also monitored, not only by the manager, but also by the software itself.

If the number of cartons of sweets ordered has dropped from one month to the next, it is Pauline's task to try to find out why.

Over a period of a week Pauline completes over 500 telephone interviews with shop managers from all over the UK.

Until this system was put in place, this task was carried out by the infamous 'travelling salesman' – a person who drove around an area collecting information that would then be passed at the end of the week to a regional manager, this manager would then report their findings to the national coordinator on a monthly basis.

It could take over six weeks for the report to be written. A total of two to three months may have passed since the shop ordered the sweets.

Obviously the telephone system is much more efficient, not only is it faster, it is also more accurate and costs less to run.

Call centres

Call centres have a high level of automation.

TASKS

1. Design a script for a call centre worker, that will enable the company to find out the name, address and query details from a customer's phone call. Develop a database for storing the results from your script.

2. Collect a range of sample data, using your script and enter it into your database.

3. Produce a report from your database that could be used by a company to send out information via the post to potential customers.

Electronic payment

By the end of this topic you will be able to:

- understand how electronic payment works

The major utility companies now allow customers to pay their bills over the telephone, through keying in their account details and credit card number using the number keys of the telephone. These details are recorded electronically, without the need for a human operator. The details are collated and sent to the credit card company electronically. These are then processed and the money paid to the company electronically.

This means that bills can be paid at any time, from anywhere in the world.

However, a proportion of customers would still rather deal with a person, even if it is over the telephone. But as technology advances, it is becoming less obvious when you are talking to a real person and not just a recorded message.

The speaking clock telephone service is a recorded message. It is made up from a number of short sound clips. When a customer dials the number the software immediately searches a database to string together the required sound files.

Sound file 1 – At the third stroke the time will be
Sound file 2 – <hour>
Sound file 3 – <minutes>
Sound file 4 – and
Sound file 5 – <seconds>
Sound file 6 – precisely
Sound file 7 – <three beeps>

The voice seems to run smoothly, but it is in fact a group of disjointed files.

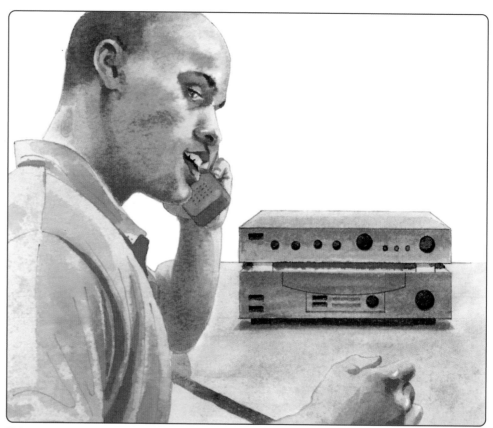

Voice messages can be recorded electronically.

Electronic payment

Voice recognition software is now enabling companies to build up a range of responses that can be recorded and played back to customers over the telephone. This makes it seem like the customer is talking to an operator, when really, as they speak, their voice is sampled and converted into a digital signal. This is then decoded by a computer, which chooses a likely response, which is converted into a sound file and played back to the customer. This happens so quickly that a 'normal' conversation can take place!

The use of email has also meant a change in the way that customer enquiries are now dealt with. Nearly all commercial websites have a contact section, where enquiries, complaints and orders can be made using email or an automated form. In many cases this is still read by a person, but some organisations are developing automated responses. The email is read electronically and a response is chosen from a database. The response is then emailed back, or posted with a scanned signature, through the traditional postal system. The customer may never know that a human has never seen their request or complaint.

Following terrorist actions in America, all mail posted to the US government is opened electronically and scanned to produce an electronic version. This is then emailed to the appropriate person, who responds with a reply. This reply may be an automated response, which is printed out with a signature, if needed, folded and inserted in an envelope and dispatched back to the original sender. Although this avoids the dangers of transmitting chemical weapons, it is also removing some of the personal touch that the public expects from their representatives.

CASE STUDY

A number of banking systems use touch tone telephone systems to record information before the customer gets to talk to a real person. On dialling the customer service phone number the caller is asked to press a button to select a particular option from a list, this moves the caller on to a new menu, with further options, one of which will be the required one.

The caller is then asked to enter their account number using the phone keys before being passed to an operator.

By the time the operator talks to the caller they have in front of them on the computer screen; name, address, bank account details, trends from the bank account data (such as salary), shopping details, general income and outgoings over the past few months.

This is supposed to mean that the operator can give more relevant advice to the caller, although a number of callers do not like the impersonality of the menu system and are distrustful of giving their account details over the telephone. This has led to a number of the major banks moving back to using staff with access to the customer's data on their computer, to answer the calls, therefore avoiding the need for the automated system.

TASKS

1. Record a sequence of questions as sound files, which could be used to carry out the survey from the previous activity.

2. Develop these sound files into a web page that 'speaks' questions to a user. Ask people to use your web page and comment on the effectiveness of your 'automated questionnaire'.

Case study

Joe runs a small convenience store in a village in Essex. Most of his customers are local people, who use the store to get groceries, newspapers and cigarettes.

Over the past few years Joe has started to lose custom to the large chain stores situated on the outskirts of local towns. This is partly due to the fact that many of his customers work in the towns and pass the stores on their way to and from the office.

He has carried out a careful survey of the prices of goods that can be bought from his store and those from the chain stores. To carry out this comparison he recorded prices into a spreadsheet. The spreadsheet software was then used to carry out various statistical analyses.

Joe also interviewed a number of his regular customers and some of the customers that now only use his shop occasionally. He recorded their responses using a word processing package.

The information from his survey and from the interviews led Joe to believe that with targeted advertising and a bit of luck he could win back some of his old customers.

He set about producing a leaflet to be posted through letterboxes around the village. He combined ideas of his own with graphs showing that his prices were often cheaper than those of the larger supermarkets. He also included some quotes from the interviews.

After distributing the leaflets he sat back and waited for the rush of customers; unfortunately it never came!

A village 'open all hours' store like Joe's.

Following numerous discussions with customers and others, Joe decided to change direction. He enrolled on a web design course at the local community college and set up an online presence. He then did a second round of advertising offering the 'new' service of online ordering.

Joe did start to get a few customers through the website, but not enough to justify the investment. However what he did find was that by offering advertising space on his website he could generate extra income to supplement the shop.

His site now gets over 1000 hits per week. He advertises the goods from his shop, but also advertises properties that are for sale in the area, holiday homes owned by local people, that are available for rent and numerous other items.

Interior of the village store with Joe working on his computer.

From an idea designed to bring in greater numbers of customers to his shop, Joe has now developed an international sales presence and is able to keep his shop open, whilst running the website. In fact he is happy that there are fewer shop customers, so that he can spend more time working on the website!

Various methods

By the end of this topic you will be able to:

- describe the scale of advertising revenue
- compare the relative costs of different advertising methods

Over recent years the role of ICT in advertising and marketing has grown substantially. The top sectors for online advertisement spending in 2001 in the USA were:

- retail ($533.3 million)
- media and advertising ($450.5 million)
- Yahoo held on to its position as the top property for online advertising revenue with more than $344 million for the year. Although this was slightly down, due to the terrorist attacks, compared to the year 2000.

Over the same period banner advertisement impressions (views by potential customers) grew 39 per cent, from 23.6 billion impressions to 32.9 billion. Which means that more people viewed banner-type advertisements on web pages. All advertising competes to get its message to as many potential customers as possible, so this has been good news for the advertising trade, even though sales have not increased by the same rate.

With over 300 million Internet users in 2002, there is a big drive for companies to try to attract custom through Internet advertising. The move to online shopping is slow, but growing – tesco.com was the second most visited website in the UK in 2001, Amazon.com being the most popular.

Although the Internet is a global system, there are still over 2 billion people in the world that do not have access to a telephone!

Advertising on the Internet can be relatively cheap for the amount of potential viewers, while television advertising can be very expensive – tens of thousands of pounds to produce the advertisement, then paying for **prime-time** broadcasting. At its peak ITV reaches approximately 20 million potential customers.

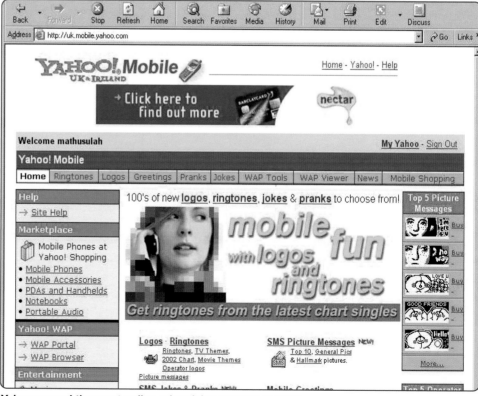

Yahoo earned the most online advertising revenue in 2001.

Various methods

In contrast radio advertising can reach 5 million potential customers; while newspapers are read by approximately 7 million households.

All of these other media can only cover a fraction of the 300 million regular Internet users, of which approximately 80 million are online at any one time!

ICT is used in all advertising, from typesetting and desktop publishing printed materials, through digital photography and video editing to Internet websites. The role of computers has become ever more important.

Tesco.com was the second most visited website in 2001.

TASKS

1. Produce a graphical representation of some of the statistics that appear in the above text.

2. Produce a description of four advertisements for similar goods, presented in a format suitable for TV, radio, newspaper and the Internet. Compare the four advertisements noting which would be most likely to make you, or your friends, choose to purchase the product.

Demographic data

Many companies employ specialist staff to produce advertising materials, others employ advertising agencies. But both systems use ICT to monitor the market. Online surveys, questionnaires, marketing statistics and other data are all collated using database and spreadsheet applications. These results are then published or presented using other software packages.

The role of ICT in this area has transformed the accuracy and speed of data collection. It is a relatively simple task to record sales, enter this information into a spreadsheet and then produce graphs showing the sales figures. This information can then be presented to the marketing department of a company; they can then use this information to make decisions regarding future products.

Demographic information is now widely used by many organisations to improve business decisions. Companies use demographic information to analyse customers, identify markets and avoid risks, enabling them to target their resources to achieve maximum effect.

Using this data it is possible to discover which customers are most profitable, where to open new stores, which branches to close and to predict how society and markets might change in the future.

The Internet has hundreds of web-based resources offering data on different sectors of society, national characteristics and particular trends that can be used to help target advertising and marketing.

www.copywriter.co.uk/resource/msource3.html#Demographic has links to a variety of sites, some produced by independent companies, some by government agencies, that supply such data.

Of course the greatest advertising and marketing will not sell a worthless product. To achieve a successful product a company must develop good products. To do this they must have the drive to do well. One such company is Nike:

Nike principles

1. Our business is change.
2. We're on offense. All the time.
3. Perfect results count — not a perfect process.
   - break the rules; fight the law.
4. This is as much about battle as about business.
5. Assume nothing:
   - make sure people keep their promises
   - push yourselves, push others
   - stretch the possible.
6. Live off the land.
7. Your job isn't done until the job is done.
8. Dangers:
   - bureaucracy
   - personal ambition
   - energy takers vs energy givers
   - knowing our weaknesses
   - don't get too many things on the platter.
9. It won't be pretty.
10. If we do the right things we'll make money damn near automatic.

Demographic data

Advertising agencies hold meetings to discuss how well their advertising is working.

CASE STUDY

Monitoring the market is essential for companies. This means not only collecting information, but acting on it. A number of high street stores not only monitor markets, they also monitor the weather, altering stock accordingly. If it is going to be a wet weekend they increase their stock of umbrellas and, oddly enough, summer clothes – people tend to buy summer clothes when the weather is awful.

TASKS

1. Carry out a survey to determine the regular shopping habits of your family. Use the results from this to predict trends in their shopping, to enable stores to stock appropriate goods.

2. Develop a set of principles for success in the Applied ICT GCSE.

ICT in the workplace

Following the Industrial Revolution people started to leave rural communities to live in towns where they could be near a major employer, such as a factory. This trend is now being reversed with the development of ICT working practices.

The main developments involving moving workers from offices to alternative workplace arrangements are:

- **telecommuting** – working from a base that is linked to the office by a telephone
- **office hotelling** – hiring an office for use when needed
- the **virtual office** – using ICT from anywhere to communicate with others, who may or may not be in an office.

This makes it possible for employees to work continuously from the field using laptops, mobile telephones and other portable devices.

There are a number of organisations moving towards more of their workers being based away from the office, however there are also companies setting up modern locally-based, shared offices offering a friendly environment, proper office infrastructure and support, close to local facilities.

These are not serviced offices, but are an entirely new concept: a permanent and sustainable workplace within a large network of mostly open-plan, shared centres, in locations close to where commuters live. By hiring these spaces for staff, a company can save thousands of pounds on salaries, travel expenses and property costs, while still having employees in a workplace with access to full office facilities.

The advantage to industry here is lower infrastructure costs and improved productivity, as the staff are able to spend more of their time working, rather than travelling in and out of the office. The technology that makes it possible is effective and gives reliable remote access to company systems, support and services.

Although working from home for some is very successful, it is not always plain sailing, especially if you are likely to be working alone for most of the week:

- Social isolation can be a major cause of stress for home-based staff.
- Not everyone has spare space at home that they can, or want to, turn into an office.
- Health and safety can be almost impossible to manage.
- Home life can be very distracting, especially if you have children.
- Costs of equipment, installation and support are high and when people leave you have to get the equipment back.

ICT in the workplace

With ICT it is now possible to work from home all or most of the time.

CASE STUDY

Bev works for a major international oil company. Until last year she had to commute to her office in London, where she was employed to monitor the traffic of oil by tanker from one country to another.

Last year she became pregnant and, after some time, found it very difficult to travel into the city. Her boss was very understanding and arranged for her to have a computer and all of the necessary equipment to work from home.

She has now had a daughter. Because of the adaptation offered by her boss, she still works from home. This means that not only is she able to carry out her work but she can also enjoy looking after her daughter.

This has proven to be a benefit for Bev in more ways than one. Her working day is now three hours shorter, as she does not have to commute. She is able to monitor the tankers at any time she wishes, rather than only during her time in the office. She also has state-of-the-art computer facilities, which she can use for her own purposes when she is not working.

TASKS

1 Produce a presentation on the office of the future: use text, images and sounds to convey what you feel office work will be like in the future.

2 Describe the advantages and disadvantages of working from home.

Support services

By the end of this topic you will be able to:

- describe how automating support services can affect employment

- discuss the impact of improvements in international communication on the manufacturing industry

Moving customer service and support from office settings to retail environments or self-service devices, means that the customer can get support or help quicker and more efficiently. An example is the ATM (automated teller machine), and the repositioning of banking services into supermarkets, enabling customers to get cash where and when they need it, rather than having to go to a bank.

Enabling technologies including point-of-sale devices, card readers and customer support terminals all offer services where they are most needed. These have led to the increase of walk-in or self-service facilities.

There is a shift from retail settings to cybersettings; this can be seen in the movement of retail sales from high street shops to websites. This has many advantages as far as the company is concerned, such as: reduced fixed infrastructure costs, reduced inventory, customised solutions, fast response, and improved customer knowledge.

Many companies have administrative operations in expensive offices that house large teams of administrative staff. Redeploying the operations to cheaper facilities can reduce costs dramatically. Doing this requires standardised order entry, billing and collection systems, and high-speed data connectivity allowing for efficient workflow.

Sophisticated customer support applications are critical in ensuring effective administrative support. By integrating ICT facilities, companies can streamline their operations, improve employee flexibility, and improve customer service and response.

This is also the case with manufacturing; materials and production costs can be reduced through redeploying operations to cheaper areas, often overseas.

With the improvements in international telecommunications, products can be designed in one part of the world, the design emailed to a production centre in another country and the product can then be freighted to the market place. All of this can be done efficiently and economically because of the use of ICT.

Broadband connections allow companies to carry out virtual conferences using video and audio, transmitted live across the Internet. This means that employees and customers can communicate directly, without having to leave their home, or office.

Combining a range of technologies to make the company and workforce more flexible can have advantages, but it may also lead to localised unemployment, underskilled staff requiring training and poor public relations when the system does not work.

Support services

Using an ATM you can access your bank account at any time and anywhere.

TASKS

1 Describe the effect that installing an ATM in a supermarket may have on:
- the customer
- bank employees.

2 Describe why standardising data requirements is important for efficient workflow.

3 Produce a map showing the location of production of one of the following:
- automobile
- training shoes
- washing machine
- vacuum cleaner.

You may wish to make this an interactive presentation.

Mobile communication and ICT's effect on work

By the end of this topic you will be able to:

• understand the effect greater reliance on ICT has had on the working patterns of some employees

• describe the advantages and disadvantages of greater use of mobile communication

Over the past decade the use of ICT in the workplace has increased dramatically. This has led to a number of differences in the way that people communicate and the work patterns followed by some staff.

Many more people can be contacted out of the office, via mobile phones and email. This has a number of advantages for the organisation:

• Maintenance staff can be passed job requests while on route to the workplace.
• Financial staff can keep abreast of the stock market out of office hours.
• Emergency services can be supported with information while attending an emergency.

The row of receptionists has now been replaced by one person using a computer.

However there can be disadvantages for the individuals concerned:

• interruption during delicate moments
• longer working days, with no increase in payment
• information overload, leading to confusion and stress.

These must be balanced for staff to feel comfortable with the increased availability of information.

Many staff now spend a portion of their day responding to emails, which can cut down the amount of time they actually spend doing their job! In many organisations, emails are used to circulate information, each employee is then expected to read the email and perhaps send a reply acknowledging receipt. In the past, information may have been displayed on a notice board, or printed on a memo and circulated. These methods did not always communicate efficiently and some members of staff may have missed the information completely.

Mobile communication and ICT's effect on work

As many companies now work with overseas partners, the use of email has proven to be a cost effective method of communication. Emails can be sent during the working day, to any part of the world. The recipient need not be at their desk, as the email will wait in their mailbox until it is called for by the email software, usually when the user logs onto the network, or accesses the Internet. They can then reply to the email and, again, it can be sent at anytime.

The cost of sending an email is a fraction of the cost of a letter, and the email can also be sent with **attachments**.

A copy of an email can also be sent to lots of people at once, enabling one person to pass information to a selection of staff in the time it takes to send it to one recipient.

Unfortunately this can lead to people sending too many emails to too many people. In business that can create problems as staff may be unable to respond to requests because they are bogged down with information that is irrelevant to them.

> **Word check** ✓
>
> **Email attachment** – this can be any file or group of files stored in an electronic format, that is attached and sent with the email.

A modern reception area, with the receptionist working on her PC.

TASKS

1. Interview a receptionist of a local firm; enquire about the way their job has altered over recent years.

2. Produce the results from the interview in a format suitable to be displayed as a poster.

Mobile technology and work patterns

Emails can now be supplemented with text messaging. Many newer mobile phones can accept WAP, SMS and email and, with the advent of 3G mobile connections, they may be able to send and receive video.

This has meant that staff can be contacted more easily, even when they are away from their desks.

It also means that staff can keep in-touch with work when they are travelling. Many commuters can be seen on their way into work using laptops, PDAs and mobile phones to check up on information they need to process before entering the office. They also use the time on the train to respond to emails, saving time when they are at work.

It is illegal to speak on a mobile phone while driving. Special in-car phones are available that do not require you to hold anything in your hand.

With the high-speed connection via a mobile phone, laptops and PDAs are proving to be extremely useful tools for accessing the Internet and email. With secure connections some employees can also log on to their company intranet and start work well before they get into the office.

Many hotels, train stations and airports now have Internet facilities for business people to use while on the move. This means that travelling need not mean losing touch with what is going on in the office.

Many larger companies have offices overseas; the ability to carry out videoconferences over the Internet has meant that, for some, travelling is no longer essential. However it also means that people on opposite sides of the world have to co-ordinate their work times, so that live conferences can take place.

The increase in mobile communication systems has also led to some worries about health – there are regular reports of the dangers of using mobile phones due to radiation, laws are being altered to make using the phone while driving an offence, while repetitive strain injury (RSI) has been linked to over-use of ICT equipment. All of these dangers have evidence to support and deny their existence, but for people working in some industries there are few alternatives. They need access to ICT all of the time and this means accepting the possible dangers.

Another side effect of the increased use of mobile technology has been the reported changes in the way school pupils are responding to examination questions – a number of examiners have commented upon the use of text message-type spelling appearing in examination answers. Although this is potentially detrimental to the use of language, it is seen by some experts as a natural evolution, as language is continually developing; perhaps 'C U l8r' will seem commonplace in the future!

Mobile technology and work patterns

Videoconferences are carried out over the Internet. Users log on to a conference in a similar way to joining a group telephone call. The computer screen shows a video of the person you are speaking to, while a webcam takes images of you and transmits them to the other person's machine. If more than two people are involved, a number of video feeds are shown on the screen, however the bandwidth can be used up, causing the images to seem very jerky. This is not normally a problem, as most videoconferencing does not require much movement on the part of the users.

TASKS

1 Describe three advantages and three disadvantages of the increased use of mobile communication devices by workers.

2 Describe the equipment you would need to be able to access the Internet while on a train.

A PDA helps you to plan your day on the journey in to work.

Training

By the end of this topic you will be able to:

- describe the changes made to staff training over recent years

- discuss the need for continual learning and improvement of skills in the workplace

As ICT has become a more important aspect in the workplace, the need to train staff in the use of ICT has become a major issue for many companies.

In the past most employers would look at the number of GCSE passes as an indicator of ability. Now with a more varied range of qualifications taken in schools and colleges, they often look for particular subjects, ICT being one of them. Some organisations expect all of their staff to achieve a minimum qualification in ICT, such as a GCSE or the European Computer Driving Licence (ECDL). As many school leavers have some qualification already, this has meant that the main thrust for training has been with existing, older staff.

Most organisations see the updating of staff skills and expertise as beneficial to the company, as well as the individual concerned. This has led to various nationally recognised qualifications being developed, particularly in the area of ICT.

Most of the training is based around typical office-type applications:

- word processing
- spreadsheets
- databases
- email and Internet use.

However many organisations use specialist software and hardware. In these situations staff will need specialist training, often carried out by the software developers.

Investors in People is a national quality standard which sets a level of good practice for improving an organisation's performance through developing its people.

Since 1991, tens of thousands of UK employers, employing millions of people, have become involved with the standard and know the benefits of being an 'Investor in People'. With the continued growth and uptake of the standard in the UK, international interest has been stimulated and continues to grow.

Many training programmes are developed 'in-house' with the trainer having been taught how to use the equipment by the developer. This person then trains others so that they can then use the equipment. However it is important that staff receive regular opportunities to update their skills. Unfortunately this can be an expensive investment, and so smaller companies often find it more difficult to find the money to train staff.

The Government has recognised this as a problem facing the country as a whole and has put together various initiatives, under the umbrella of 'Lifelong Learning', to try to support all workers in their endeavours to continually improve their performance, and therefore the performance of their companies, through regular training.

ECDL

The European Computer Driving Licence (ECDL) is an educational ICT course based around seven modules:

- Basic concepts of Information Technology
- Using the computer and managing files
- Word processing
- Spreadsheets
- Database
- Presentation
- Information and communication

Training

Training continually helps you to improve your performance.

> ## TASKS
>
> **1** Produce a list of skills and abilities that you feel would constitute a minimum competence in using the following applications:
> - word processing
> - spreadsheets
> - databases
> - email and Internet use.
>
> **2** Investigate the training of staff in a local organisation; take note of induction training, on-the-job training and specialist training.
>
> **3** Produce a training pack that would guide an employee through how to carry out an operation from one of the following:
> - cut and paste in a word processor
> - scan an image and insert it into a DTP document
> - set up an email account using a web-based email client (for example Hotmail, Yahoo).

Types of jobs

ICT has automated many of the jobs that people used to do manually. This has affected all sectors of employment. Below is a set of examples.

Type of work	In the past	Modern equivalent
Office work	Companies used to employ a number of typists to cater for the volume of letters	One typist using a word processor and predesigned templates with data saved ready to be imported into a document
	Each typist could type one letter with carbon paper allowing two or three copies	One typist can produce a 'form letter' which the word processor can then automatically generate and print any number of letters
	A spelling mistake could only be rectified with over typing, or retyping the whole document	All word processors have spelling and grammar checks, that can ensure that mistakes are avoided, if an error is spotted it can be rectified on the screen and corrected before printing
	Colour was limited to two, usually black and red, due to the inked ribbon in the typewriter	Unlimited colours can be reproduced, however printing can be expensive
	Letters, once printed, had to be signed, folded and put in envelopes, addressed and stamped	Signatures can be printed from scanned files, printing facilities can fold and place the letter in a pre-addressed and franked envelope, and dispatched automatically
	Letters were posted using standard mail distribution system	Email can be used as an alternative to post, or private delivery companies can be employed
Manufacturing	Large labourforce carrying out manual tasks	Small number of highly trained technicians manning automated workstations
Stock control	Paper-based ledgers, completed by stock managers	Bar code systems read automatically
	Goods moved by manual means	Robotic conveyor systems, automatically moving stock to required position

Types of jobs

This move to greater automation has meant that one employee now produces more work than in the past, however what they produce has changed.

As production and manufacturing costs are related to staff costs, many companies have moved their factories to where labour costs are less. This has meant that there has been an increase in other specialist jobs to service the ICT requirements of these companies.

The greater reliance on ICT has led to more people moving into software and hardware engineering, website design and so on. ICT also ensures that the goods produced by the manufacturing companies are made in a cost effective manner and are distributed efficiently.

The old-fashioned typing pools used typewriters. These have now been replaced with PCs.

TASKS

1. Carry out an investigation of work practices at a local employer.

2. Produce a table similar to the one opposite for the tasks carried out by employees of the local company.

CASE STUDY

On a recent visit to Kenya, an ICT teacher was surprised to see how high the standard of ICT was among some school pupils. After some investigation he found that it was because some of the pupils were being taught a high level of programming skills, as the local economy was moving towards a more ICT-based economy.

The local teachers had seen that one way to avoid the poverty that threatened many areas of Africa was to embrace the new technology. However they still had to be careful that traditional skills and values were maintained, otherwise the agricultural and manufacturing base that supported the new technology would collapse. This was why only a relatively small group were being taught ICT to this higher level.

Legislation (1)

The Data Protection Act

The Data Protection Act 1998 came into force on 1 March 2000 and with it came a new set of requirements, which are imposed upon almost every firm in the country.

Basically it is the legislation that covers the use of data about a person. Information cannot be collected and used for unlawful practices. Any data that is collected must be kept secure and accurate, and be destroyed after use.

Protecting data means ensuring that personal data about an individual is processed in accordance with legal requirements in particular with the principles established in the 1984 Act and further developed in the 1998 Act, in order to protect the rights of the individual.

The effects of the Data Protection Act are far-reaching. Companies and other organisations must develop strategies in order to avoid disruptions, or in the most severe cases court actions!

The Data Protection Act contains eight data protection principles.

They state that all data must be:

- processed fairly and lawfully
- obtained and used only for specified and lawful purposes
- adequate, relevant and not excessive
- accurate and, where necessary, kept up-to-date
- kept for no longer than necessary
- processed in accordance with the individual's right's
- kept secure
- transferred only to countries that offer adequate data protection.

The Data Protection Act requires that appropriate security measures are in place to safeguard against unauthorised or unlawful access/processing of personal data.

This means that all data collected about something, or somebody, is controlled by the Act. This means that if data is collected about an individual, it must be held securely and not passed to others without their permission, except in particular circumstances.

However statistical data collected from individual records can be used – if a member of the public takes part in a survey the results from the survey can be passed to others, as long as the individual cannot be singled out.

There are various exceptions to the Data Protection Act, for example information about an individual's medical history can be passed to a hospital casualty department treating the individual after a serious road accident.

In most cases, anyone giving an organisation information about themselves should be aware that the organisation can use that information. The organisation may also pass the information to someone else, a 'third party'. Although this is only allowed with permission – in most cases permission is granted by the giving of the information, and the individual should make it clear if they do not want their information passed to anyone else by actively withholding their permission.

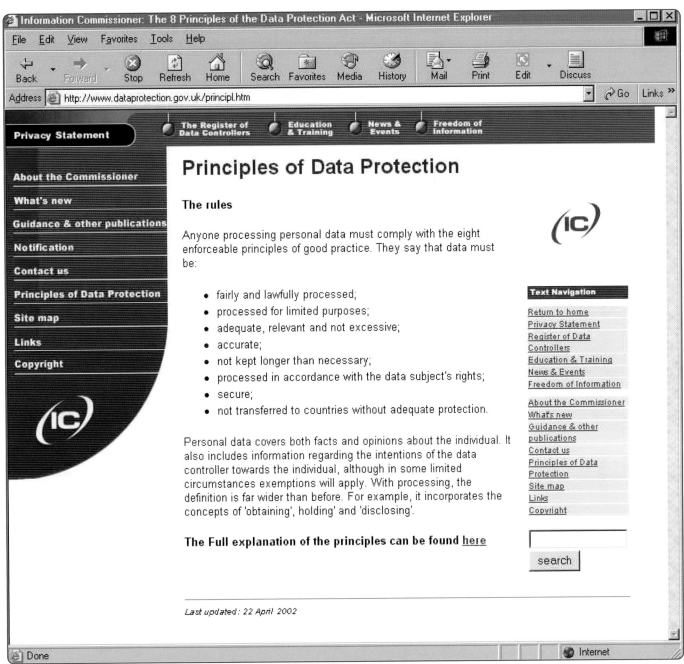

The Data Protection Act website

TASKS

1 Investigate a local company's policy on data protection.

2 Produce a summary of your investigation highlighting the roles of the employees and the rights of individuals.

Legislation (2)

By the end of this topic you will be able to:

- describe the basic elements of a range of legislation relating to the use of ICT

ICT is a relatively new field for legislation. However there are a number of laws that have been passed that cover the appropriate use of ICT software and hardware.

Regulation	General principles	Reason for regulation
The Computer Misuse Act 1990	This covers 'securing computer material against unauthorised access or modification; and for connected purposes'. Meaning that an individual may not access a computer, or a file on a computer, without permission.	This came about to stop 'hacking' where an individual or group breaks into a computer file structure to collect or change information.
Copyright, Designs and Patents Act 1988	This covers the rights of individuals or groups who produce new materials. This means that people have to seek permission before using someone else's materials – including web-based materials – although the producer may give up their rights by making materials freely available to the public.	This has existed for many years, but has been updated to cover electronic communications, ensuring that people can protect their work, although by making it available over the Internet, it would be difficult to claim that you hadn't given permission to use it. However, permission should still be sought before materials are used to avoid accusations of 'copyright infringement'.
Health and Safety at Work Act 1974	This covers the health, safety and welfare of persons at work. It also protects others against risks to health or safety in connection with the activities of persons at work, for controlling the keeping and use and preventing the unlawful acquisition, possession and use of dangerous substances, and for controlling certain emissions into the atmosphere. This means that employees and employers have a responsibility to ensure that the workplace is as safe as it can be, and that nobody is put at risk because of the operations carried out in the workplace.	This has existed for over 100 years. It protects workers from being put in dangerous situations. There are still hazardous operations carried out in the workplace, but they should be carried out as safely as possible, or not at all.

Legislation (2)

Regulation	General principles	Reason for regulation
Health and Safety Regulations 1992	There are a wide range of regulations covering the use of ICT equipment and materials, particularly the use of VDUs. It also covers the working environment of all workplaces to ensure that people are not injured due to poor workplaces rather than the practices of the workplace which are covered in the Health and Safety at Work Act.	These complement the Health and Safety at Work Act, covering the materials and equipment, rather than the operations carried out.
Regulation of Investigatory Powers Act 2000	This covers the lawful, or unlawful interception of communication by post, phone or Internet. Certain bodies do have permission, such as the Police or Government Agencies, but generally this law makes it illegal to read other people's post or email, or listen into telephone calls without permission.	Electronic communication can be intercepted relatively easily; these regulations make it clear who does, or does not, have permission to intercept any form of communication.

Word check ✓

EU regulations – rules set by the European Parliament which, although many of them are similar to UK laws and regulations, are often newer and sometimes contain more detail. By following them in the UK it means that services and products produced in the UK can be sold in Europe with very little adaptation.

There are also various **EU regulations** and Internet Codes of Practice, which may not be Law in the UK, yet many organisations do adhere to them.

It should also be remembered that even if a law does not exist at present which is directly related to the use of ICT there are many general laws, which cover the rights and responsibilities of individuals.

TASK

1 Produce a set of notices that could be displayed in the workplace to remind staff of their role, rights and responsibility for each of the Acts listed.

Aside from health and safety acts and regulations, you should take care of your health by taking regular breaks and doing stretching exercises.

229

The downside

ICT has delivered many benefits to groups and individuals, however it has also created opportunities for misuse.

With the advent of Internet shopping, the ability to get hold of someone's credit card details and then use them for illegal purposes has become more common.

In 2000 over £100 million was spent using counterfeit credit cards! This was a rise of over 50 per cent on the previous year.

Over £300 million was spent fraudulently using credit cards. However less than £10 million was fraudulently spent over the Internet, the majority of this through online auctions. The greatest illegal money transfers were made using false details to obtain money orders. People in the UK carry out less than 1 per cent of Internet fraud, whereas over 85 per cent is perpetrated in the US.

ICT can, however, be used to carry out other fraudulent activities – images can be scanned and printed to produce counterfeit money, identity cards, credit cards and so on. The data contained on the magnetic strip on the reverse of a credit card can be copied and duplicated onto false cards and using high quality image manipulation software can allow a user to alter a document or an image electronically before printing.

The misuse of personal information is also a growing concern for many people. There are Internet sites that offer 'legitimate' replacements for missing documents. The user passes on their details and the company reproduces the document, for example, a driving licence, or insurance note. However some of these companies do not carry out checks on the user and so could be producing documents containing the details of some other person.

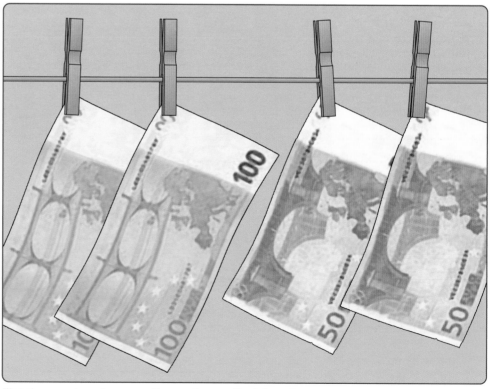

Illegal money transfers are often made over the Internet.

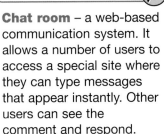

The downside

A number of organisations collect data about an individual, then pass this information on to a third party without permission, regardless of the Data Protection Act. Although this is illegal, the victim may not be aware that it has happened until it is too late. The storage of so much information, which can be searched through quickly and easily has created a problem for data security.

Email has also become a target for illegal activity. The second largest area of Internet fraud is the 'Nigerian Letter Fraud'. This concerns an email that has been sent to millions of Internet subscribers, requesting bank account details and financial support to enable a prominent Nigerian politician to get their money out of the country! The email promises millions of pounds to the recipient. When the money or bank account details are sent the original sender disappears, there are obviously no millions of pounds coming, and the recipient often finds their bank account emptied.

Other aspects of ICT and Internet misuse include 'spam' email, which can be annoying to organisations as well as individuals. This involves a form of junk mail sent via email to thousands, sometimes millions of users. The traffic this creates can cause networks to get jammed. It also fills up mailboxes and takes time to clear.

Chat rooms have also been cited as potential areas for concern. Due to the anonymity of the users, it can be impossible to tell who you are communicating with, and this can put people at risk. It can also lead to abuse via email.

> **Word check** ✓
>
> **Chat room** – a web-based communication system. It allows a number of users to access a special site where they can type messages that appear instantly. Other users can see the comment and respond.

Data on the magnetic strip is read by the card reader.

TASK

 Carry out further investigation into one of the following:
- credit card fraud
- misuse of personal information
- spam
- chat rooms.

Then develop a set of rules that could be followed to avoid some of the pitfalls.

Use these rules as a basis for a web page.

Viruses

By the end of this topic you will be able to:

- describe how an ICT system can be infected with a virus

- describe the effect viruses can have on ICT systems

Almost every computer user in the world has heard of computer viruses. Many have even had the misfortune of experiencing a virus attack at some point.

Virus attacks are becoming more prevalent than ever before. Thousands of people suffer often-irrecoverable damage to their systems and data. Yet many do not even know what hit them let alone what they can do to avoid a recurrence.

A computer virus is most often defined as 'a malicious code of computer programming'. What this means is that a computer virus is a program – only written to cause damage to the system it is installed on. A computer virus is designed to install, propagate and cause damage to computer files and data without the knowledge or permission of the user. Viruses only work on the memory of a system – the RAM and disk storage, they do not affect the monitor, keyboard or your own blood stream!

The first step in any virus attack is always the invasion. This is when the virus actually enters the computer system from an outside source. Much of the effort in preventing a virus attack lies in understanding what the entry points are and how best to monitor and block out any possible intrusion. All viruses enter the computer system through two main entry points: the disk drives and the network adapter cards. This makes any disks or CDs that you insert into these drives a possible source of virus infection.

The network adapter card is most likely your computer network or modem connected to the local intranet or the Internet. Viruses entering through this point are often disguised in the form of attachments in emails. These attachments are often program files and office documents containing macros. Some web pages may also contain harmful programming codes that might transfer virus or virus-like codes into a system.

Most anti-virus software scans emails and disk-based files before they are used by the system.

Infection often begins with opening the file containing the virus. Once the virus has been activated it installs itself into the computer's memory. It is essential, therefore that files are not opened if the user is unsure about what the file is or where it came from.

After entering the computer memory, a virus can then multiply and spread copies of itself across the main data storage device, usually the hard disk drive. It does this by copying itself into other files. Later when users transfer or copy these files to another machine, the virus gains entry to more systems.

This can cause massive damage to a system – whether it is a computer at home or a major organisation, the effect can be the same – total loss of data!

Anti-virus software can stop this occurring, but it must be updated regularly as a virus can actually use the anti-virus programs to infect an even greater number of files.

Unfortunately a security guard cannot protect you against viruses.

Other security software can also be employed to protect data – a firewall can stop others accessing a machine through the Internet; it can also stop malicious programs such as a virus from sending data from a machine without permission.

It is also important to back up data regularly in case of a virus attack – anti-virus software can only deal with viruses it recognises and as new viruses are developed continually it is possible for a system, even with updated software, to get infected.

TASKS

1 Check your virus protection.

2 Produce an on-screen representation of how a virus works.

Personal communications

Many aspects of personal communication have already been covered in previous sections; the major development of ICT is in this field. Below is a summary of some of the major changes that have taken place in the ways in which individuals use technology to communicate.

The Internet

The Internet has made many differences to the way the public retrieve information about products or companies:

- People have a wider range of products and services to choose from; the Internet has brought access to millions of informative pages of data into the home. News agencies are able to stream information, giving instant access to the latest headlines, shops can advertise their latest products for a fraction of the cost of 'traditional' advertising and entertainment sites can be used for relaxing or competing in international competitions.
- International boundaries are ignored, as businesses are able to transfer information on a global scale. Employees can access intranet sites to keep abreast of company activity; the public can find information about companies, without expensive postal searches or visiting in person.
- Many online stores are able to offer discounts over the Internet, as their overheads are lower.

Mobile phones keep you in touch with your friends and family.

Mobile phones

The advent of mobile phone technology has made a dramatic difference to personal communication:

- People can be contacted 'on the move'.
- People feel safer as they can access the emergency services, or friends and family when needed.
- WAP technology has enabled access to the Internet while on the move; this will improve in the future as 3G technology becomes available and affordable.

Entertainment and leisure

The world of entertainment has now moved into the ICT field. Until recently people were passive observers of entertainment devices, now greater **interactivity** is being incorporated into devices and media:

- DVD and other storage devices have enabled production organisations to include 'extras' with films and music – games, interviews, still images, music soundtracks.
- The greater interactivity has led to more discernment on the part of the consumer; games must have realistic graphics, films and TV programmes have 'user defined endings', digital broadcasting can allow viewers to choose their own camera angles or soundtracks.

Personal communications

Education and lifelong learning

These technologies have had far-reaching impact on all aspects of education:

- Teachers and learners can communicate from different locations, at different times, using the Internet, mobile phones or email.
- The range of media, appealing to different teaching and learning styles has increased, giving more opportunities for learning to take place.
- The Internet has enabled learners to access up-to-date and comprehensive research materials. These materials have enabled teachers to make their lessons more relevant to today's educational needs.

Word check

Interactivity – is the ability for a user to alter what they see or hear, or to take part in an activity, rather than being a passive observer.

CASE STUDY

Until recently cinemas used standard film shown through a traditional reel-to-reel projector. In the summer of 2002 the latest Star Wars film was released to some cinemas on DVD. Unlike the DVDs used in home systems, this film was on five long special quality DVDs.

The cinema had a special multimedia projection unit installed with five players, each one synchronised so that as one disc finished the next would start without the viewer noticing.

The trial went well, the discs were capable of delivering a better quality picture than the traditional film and they would not degrade as quickly as film.

This has also opened up new possibilities; a multi-screen cinema would be able to show the same film on all screens, with only one set of discs. Also the transportation of the discs can be done by post, rather than film, which is bulky and could easily be damaged.

TASK

1 Carry out an investigation into the way that the television at home has changed in the last 30 years.

Use the results from this investigation to produce a graphical comparison of how TV has altered.

Make a list of the ICT equipment you use in one day. Categorise it into:
- Internet
- mobile phone
- entertainment and leisure
- education and lifelong learning.

There will probably be a number of overlaps, so think carefully about how to present your data.

Community activities

Although the development of ICT has benefited business and education, it has also made a difference to the way the support systems of public services function.

The UK Government has promoted and helped fund public access to the Internet, through the use of libraries and post offices with Internet terminals. Private organisations have also seen public access as an important revenue stream – the cybercafé on London's Oxford Street, is one of the busiest shops in a very busy shopping area! This improved access enables people to not only access the Internet, but also send and receive email, giving people the ability to communicate with friends and family worldwide in a cost effective manner.

The use of the Internet has also been incorporated into the way public services are organised. Local and national government hold online discussions, where the public can voice their concerns regarding particular policies; email is also becoming an effective method of contacting councillors and MPs. Independent interest groups cover every imaginable hobby or pastime, as well as serious issues, through the use of message boards and chat rooms.

Public services such as museums and galleries have also moved into using the Internet to promote themselves. The public can view extracts from the displays, check opening times, get directions on how to get there and arrange the necessary tickets, all carried out online.

Public transport and private travel organisations also list their services on the Internet, allowing the public to browse through availability and times, arrange their itinerary and then make a booking. All without having to leave their own home to do so.

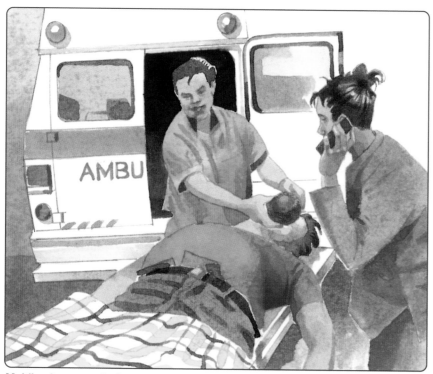

A less common use of these worldwide services has been the ability to use systems such as the **Global Positioning Systems (GPS)** to locate and assist with navigation. Many sports have benefited from this technology, such as sailing and car rallying, but as with other aspects of ICT, the price has been too expensive for public use. However, this is changing, as portable navigation systems are now fitted in many cars. There are also portable devices for use by walkers and other outdoor pursuits enthusiasts and many mobile phones can be accurately located to enable WAP systems to be used as positioning systems. This technology can also be very helpful to the emergency services.

Mobile phones make it easy to report an accident, while the emergency services use GPS to locate the scene of the accident.

Community activities

All of this has meant a dramatic change in the way that everyday life is affected by ICT. It is no longer something that is taught in school and sometimes used in the workplace; it is a support system for the whole community. It would be impossible for the western world to function without the extensive ICT facilities it now employs.

Local governments have their own websites, where online discussions may be held, like the one above of Essex County Council.

CASE STUDY

The driving test has changed quite a lot over recent years. One of the more recent innovations has been the inclusion of a written test. Another idea has been to include some form of simulation to help assess drivers without the need for them to actually drive on the roads.

The British School of Motoring has worked with a number of software developers to produce a simulation device to help learners to develop certain skills prior to trying to drive on the busy UK roads.

The simulation covers visual scanning ability, hand/eye co-ordination and risk avoidance skills.

There's also a MAP (Mind Alertness Program) CD-ROM which allows the learner to continue making progress through a range of computer exercises at home.

The system, already installed in some BSM centres, is made up from a PC, running a high quality digital video over a number of screens. The learner sits in a model driving seat with the full range of controls and dashboard clocks as would appear in a real car. The windscreen and side windows are replaced with video screens.

As the program runs, various scenarios can be played through, putting the learner into potentially dangerous situations, where, in the real world, someone could be hurt or an accident may occur.

This has proven to be a successful way for some people to take the first steps in learning to drive.

TASKS

1 Carry out an investigation of your local council website: list the various sections that may be of interest to the local community.

2 Produce a report on how to check the train timetable for your local railway station.

3 Describe how GPS can be used by the emergency services.

ICT and people with special/particular needs

By the end of this topic you will be able to:

- describe a number of strategies that ICT can offer to enable people with special/particular needs to help them in their everyday lives

ICT can improve the quality of life for all individuals, but for those with special/particular needs it can be used to dramatically improve their quality of life.

There are a range of hardware devices and software adaptations that can be incorporated into systems to improve access for individuals with:

- **sensory impairment**
- physical disability
- limited mobility
- learning difficulties
- language difficulties
- multiple disabilities.

The majority of ICT systems require visual interactivity with limited physical movement; this can be a great advantage to those who find manual systems difficult to operate.

People with limited physical movement can use adapted equipment to move a mouse pointer around a screen and therefore control software. Visual and hearing difficulties can be overcome with various software and hardware adaptations.

Educational software has been developed for use by people with learning difficulties to allow them to learn in a more appropriate manner. This allows them to access knowledge and information to improve their choices in life.

All of these facilities have been made possible due to the improvements in the flexibility and power of modern equipment. To support these developments, laws have been passed to ensure that companies consider those with difficulties when designing equipment, software or websites. This has led to greater inclusion of all sectors of society in the future developments of ICT.

Devices that have been developed for one purpose have also been found to be useful in overcoming difficulties experienced by other ICT users:

- Vibrating phones and pagers have been designed for mainstream use. They have been developed for use by people with hearing difficulties, flashing displays on phones showing when a call is received have also been found useful.
- Video conferencing has enabled those with hearing or other difficulties to take part in discussions through the use of sign language and lip reading.
- Text messaging has obvious uses for people with speech difficulties; the ability to generate text without a standard keyboard has also proven advantageous.

The use of the Internet for shopping has enabled those with physical or mobility difficulties to select goods, pay for them and arrange delivery, without the need to leave their homes.

There are also many ICT developments that have been used to design new and improve existing equipment and facilities. Building and vehicle design also now take into account people with special/particular needs. This has led to great improvements in many people's lives.

ICT and people with special/particular needs

Stephen Hawking is probably one of the most famous disabled people. He is totally reliant on ICT in his work as a scientist.

Word check

Sensory impairment – this covers a range of conditions where a person has difficulty with one or more of their senses. It is usually limited to hearing (deafness) and sight (blindness), however difficulty with the other senses can also be a problem to the sufferer. Lacking a sense of taste or smell may not seem very debilitating, but, to those who suffer from these conditions, they can be very serious.

TASKS

1. Make a list of disabilities and possible ways of overcoming the difficulties faced by those with disabilities.

2. Carry out an investigation into the availability and costs of accessibility aids for those with special/particular needs.

3. Use the results of these investigations to produce a web page with strategies for overcoming problems faced by people with disabilities.

Incoming speech amplifiers and induction loops

By the end of this topic you will be able to:

- explain the purpose of amplified speech and induction loop systems

- describe the advantages and disadvantages of installing an induction loop in a public building

People with poor hearing find their situation worse in crowded or noisy environments. To overcome this, many hearing impaired people use hearing aids. Conventional hearing aids are electronic amplifiers with an in-built microphone and an earpiece. They also have a 'T' switch for converting the signals from an induction loop system to amplified audio, enabling the user to hear a transmitted signal.

Induction loop systems for the hard of hearing are now becoming mandatory in many public buildings. Apart from serving as a means of communication, they also support the emergency evacuation protocol of the venue.

Most hearing aids nowadays have a switch marked M and T. Some even have M, MT and T. The M (microphone) position is for 'normal' listening, that is, receiving airborne sound via the microphone built into the hearing aid. The T position is for receiving the sound via an induction coil, which is built into the hearing aid. For the induction coil to provide sound, a magnetic field is set up by a loop of wire around the area concerned, powered from a special loop driver amplifier. The MT position, which is provided on some hearing aids, allows listening simultaneously to both airborne sound via the microphone and inductively transmitted sound via the induction loop.

In a noisy environment, a person with impaired hearing, wearing a hearing aid, can find it almost impossible to hear the speaker clearly. It is for this reason that more attention is now being given to assisting hearing-aid users by installing induction loops in churches, public buildings and in some cases, the workplace, where announcements can then be made over the system.

Induction loops and **infrared systems** replace the sound path between the sound source and the listener with either an inductive (magnetic) or infrared signal that is not affected by acoustics or other sounds. The listener uses a receiver that converts the signal back to sound. For loops, this is normally the listener's own hearing aid, but infrared systems use special receivers – which are lent to people who want to use the system. Both systems enable users to hear from anywhere in the area the system covers. What other people hear without a receiver is unaffected.

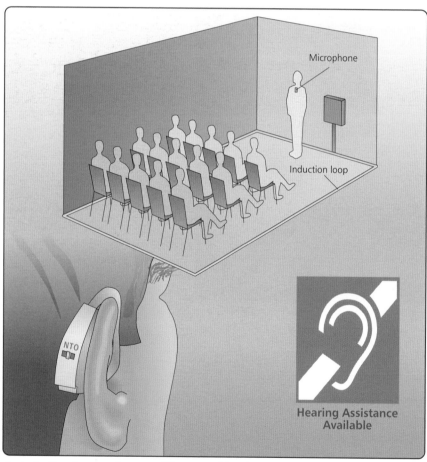

An induction loop system amplifies sound for the hard of hearing.

Incoming speech amplifiers and induction loops

Whichever system is installed, the quality of the sound it produces can only be as good as the signal it receives. Neither loops nor infrared systems improve signal quality, they simply reproduce what is fed into them. It is easy to get a clear signal when this comes from a person speaking directly into a microphone. The further the sound has to travel to reach the microphone, the more it is corrupted by room acoustics and background noise. The microphone must therefore be placed where it can receive sound well. Usually this is as close as possible to the person speaking.

One particular drawback to the induction loop is that the signal transmitted can be picked up outside the area it services – hearing-aid users outside the room can overhear conversations if their hearing aids are switched to 'T'. Adjoining rooms and rooms directly above and below one another are also affected by this, creating difficulties for people in those rooms. For this reason one loop may be unsuitable for confidential meetings. Fitting more than one loop may solve the problem, as the signal from one loop will interfere and overpower the signal spilling over from the adjacent room.

> **Word check** ✓
>
> **Induction loop** – a system with a microphone positioned to pick up the voice of a speaker, this is then transmitted via a loop aerial to any device that can pick up the specified frequency.

CASE STUDY

Josy has a hearing impairment, she is deaf in one ear and only has partial hearing in the other.

For a number of years she has been wearing a hearing aid, which has M and T settings.

She has also learned to lip read and does know some sign language, although she rarely uses it.

She applied for, and successfully got, a job as a nurse without mentioning her disability. Most of the patients and staff of the hospital are unaware that she has any difficulty in hearing.

The hospital has a full induction loop system for the benefit of the patients, and by using her lip reading skills she has very rarely been in any way disadvantaged.

The only problem she has is with the alarms used by the patients when they want to get the attention of the nurse. Although she doesn't mind not hearing the alarms as it means that the other nurses respond, and she doesn't have to run around quite as much!

TASKS

1. Describe, in detail, how a hearing aid and induction loop works. Use diagrams and pictures to help explain your answer.

2. Describe how a classroom could be equipped with a system that would help people with hearing problems to listen to the teacher.

Speech synthesisers and voice recognition systems

By the end of this topic you will be able to:

- describe how speech synthesisers can help ICT systems communicate with users

- describe the operation of data entry systems that use voice recognition systems

A software speech synthesiser is a program which converts text to speech and which produces its voice using a sound card. It must comply with standards as used by **SSIL** and **MSSAPI**.

Traditionally, speech synthesisers were either hardware cards, which were placed into slots inside a computer, or boxes connected to a computer via a serial or a parallel port, which produce the voice using special chips.

With the price of CPUs and memory falling, and with the increased capabilities of sound cards (such as being able to play several wave sounds at once), software synthesisers are easily obtainable. Many sound cards can still only play one wave sound at once and since the software synthesiser requires this channel to produce its voice, other sounds or recordings cannot be played at the same time as text is being spoken.

One other advantage of software synthesisers is that their text to speech capabilities and voices can be enhanced relatively easily. This is because it is easier to update software than it is to redesign a chip.

A speech synthesiser converts text to speech.

Speech synthesisers and voice recognition systems

Voice recognition technology has two basic elements: finite command recognition and true dictation recognition.

Finite command recognition

technology matches the speech pattern of the spoken command with a stored set of known commands. This simple command recognition is also extended to implement a crude sort of speech recognition. This kind of speech recognition is really only a command recogniser that is programmable, in other words the user creates the commands that are later searched for execution.

True dictation recognition analyses the voice to recognise parts of speech, grammar and language.

Dictation software can be divided into two categories, discrete and continuous. Discrete recognition requires the user to pause between each word, while continuous recognition actually understands natural language.

Dictation software is far more interactive and dependent on visual cues and feedback and is impractical for blind users who rely on a screen reader to access the computer. Dictation software requires training which necessitates the user having to read text and prompts off the screen in response to the computer in order for it to recognise the way the user speaks.

Examples of continuous recognition software include IBM *Via Voice Gold* and Dragon's *Naturally Speaking*. These packages can also be purchased with extra modules to handle specific vocabulary such as medical or legal terms. Dragon's *Naturally Speaking* has a number of different versions to accommodate specific vocabulary types.

CASE STUDY

Large portions of this book were written using voice dictation software.

Although to a non-typist it appears to solve the problems raised by not being able to type properly, it does require time to be spent on training the software. Due to the intricacies of the spoken language, the software has a variety of settings that need fine tuning to make the system work at its optimum.

It is also important to proof-read, or check, the text after each section.

This should avoid the following:
Sum people can half difficulties wither tie pin.

Or as it should read:
Some people can have difficulties with their typing.

Neither sentence will show any errors after spell checking, or simple grammar checking, but they obviously have very different meanings.

TASKS

1. Produce a web page describing the benefits of using a speech synthesiser to read out text to a user, and then use a screen reader to read it back to you.

2. Use a dictation program to input data into a word processor. This will mean training the software by using the associated materials.

3. Describe why a dictation program would not be much use for a blind computer user.

Word check

SSIL and **MSSAPI** – software synthesisers must comply with one of two major standards used by the majority of products on the market. The two standards are MSSAPI (Microsoft® Speech Application Programming Interface) and SSIL (Speech Synthesiser Interface Library). This means that the software synthesisers use similar technology to decode and recode speech, making it easier for the hardware manufacturers to ensure that their products will be compatible.

Environmental control systems

By the end of this topic you will be able to:

- describe the main hardware elements of an environmental control system
- explain how the process of environmental control works

One of the most common systems of computer control can be found in **environmental control** – central heating and air conditioning are the two main systems, but there are others.

Environmental control is a system that permits remote control of devices in the immediate surroundings. A person can independently turn lights, radio and television on and off, answer or initiate phone calls, and unlock a door. Essentially any aspect of the environment can be controlled depending upon the system's complexity.

This involves a hardware or software system allowing the user programmed or spontaneous control over remote, electrically operated appliances.

This means that a user can set up manual or automatic operation of electrical appliances. This is done through the use of a hardware or software system; for example a central heating system.

Although this has a practical application for anyone, it has proven particularly useful to people with disabilities, allowing them greater autonomy and control over their household devices.

Over recent years a number of companies have begun marketing complete systems to home users, previously this sort of arrangement was generally only found in the workplace.

When deciding to install and use an environmental control system, there are different levels of complexity to be considered, and each level has an associated price increase.

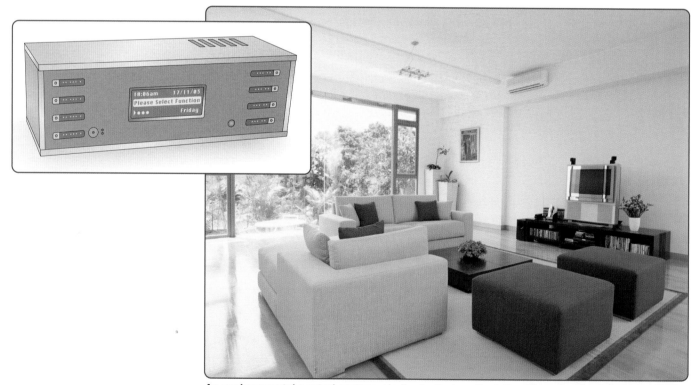

An environmental control system, similar to that on the left, will control the television, DVD and CD player, turn the lighting on and off and control the temperature.

Environmental control systems

Many households have now installed a **security alarm** – consisting of a range of **passive sensors**, a **control unit**, an output unit, possibly linked to the local police station, and a remote switching system.

This system may be expanded to include thermostatic temperature controls that are linked to the central heating and timers to control lights. Both of these still have a use in making a house appear occupied while the owner is away.

There are other systems that can be added, such as hardware and software that allows you to monitor and adjust settings for lighting, heating and air conditioning, security, and appliances such as TVs and videos, via Internet or intranet, with the added benefit of wireless access, video surveillance, and email notification of programmed events, making a **total home automation system**.

TASKS

1 Using the following table as a starting point, make a list of all of the devices you could control in your home.

Input	Control	Output
Keypad	CPU	Lights
Light sensor	Timing system	Water heater
Temperature sensor	Memory storage	Air conditioning
Passive infrared sensor		Alarm
Timer		Curtain motor
Weather sensor		Shower/bath taps
Internet link		Video display
		TV/video
		Music centre

2 Describe the daily routine of a household control system. Use the Internet to find out how much the system you have described would cost.

Case study

Over the past few years, the Government has been developing various initiatives with public and private organisations.

One such initiative is an online learning activity. A group of educational organisations have been working together to provide ICT facilities for the community.

The project started in 1998, with various meetings between the different partner organisations. These consisted of a number of colleges and industrial training providers getting together to try to sort out what they thought would be a good and successful way of tackling the need for educational facilities in a range of different venues.

The solution was thought to be a number of computer rooms with networked machines spread all over the town.

The funding for the project was to be arranged through a bid to the Government; if successful the Government would pay for the majority of the equipment, with smaller bids to other agencies, including the European Social Fund, to generate the remainder.

Wheelchair users are able to work from home.

A detailed plan was drawn up involving all of the partners. This involved visits to potential sites, including factories, libraries, schools and colleges. The initial estimate was for 200 networked PCs with each site also having a server, printer and other peripherals.

With this equipment list the bid also had to include furniture – 200 workstation desks, 200 chairs, filing cabinets, plug sockets and everything else that could possibly be needed.

The total bill for the equipment was almost £2 million!

This was put into the bid along with staffing costs, technical support costs and so on. The bid was successful and so the money was made available to set up the community facilities.

The computer suites were located in 15 locations around the town each with between three and 20 workstations, linked to the local college's host computer.

A variety of learning program-related courses were developed and software was written and installed onto the system. Other software applications were also installed, Microsoft® *Office*, Internet and email software and some other packages.

This was thought to be a broad enough selection to allow all members of the local community to benefit from the facilities.

In addition, the centres each offered access to the Internet and had a range of special equipment and software to meet the needs of learners with different requirements. All centres were designed to accommodate people with special needs and some had full disabled access.

But, the important part of such an initiative is the involvement of the community and continued development of the facilities.

At the outset the partner organisation's main aim was to work together to build a better future for the residents and workforce of the town and local villages by broadening the possibilities for learning.

Case study

Over three years the project has continued to develop and grow. The people in charge have continually sought new equipment: linking the out-centres with telephone lines proved difficult and the connection speed was slow, fibre-optic systems were developed and later wireless networking was employed to allow fast access from any terminal.

Staff have been employed to co-ordinate the use of the rooms with the various demands, public access was arranged for certain times, classes were taught at others. In the suites that were housed in business premises, the company ran private training sessions for their staff and so on. Each suite has been developed further over the past few years to cater for a wider cross section of the community.

All this has meant that the town now has a state-of-the-art computer network, that they can use for free, or a minimal charge, at various times and in various centres. This provides the means for anyone and everyone to improve their knowledge, skills and employment prospects, when they want to, and at a pace that suits them.

You're never too old to learn.

This continued development has had funding implications. The cost of renewing equipment, due to damage, breakdown, or obsolescence has now become a large part of the running costs. To try to overcome this, a team of technicians have been employed that travel from suite to suite, carrying out maintenance, servicing machines and repairing them where possible. The development of more robust software has also helped to lower the need to replace equipment.

This has allowed more of the funding to be spent on newer technology, which will hopefully, in time, mean that even more use is made of the facilities by the local community. Some of the suites now have videoconferencing facilities, others have digital photographic equipment and other forms of technology are being investigated to provide the widest possible arrangement.

There are many learning packages available on the Internet. Below is a typical page from the Electric Paper website (www.electricpaper.ie), who specialise in interactive educational products to help people learn about computing.

All of this came about because the Government wanted to support the idea of people continuing their education after leaving school and college, 'Lifelong Learning'. But this partnership saw that just offering classes to local adults at traditional education centres would not really help. They decided to take the classes to the public and sited their classrooms where the public could attend when and where they felt the need.

This has been, and continues to be, a success story. More people from all sections of the community now have access to ICT facilities, to support them in learning, finding employment, using the Internet, or just sending an email.

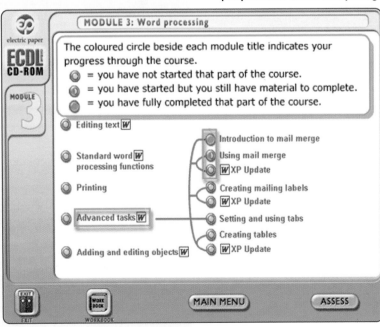

Glossary

Absolute cell reference – putting a $ sign in front of a cell reference in a formula will make sure that the reference remains the same if the formula is replicated. This is an absolute cell reference.

Add to favourites – see Bookmark this page.

Access right – allows only certain people to view certain parts of the computer, for security reasons.

Annotate – notes that are written onto screen prints to explain what they show.

Attributes – the name for a field, when designing a relational database.

Automatic processes – processes that the computer can perform, such as spell check and mail merge.

Back button – a button on your browser that will take you backwards along the chain of sites that you have visited.

Back-up – the copying of data from a computer onto a magnetic tape or another computer, in order that it may be kept safe.

Balance Sheet – a sheet showing the difference between the profit and loss, as shown on the profit and loss account.

Banks Automated Clearing System (BACS) – a system whereby the bank transfers an organisation's money into an employee's or supplier's bank account direct. It avoids having to write a cheque.

Binary data – the system of numbers using combinations of the digits 1 and 0. All information entered onto a computer system is converted into binary codes.

BIOS (basic input-output system) – is the program that enables the computer and the operating system to function. When you switch on a computer the BIOS is the program you see running before the operating system becomes active.

Bluetooth – a recent form of wireless technology that lets you transmit data between two hardware devices, safely and quickly.

Bookmark – a facility in browser software that lets you keep a list of your favourite websites, in order that you may access them quickly.

Bookmark this page – an option in the browser that adds the website you are looking at to your list of favourites.

Browser – enables the computer to convert the signal from the modem into a structure with which you can interact.

Business letter – an external document sent from one business to either another business or to a client.

Bytes – the unit that data is transmitted at.

Calculated field – the field, in a database, which you should not enter data in, as the computer will determine the correct value from the formula entered.

Call centre – an office with a team of staff answering telephone queries.

Cathode-ray tube (CRT monitors) – work in the same way as a television. They are the oldest type of monitor and are large and bulky.

Central processing unit (CPU) – the main processor that is used in computer systems.

Clipboard – a part of the computer that holds text that you have cut until it is required. You cannot see the text on the clipboard until you paste it.

Closed-loop – a system that requires no human intervention.

Colour – in printing, colour pictures are made up from four colours – cyan (blue), magenta (red), yellow and black. On a computer screen colour is made up from only three colours – red, green and black.

Component – a piece of equipment that is used to form part of a larger piece of equipment. For example combining together a number of different electronic components will make a mobile telephone.

Computer system – a collection of hardware and software that enable information to be entered, processed and communicated to a person or device.

Conditional formatting – used in spreadsheets to make important information stand out.

Configuration – the way that different combinations of hardware and software are used.

Control unit – part of a security alarm, that lets you turn on or off the alarm. It also has a keypad for you to key in your personal code.

Convergent technology – where all digital devices (such as digital radio, computer and television) are built into one home entertainment system, so that the devices do not pick up on the frequency of another.

Copy – to use exactly the same text in a different position.

Corrupt – the existence of errors in a set of data, or in a computer program. Corrupted programs or data may not work and might have to be deleted and reinstalled.

Countersigned – a second signature on an important document, such as a cheque or an order, normally by a senior manager.

Cursor – the symbol on the screen, which shows you where you are on it.

Customs and Excise – the government department that keeps files on how much VAT an organisation pays, or how much duty it pays on importing goods from other countries.

Cut – to take a piece of text from its position on the screen to put (or paste) it elsewhere.

Data collection sheet – a questionnaire used to capture the information that will be entered onto a computer system.

Data types – text, numbers, date or time.

Data validation – a way of checking that data, which has been input, is correct.

Design – decide how something is going to look or work.

Diary entry – an entry onto a PDA, taking the place of a paper-based diary.

Dictation software – divided into two categories: discrete and continuous. Discrete recognition requires the user to pause between each word. Continuous recognition understands normal language.

Digital video camera – a video camera that takes pictures digitally. Potentially this gives everyone the ability to produce TV programmes.

Discussion – an informal talk to find out information.

Dumb terminal – a computer workstation that is connected to the main computer server, but has no processing power of its own.

DVD player – a machine that plays DVDs.

Edit – decide how something will look before it is inputted.

Electronic data interchange (EDI) – a system that automatically sends data directly to another computer.

Electronic point of sale (EPOS) – a large system that keeps track of goods going in and out, using bar codes to track everything.

Email address – a unique address that enables you to receive and send emails.

Email account – an account that you open with your ISP, so that you can register your email address.

Enabling technologies – include point-of-sale devices, card readers and customer support terminals. They allow customers quicker and more efficient purchasing.

Entities – a table that is inserted into a relational database.

Environmental control – a system that permits remote control of devices in the immediate surroundings, such as unlock a door or turn on a television or radio.

Ergonomic keyboard – with specialist key layout, designed to make them easier to use.

Error message – a message that appears on your screen to let you know that one of the programs or devices are not working properly.

External – outside of an organisation.

External communication – when an organisation exchanges information with someone outside the organisation.

Extranet – an intranet that is also made available to specified users outside of the organisation.

Eye-strain – eyes can suffer with tiredness if you look at a computer screen for too long a time.

Favourites – a list of the websites that you visit most frequently.

Fieldname – the name given to a field.

Field – a single piece of information in a database.

File – a collection of records.

Finite command recognition – matches the speech pattern with a stored set of known commands.

Foreign key – fields in a database that are common to another table in the same database. They are used to link each table.

Formatted – the way that the text should look, for example the font style and size.

Formulae (plural)/formula (singular) – an equation or way of producing a result in maths.

Forward button – a button on your browser that will return you to an earlier web page or site that you have been looking at.

Frame-based – a page that has been built up as a series of frames, using a DTP package. Each frame contains one type of data – for example text, photo, or drawing.

Fuser unit – generates heat in a printer, so that ink is fused onto the paper.

Gateway – email that is to be sent by SMS has to go through a gateway, which will convert the signal.

Global Positioning System (GPS) – locates a position and assists with navigation, now found in many cars and boats.

Graphical user interface (GUI) – the main operating system used by personal computers.

Head pointer – a device worn on the head, that allows control of the on-screen pointer, either through radio, infrared or light emission.

Headaches – can be suffered if you look at a screen for too long.

History – a list of the websites that you have visited recently.

Homepage – the first page in a browser or on a website.

House style – a design that is developed for an organisation so that all of their documents look the same.

Image – a picture of some kind. It could be a photograph or a drawing.

Implement – putting a new computer system into action.

Industry standard – the usual and most accepted way that an industry works.

Infrared system – see induction loop.

Inland Revenue – the government department that keeps note of how much you earn and how much tax you have to pay.

Input devices – the hardware that enables data to be entered onto the computer system.

Interface – an electric device that acts as a buffer between two pieces of equipment.

Internal – in-house or within an organisation.

Internal communication – when communication is between two members of the same organisation.

Internet – a way of sharing data from one computer to another.

Interview – a formal meeting, to discuss things and find out information.

Intranet – the same as the Internet, except that viewing of the network is limited to people within the organisation.

Key data – the most important data in a database. It can be used to extract information from a computer.

Keypad – the keys that are pressed to input information.

Layout – the way that a document looks on the page.

Light pens – used directly on the screen, having a similar effect to touch screens.

Liquid crystal display (LCD monitors) – display the image by manipulating a liquid crystal display board.

Local area network (LAN) – a network where the computers are all located within one building or site.

Logical operators – words, such as and, or and not, that that you can add to a search when looking for things to match more than one criterion in a database.

Loyalty cards – a card that is given to a customer by an organisation that stores data on a magnetic strip, which helps the organisation to know what each customer is buying. In return, the customer collects 'points' and when they have sufficient points they may have a free product.

Macro – a small program that you can create, to act as a shortcut or time-saver.

Maintain – to look after a system.

Memo – short for memorandum. It is an internal document that is used to send short messages around a company.

Microprocessor – a computer chip.

Moderator – someone who ensures that the rules of a discussion group are kept. They usually have the power to ban from the group any person who breaks the rules.

Modem – a machine that links the computer to the Internet, through a telephone line.

Monitor – checking how a computer performs. Also another name for the computer screen.

MSSAPI – see SSIL and MSSAPI.

Multi-tasking – doing several things at the same time.

Network – a group of computers.

Network file server – a computer that acts as a focal point for a network. It runs the operating system that controls the workings of the network.

Notebook – a small portable computer.

Numeric – data that can only contain the characters 0,1,2,3,4,5,6,7,8,9.

Off-list – used in discussion groups, when a message is sent to a group member rather than to the whole group.

Office hotelling – hiring an office for use when needed.

One-handed keyboard – allows a pointer to move around a screen, with buttons to carry out commands.

Operate – another word for work.

Operating system – the main computer.

Optional field – a field in a database that you can leave blank.

Order form – can be paper based or screen based. A way of ordering goods or services.

Output devices – the hardware that enables data to leave the computer system.

Palmtop computer – a very small portable computer. Powerful enough to run applications software but too small to run input and output devices.

Passive sensor – part of a security alarm. It can be an electronic beam that is broken, or a change of weight on a window sill as it opens, which sets off an alarm.

Payslip – a slip that is given to an employee every payday, detailing how much they have earned and how much tax and national insurance they have had to pay.

Peripherals – input and output devices that do not form part of the main computer system.

Personal Digital Assistant (PDA) – see palmtop computers.

Photo editing – changing the look of a photograph or picture using a photo-editing program. For example to make it smaller or darker.

Portfolio – a collection of your best work.

Presentation – a talk given to people that is illustrated with slides.

Primary key – a field within a database that holds data that is unique to a certain record.

Print head – the main part of a dot-matrix printer. A matrix of either 9 or 24 pins, which move to form individual characters.

Profit and Loss Account – a report showing how much money has been made by an organisation and how much it has lost.

Program – the computer software that allows the computer system to operate.

Protecting data – ensuring that personal data is processed in accordance with legal requirements, in particular the rules as set by the Data Protection Act 1998.

Protocol – an agreed set of standards that enable data from one computer system to be exchanged with another computer system.

Puck – a type of pen for drawing on graphics tablets.

Query – ask the database to find certain information.

Relational database – consists of a customer data file and a product data file, which you can search to find information.

Relational operator – symbols, such as =, < and >, that you can add to a search when looking for things to match more than one criterion in a database.

Remittance advice note – a confirmation that payment has been received.

Repetitive strain injury (RSI) – problems with the forearms after using a keyboard for too long a period of time.

Report – a printout of certain data that is stored in a database.

Required field – a field in a database in which you must enter data.

Search – to look for a certain record.

Search engine – helps you to find the information you require on the Internet. It contains enormous databases detailing all the websites that have been listed.

Secure server – a server that allows customers to enter orders directly onto their computer system, in a secure and safe manner.

Security alarm – a device that sets off an alarm should someone attempt to break into a house or office.

Servo-motor – moves a device with force and at high speeds, such as fork-lift trucks.

Sign-up – register to use a part of a website, such as a discussion group.

Sort – to put the data into either alphabetical or numerical order.

SPAM – unwanted advertisements that can flood an email account.

Standalone – a computer that is self-contained.

Stepper-motor – moves a device in a number of small but accurate steps, such as a drill.

Storyboard – a tool to assist in the planning of a multimedia presentation. It consists of a series of boxes that represent the slides/screens in the presentation. You can use them to indicate what will appear on each one.

Structure diagram – used to show how slides/screens link together in a presentation.

Systems analyst – the person whose job it is to develop new ICT systems.

Telecommuting – working from a base that is linked to the office by a telephone.

Test data – is used to test data validation rules. There are three types of test data: normal data, extreme data and abnormal data.

Text – the information that is entered into a computer is treated as text, even if it contains numbers.

Text messaging – a cheap form of communicating over the mobile phone. Useful for people with hearing difficulties.

Toner cartridge – the place where magnetic ink is stored before it passes over the drum, which then passes it on to the paper.

Trackerballs – in effect, a mouse turned upside down. You move the ball with your fingers, which moves an on-screen pointer.

Troubleshooting guide – a list of common error messages and what they mean.

True dictation – analyses the voice to recognise parts of speech, grammar and language.

URL (Universal Resource Locator) – see web address.

Unique reference number (URN) – a number that is given to a product in order that it may be easily traced or found on a computer.

Validation rule – a rule that you set up to check that data entered on a spreadsheet is valid.

Validation test – the test that you carry out to ensure that data is valid.

Vibrating phone – developed for use by people with hearing difficulties.

Videoconferencing – a discussion that takes place live over the computer. Particularly useful for people with hearing difficulties, as they can take part in the discussion through sign language.

Virtual office – using ICT from anywhere to communicate with others, who may or may not be working in an office.

Visual display unit (VDU) – another name for a computer monitor or screen.

Voice recognition technology – a way of inputting information into a computer using speech.

WAP (wireless application protocol) – a way of sending information to and from mobile phones.

Web address – the address of an Internet site. It will nearly always begin with www.

Web page – a website is normally made up of several pages, including the homepage.

Wide area network (WAN) – a network that connects computers in different towns, cities or countries.

WIMP – an operating system that makes use of Windows, Icons, Menus and Pointers.

Worksheet – the grid that data is entered into when making a spreadsheet.

Word string – a word or phrase that will help you find on the Internet the information you are looking for.

World wide web (www) – a way of accessing information that has been posted by a person or organisation, which may be accessed by any other computer connected to the web.

World Wide Web Consortium (W3C) – a group of experts from all over the world, who work to improve the quality of the Internet.

Index